Iraq, Afghanistan and
The Imperialism of Our Time

Iraq, Afghanistan and
The Imperialism of Our Time

AIJAZ AHMAD

LeftWord

Offset edition first published in India in January 2004.
Reprinted in March 2005.
Digital print edition, March 2020.

LeftWord Books
2254/2A, Shadi Khampur
New Ranjit Nagar
New Delhi 110008
India

www.leftword.com

LeftWord Books is a division of
Naya Rasta Publishers Pvt. Ltd.

© 2004, LeftWord Books

ISBN 978-81-87496-38-0

Contents

Preface   **vii**

Frankenstein and the Monster: Saddam in US Captivity   **xvi**

I

In Lieu of an Introduction   **3**

II

1. 'A Task That Never Ends': Bush Proposes Perpetual War   **39**

2. Re-mapping the Globe   **55**

3. In the Shadow of Permanent War   **72**

4. US Design and Global Complicity   **90**

5. World Peace in the Balance   **104**

6. Imperial Overreach and the Resisting Multitude   **118**

7. War, Oil and the Dollar   **134**

8. War of Occupation Begins   **149**

9. Barbarians at the Gate: The Battle for Baghdad Begins	**166**
10. Wars Yet to Come	**181**
11. Resistance in Iraq, Disarray in the US	**196**
12. Afghanistan: The Forgotten War	**211**

III

The Imperialism of Our Time	**229**

Appendices

1. Sanctions and Their Effects on Iraq	**272**
2. Ramsey Clark's Report to UN Security Council	**274**
3. WMD: Who Said What When	**282**

For
N. Ram
&
in memory of Taimur Khan

Preface

This book brings together two kinds of writing. The bulk of it consists of twelve essays published in *Frontline* between October 2001 and September 2003, on the wars of occupation that the US has waged against Afghanistan and Iraq during this period, as the beginning of what is, by its own declaration, a continuing and never-ending global war.[1] These essays remain virtually unedited but the factual narrative has been updated in some cases, here and there, with the device of footnotes. These are then followed by a lengthy essay, 'The Imperialism of Our Time', first published in *Socialist Register 2004*[2] and re-printed here with substantial revision of some sections. The *Frontline* essays are essentially fact-laden and empirical in nature, largely journalistic in their presentation, with the intent to analyse the unfolding US policies, the two wars and a whole array of related issues in the perspective of the larger geopolitical events during these two years. 'The Imperialism of Our Time' is a much more theoretical piece on the current phase of imperialism which emerges after

---

[1] I published a total of seventeen essays in *Frontline* on this subject during those two years. Twelve are included here and the other five have had to be excluded, for reasons of space. I specially regret excluding the three essays on Israel and the US-Israeli axis without which the strategic design for the Middle East remains unintelligible.

[2] Leo Panitch and Colin Leys (eds), *Socialist Register 2004*, Merlin Press for UK, Monthly Review Press for the US, October 2003.

the dissolution of the communist states in the erstwhile Warsaw Pact countries and the forced dismemberment of Yugoslavia; on the shifting character of imperialism in the colonial and post-colonial eras; on the special place of the US in the history of colonialism as a whole; the dangerous novelty of the Bush regime within the continuity of the US imperial design. This essay is not on Afghanistan and Iraq *per se* but aspires, in part, to lay the foundation for a theoretical understanding of these wars of occupation not as discrete episodes but as key events in a new and global imperial offensive.

The first two of the *Frontline* essays were written soon after a group of hijackers rammed passenger aircrafts into the two buildings of the World Trade Centre in New York and an outer building of the Pentagon in Washington DC, causing the death of close to 3,000 people of roughly 60 different nationalities living and working in the United States, including a very large number of Muslims. The US Senate responded by bestowing upon the US President historically unprecedented war-making powers, and, on 20th September 2001, President George W. Bush addressed a joint session of the US Congress to announce a comprehensive policy of what was now called 'war against terrorism with a global reach' which, he said, would be fought in dozens of countries, overtly and covertly. Moreover, the war was going to be *permanent*: 'a task that never ends', in his own chilling words. In the article I published immediately after that, I became one of the first writers to say that this was neither bluster nor expression of a passing fury but a Presidential announcement, backed by the entire US Senate, of a long-term policy aimed at the conquest of the planet for the American imperium through a globalized militarism to supplement the neoliberal globalization. I suggested that the tragedy of the World Trade Centre victims was being used now pretty much on the model of the burning of the Reichstag which helped consolidate Hitler's power in Germany and paved the way for the Nazi bid for global empire. By the time I drafted the second of these pieces the invasion of Afghanistan had begun. I was virtually the only commentator anywhere in the world at that time who suggested that the Taliban would not be defeated so easily and that resistance will emerge sooner or later, as has indeed happened.

Those two essays, on what we may call the Bush doctrine and on the early phase of the invasion of Afghanistan, are then followed by nine articles on Iraq which were published between September 2002 and August 2003, starting from the time that prospects for a full-scale invasion of Iraq became palpable, covering the build-up toward that invasion and the global opposition that arose against it, then the war itself, the occupation of that long-suffering country, and the emergence of Iraqi resistance and the consequent disarray in US policies. Inter alia, these articles also cover a number of related topics: the regime of genocidal sanctions and ferocious bombings by the US-UK alliance which had sought to destroy the very fabric of Iraqi society over roughly twelve years, prior to the invasion of 2003; the dastardly role of the UN; the ambiguous role of the European Union and the currency war between the dollar and the Euro; the politics of oil, not only in Iraq but also more widely in the Middle East and the Caspian Sea basin; and so on. These articles are then followed by a concluding piece on Afghanistan, written almost two years after the initial invasion and imposition of the client Karzai regime there, which reports on the re-emergence of the resistance in Afghanistan and seeks to draw certain parallels as well as contrasts between the modalities of occupation and the dynamics of resistance in Iraq and Afghanistan respectively.

Each of these texts falls somewhere between a journalist's reportage of particular events and an essayist's intent to understand the available empirical facts in terms of the motion of the whole at that specific juncture, however contradictory or even opaque that larger motion may be on a given day. Since each of the essays was bound by the word-limit on what can be printed and by the immediacy of the events getting reported, each is essentially fragmentary, merely a figure in the carpet that got woven, essay by essay, over two years. This is not the book I would have written if I were to write it now, with the wisdom of hindsight. Rather, this is the chronicle of how some of the great crises of our time appeared to an observer, located largely in Delhi, as they unfolded, week after week, without any firm knowledge of the shape events would take after the essay had gone to print.

This kind of writing involves at least two processes of repeated self-correction. One is the obvious kind where one makes an error of judgement, thanks to excitement of the moment, fragmentary nature of factual knowledge, and speculation where facts are not available, not to speak of one's own prejudice and disposition. One then uses the latter essay to correct the errors of the former; the respective essays can then be seen both as discrete reports on preceding events as well as so many stages in, so to speak, a pilgrim's progress. I have left virtually all such errors intact, resisting the temptation to revise and only adding footnotes, here and there, for updating and clarification. The other kind of self-correction is actually the more interesting one. One reports a fact, offers an analysis, then some time later (weeks, months) one comes upon some other body of evidence which can then give one a richer, more complex understanding of those same facts which had been understood not incorrectly, in the strict sense, but superficially. For example, I was certainly one of the first to say that Bush's speech of 20th September 2001 was not just a response to the events of nine days earlier but a historic statement of a new imperial design to which he was committing the US for many years to come, in various parts of the globe. That was certainly correct. However, I had not until then actually read the key documents of the neoconservative establishment, and did not have any clear grasp of the whole background of the key players such as Cheney, Rumsfeld, Wolfowitz, Richard Perle, and Condoleeza Rice, so that I initially had little sense that the intellectual foundations and programmatic forms of what Bush was now enunciating had been in the making, on a very elaborate scale, for well over a decade by a well-knit and increasingly powerful group with neoconservative strategic vision, militarist ideology and Zionist affiliation. Nor had I thought seriously until then about exactly where to draw the line between the strategic thinking of the Clinton and the Bush administrations. The latter essays were thus better informed than the earlier ones, even on issues which were not entirely new, so that the writing of these essays has been for me something of a prolonged apprenticeship.

My biggest debt, by far, is to N. Ram, Editor of *Frontline*, which is in my opinion the best news-magazine in the English language, anywhere in the world. His own project is greatly aided by the fact that India has an extraordinarily lively political and intellectual culture of the Left, which demands and sustains so serious an outlet of current news and political analysis. He has afforded me two unusual freedoms: the freedom to write whenever and on whatever topic I please, thus releasing me from the obligations of a regular column; and the freedom to write 4,000-5000 word essays, unedited by anyone else, which makes it possible not only to combine reportage and analysis but even to take off on brief theoretical forays. This also means, however, that the responsibility for each word and phrase in these articles is entirely mine.

Beyond that, I have learned much from discussions with friends and colleagues too numerous to name, and from audiences in India as well as North America who listened to what I had to say and enriched my understanding through their comments and interrogations. The Internet has been an indispensable source of information which provides the opportunity to *read* and build one's own archive from a wide variety of sources, official as well as oppositional, which then releases one substantially from the unpleasant duty of watching too much television. All of us who are intellectual workers and participants in socialist and anti-imperialist politics owe an incalculable debt of gratitude to all those individuals, virtually around the globe, who give so much of themselves to building an alternative media comprised of hundreds of websites and mailing lists, with no cost to us but at great cost of time and energy to themselves. Among the mailing lists that have regularly fed me with indispensable information and analyses I must mention two in particular, both organized by former colleagues and students in the Department of Political Science at York University in Canada, where I have had the pleasure of teaching: the list maintained by the group for 'Discussions on the Socialist Register and its articles', and another maintained by the Middle East Socialists Network (MESN). A word of thanks in particular to Mr Sid Shniad, who does not know me personally, and to Khashayar Hooshyar, a former student and now a dear friend, for posting innumerable news items and essays on these two lists without which my own writing would have been much the poorer.

I am also indebted to Leo Panitch and Colin Leys, editors of the *Socialist Register*, who made a more compact essay out of the text I had given them, for publication in their journal. In preparing the version for inclusion in this book, I have often gone back to the original text, re-written some sections and added fresh material here and there; some marks of their editing remain, however, which I am glad to acknowledge. I am similarly indebted to Sudhanva Deshpande of LeftWord Books for preparing and seeing this book through the press.

Dates of publication for all the *Frontline* essays have been provided here. Those are not the dates of composition, however. Like most news-magazines, it too has an idiosyncratic system of dating its respective issues. Typically, an article was written two to three weeks prior to its date of publication.

Aijaz Ahmad

A NOTE
Frankenstein and the Monster
SADDAM IN US CAPTIVITY

On 14 December 2003, a day before this book was to go to press, the Anglo-US occupation authorities announced that they had captured Saddam Hussein the evening before and the TV networks, notably CNN and BBC, the two principal echo-chambers of the empire, took to dutifully showing the footage of his humiliating dental examination over and over again, for hours on end, ritualistically, pretty much as they had shown, in infinite repetition, the falling of the Twin Towers of the World Trade Centre on 11th September 2001 and for some days thereafter, so as to fix a certain image in the minds of the TV-watching world: *progress* from American tragedy to American triumph, in just over two years, and from the majesty of those tottering towers to the hapless surrender of the man the US has been demonising as the most gruesome of the demons behind all things Arab and Islamic. In the political unconscious of the US public these two images undoubtedly got intertwined, in an eternal battle between Good and Evil. For much of the rest of the world, hours and hours of this televised spectacle of an exhausted, lonely, elderly, dishevelled captive by the greatest imperial power on earth was simply disgusting.

Saddam's daughter in Amman and his sister in an unnamed Arab capital had identical, and highly plausible, reactions in their respective interviews: Saddam seemed drugged. For all one knows, he might have been tortured. They demanded that he not be tried by either the occupiers or their puppet regime in Baghdad. Both demanded trial by a competent international authority while the daughter, Raghad, announced that the family shall soon be appointing a lawyer to defend her father.

CNN and BBC showed miserable little groups in Baghdad celebrating and individual shopkeepers firing their guns in jubilation. They did not show the many pro-Saddam demonstrations that erupted throughout northern Iraq right under the guns of the American occupiers. In one such demonstration, US soldiers killed three Iraqis.

By any standards of international law, the American occupation of Iraq is illegal. Any trial of Saddam in a court with international jurisdiction would bring up the question not only of his crimes but also the legal status of those who have held him in captivity. Such a trial may turn into a trial of the lawless occupiers and their war crimes. Knowing this, Bush and Blair announced quickly that the trial shall be held by an Iraqi court and pointedly excluded any role for the UN. Everyone knows that such a court shall be beholden to the Americans and their puppets in the so-called Iraqi Governing Council (or whatever is put in its place in the coming months), and that it would sentence Saddam to death. To circumvent this foregone conclusion, Kofi Annan, the UN Secretary General, immediately went on record demanding trial by a competent international court and, in keeping with the extremely widespread European sentiment, he refused to condone any proceedings that would include the possibility of death penalty. The UN has never set up a court which carried the death penalty, he said, and 'as Secretary General . . . I am not going to turn around and support a death penalty'. He clearly had in mind something resembling the Hague tribunal where the former Yugoslav head of state, Slobodan Milosevic is currently on trial.

This puts in perspective the uses of Saddam Hussein captured alive rather than dead by his own bullet or someone else's. Much moral indignation has been expressed all around, from Right to the Left, about Saddam's 'cowardice' in not killing himself instead of allowing himself to be captured. He probably is a coward; tyrants usually are. But that's not the issue. In eluding the Americans for eight months, on his own soil, despite all the American gadgetry which sees through mountains and oceans, Saddam has proved that even an individual, stripped of all his powers, can resist; and he can do so because he is among his own people. Second, corpses cannot speak for themselves, especially when enemies of the dead man have custody of the corpse; a living person has at least a chance of speaking, if he can survive the torture which Saddam is likely to be facing, now and in the months to come. Battle over the modalities of his trial shall keep alive the whole issue not only of his rights but also, crucially, of those who occupied his country barbarically and now hold him captive; he may have some rights, they have none, if the letter of international law is observed. Triumphant tyranny of imperial proportions putting on trial a local, broken tyrant who may yet tell the tale of the profound collusion between these two tyrannies, the American and the Ba'athist, can be a chastening drama for the world to watch. I would rather hope that the Americans fail to break Saddam's will entirely, and that in exposing himself he also manages to expose the crimes of his prosecutors who were for long his benefactors and then turned against him only when their own interests began colliding with his ambitions.

For that reason, there should be an international movement for the protection of Saddam's rights as a prisoner of war, his right to a lawyer, his right to immediate and continuing access to the Red Cross and other agencies which are internationally entrusted with the duty to make sure that prisoners of war are treated in accordance with the Geneva Conventions and the Hague protocols. We need a healthy, defiant Saddam in open court, for reasons not narrowly moralistic but profoundly political which are then subject to a much more complex understanding of public morality.

In the process, we should avoid two mistakes.

One, we should never trust the Anglo-American version of events. They say that Saddam was captured on the evening of 13th December 2003, that he had $750,000 dollars but not even a radio or any other communication equipment, that he had a loaded pistol which he did not use, that there were two AK-47 rifles and two men who tried to run away without using those rifles, that Saddam was living in what they call a 'spider hole' – and they have given gory, rather implausible details of the conditions in which he lived in and around that 'hole'. Maybe, maybe not; all of it may be true, or some of it, or none. Only time will tell, and that time may not come for quite a while.

Second, one ought not forget even a little of the sort of monster Saddam Hussein is and has been for over forty years. His career as an assassin – and an assassin of communists in particular – began early, and began, appropriately enough, with his killing in 1958 of a brother-in-law who was a communist. Before finally capturing him in 2003, Americans 'captured' him early, in 1959, when he was recruited into a squad to assassinate Gen. Kassem, the progressive anti-monarchist who was accused of being close to Iraqi communists (for the US, radical third world nationalism is 'communist' by definition). He participated in all the coup attempts between 1963 and 1968 which the US sponsored and the Ba'athists carried out, and in which the Ba'athists killed communists – based, in part, on information provided by the CIA. After the last of these coups, in 1968, which led to continuous Ba'athist power until 2003, Saddam took charge of internal security and created the institutional framework of the dictatorship; the question of Israel was the only point of friction between the US and the Ba'athists even though, unlike Syria or Egypt or even Jordan, Ba'athist Iraq never fought a war with Israel. For the rest, Saddam remained a close ally of the US upon whose promptings he invaded Iran in 1980, in a savage war which cost the two countries a million lives and in which the US-UK alliance supplied him with satellite photographs, equipment and weapons, including the capacity to manufacture chemical weapons (and use those weapons against Iran). The US turned against him only after he invaded Kuwait and threatened Saudi Arabia, the monarchies the US loves next only to Israel. If Mary Shelley were to write the story of the love-hate relation between the US and Saddam, she would probably call it 'Frankenstein and the Monster'.

Finally, how significant is the question of Saddam's arrest for the foreseeable future of the Iraqi resistance? The short answer is: not much. I wrote immediately after the capture of Baghdad, and I have never tired of saying, that the removal of the top echelon of the Saddam regime is a precondition for the real emergence of a national liberation struggle in Iraq. From inside the Iraqi army and the Ba'ath party, resistance was always more likely to come from the middle-ranking officers and the rank-and-file, not the predatory top. Equally important is the fact that most groups currently engaged in resistance seem not to have arisen from among even those elements; many are secular nationalists, leftists and Islamicists. Various groups either operate autonomously or cooperate for patriotic reasons, against a common enemy. Removal of even the pretence of a Saddam-led resistance is likely to facilitate greater convergence between these various groups and the Ba'athists now released from a charismatic relationship with a hidden leader. Many among the Shia who have been on the sidelines shall be less fearful of the restoration of the Saddam regime and may cooperate with the armed resistance more closely. Saddam was a symbol; his arrest shall demoralize some, energize others. In the meanwhile, the arrest of Saddam deprives the imperial occupiers of their last fig leaf. They gave all sorts of reasons for their invasion and occupation, all of which were transparently false; the very last one was that they were liberating Iraq from Saddam. Well, he is now in their custody. Why are they still in Iraq? And, as the resistance continues and grows, they can no longer pass it off as 'Saddam loyalists', Ba'athist 'remnants', etc. With Saddam in captivity and the occupation getting more and more ferocious, the emperor is naked – cannot find his clothes, not even his fig leaves.

Just as the US failed to garner even a semblance of backing in international law for its invasion of Iraq, it dare not put Saddam on trial in a court that has international jurisdiction. It has too may skeletons in its own closets. So, it will prefer to go on 'interrogating' and will then prefer to arrange for a quick trial and an even quicker execution. Donald Rumsfeld said on TV that Saddam shall be treated as a war prisoner and in accordance with the Geneva Conventions. Why then does he not have immediate Red Cross protection and access to legal aid? By what right does the US hold him in an undisclosed place while he gets infinitely 'interrogated' by CIA and Co.?

One of course wishes that the democratic forces in Iraq had managed to kill Saddam a long time ago; the world would have been the better for it. Under the circumstances, though, it is perhaps all for the good, possibly for the wrong reasons, that Saddam did not kill himself. And, as resistance to imperialism unites more and more Iraqis, real democratization of Iraq may yet come about in consequence of this invasion, not as a gift *of* the Americans, but in the form of a popular unity and uprising *against* them.

I

I firmly believed we should not march into Baghdad. . . . To occupy Iraq would instantly shatter our coalition, turning the whole Arab world against us and make a broken tyrant into a latter-day Arab hero . . . assigning young soldiers to a fruitless hunt for a securely entrenched dictator and condemning them to fight in what would be an unwinnable urban guerrilla war. . . . Furthermore, we had been self-consciously trying to set a pattern for handling aggression in the post-Cold War world. Going in and occupying Iraq, thus unilaterally exceeding the United Nations' mandate, would have destroyed the precedent of international response to aggression that we hoped to establish. Had we gone the invasion route, the United States could conceivably still be an occupying power in a bitterly hostile land.

Bush Sr., former President of the United States, in his 1998 book, A World Transformed, *on the Gulf War of 1991*

The United Nations served as an imprimatur for a policy that the United States wanted to follow and either persuaded or coerced everybody else to support. The Security Council thus played fast and loose with the provisions of the UN Charter.

Stephen Lewis, Canada's Ambassador to the UN at the time, about the Gulf War

Lesley Stahl: 'We have heard that a half million children have died [because of sanctions against Iraq]. I mean, that's more children than died in Hiroshima and you know, is the price worth it?'
President Clinton's Secretary of State Madeleine Albright: 'I think this is a very hard choice, but the price . . . we think the price is worth it.'

On American TV programme 60 Minutes *in May 1996*

II

Dear President Bush, I'm sure you'll be having a nice little tea party with your fellow war criminal, Tony Blair. Please wash the cucumber sandwiches down with a glass of blood.

*Harold Pinter, British playwright,
in an open letter published in* The Guardian

George Bush was not elected by a majority of the voters in the United States, he was appointed by God.

*General Jerry Boykin, Deputy Undersecretary of Defence for intelligence,
in charge of facilitating intelligence information for
Donald Rumsfeld's 'High Value Target Plan', aimed at hunting down
Saddam Hussein, Osama bin Laden, and Mullah Omar*

[President George W. Bush is] the greatest threat to life on this planet that we've most probably ever seen.

Ken Livingston, Mayor of London

And, before it is all over, democracy, noble and delicate as it is, may give way. . . . Indeed, democracy is the special condition that we will be called upon to defend in the coming years. That will be enormously difficult because the combination of the corporations, the military and the complete investiture of the flag with mass spectator sports has set up a pre-fascist atmosphere in America already.

Norman Mailer, American novelist

Fascism should more properly be called corporatism, since it is the merger of state and corporate power.

Benito Mussolini, founder of Italian fascism

III

You call Donald Rumsfeld and tell him our sorry asses are ready to go home.
*Pfc. Matthew C. O'Dell, a US infantryman serving in Iraq,
as quoted in* New York Times, *June 15, 2003*

We lack the metrics to know if we are winning or losing the global war on terror.
*US Defence Secretary Donald Rumsfeld,
in a confidential memo, 16 October 2003*

The message is that there are known knowns, there are things that we know that we know. There are known unknowns that is to say, there are things that we now know we don't know. But there are also unknown unknowns . . . things we do not know we don't know. And each year we discover a few more of those unknown unknowns.
*Donald Rumsfeld, on why US charges against Saddam
turned out to be false*

IV

The trumped up reasons for going to war have collapsed. All the Administration's rationalizations as we prepared to go to war now stand revealed as 'double-talk'. The American people were told Saddam Hussein was building nuclear weapons. He was not. We were told he had stockpiles of other weapons of mass destruction. He did not. We were told he was involved in 9/11. He was not. We were told Iraq was attracting terrorists from Al Qaida. It was not. We were told our soldiers would be viewed as liberators. They are not. We were told Iraq could pay for its own reconstruction. It cannot. We were told the war would make America safer. It has not. . . . Before the war, week after week after week after week, we were told lie after lie after lie after lie.
US Senate Statement by Senator Ted Kennedy

Every ten years or so, the United States needs to pick up some small crappy little country and throw it against the wall, just to show the world we mean business.
Michael Ledeen, holder of the Freedom Chair at the American Enterprise Institute

You've got to go where the oil is.
US Vice President Dick Cheney

After all, this is the guy [Saddam Hussein] who tried to kill my dad.
President George W. Bush, at Houston, September 26, 2002

I

5 DECEMBER 2003
In Lieu of an Introduction

I had arrived in Toronto three days earlier and was now sitting in a physician's chair, struggling with bad sinuses, when he came in, pale and hysterical, to announce that the Third World War had begun. 'They are bombing New York', the physician was shouting. I was stunned, but also puzzled. 'Who are *"they"*?' I asked. He couldn't tell. I thought he had taken leave of his senses and tried to joke: 'Is it Putin? Not the Israelis, surely?' But he was to be neither cajoled nor consoled, and we decided amicably that my sinuses could wait. I noticed mayhem in the corridors and rushed back to where I was staying. I tried to call a close relative who lives in New York – at home, then in her office – but could not get through; tried to call friends in New York, with no more luck; in desperation I even tried calling the New York Police. Frustrated, I turned on the TV and began seeing the Twin Towers of the World Trade Centre crumble and fall, enveloped in gigantic flames, again and again, in a ritual repetition of the ghastly event as one seasoned commentator after another did their best to invest the event with apocalyptic significance, assuring us that this was the biggest attack on mainland USA since Pearl Harbor. It was 11th September 2001.[1]

That analogy with Pearl Harbor must have been repeated

[1] The text of this introductory piece is essentially narrative. A wealth of factual detail has been relegated to very ample footnotes.

4 / Iraq, Afghanistan and the Imperialism of Our Time

a couple of hundred times that day, until it sank into every American's consciousness, deeper than any conscious thought.[2] And that bold caption 'Attack on America' (with variants, viz. 'America under Attack', 'War on America') which had been put there quickly, with deliberate precision, just stayed on the TV screen for days on end. I did not then know that the US government itself had jammed most of the phone links to New York for security reasons, so I kept dialling for some hours. Some dear ones lived in that city, and I knew some who even worked in the World Trade Centre, so I could feel my own very personal hysteria rising alongside the political fear of the manner in which the US was likely to eventually retaliate with characteristically excessive zeal and brutality. It was only later, when the phone links had been fully restored, that I found out that the son of a dear friend had been on the 92nd floor of the blasted Towers that day and that the daughter of another close friend had survived only because she had an early morning appointment elsewhere in the city and was still about a hundred yards away when the building she was planning to enter got hit, caught fire and starting crumbling.

For that one day at least, the TV was one's only effective interlocutor, as tragedy was predictably turned into spectacle. At

---

[2] I was to later read 'Rebuilding America's Defences: Strategy, Forces and Resources' of September 2000, the key document of the chief neoconservative think-tank, Project for a New American Century (PNAC) which was authored by a group which at that time included Richard Perle and Paul Wolfowitz, who were to then emerge as chief strategists at the Pentagon under Bush. In that document the authors contend that the kind of radical changes in US strategy they were proposing may take some time to unfold unless hastened by 'some catastrophic and catalyzing event, like a new Pearl Harbor'. This analogy was revived recently by none other than Gen. Tommy Franks, who led the US assault on Iraq in March and was now quoted as saying that another 'Pearl Harbor type event' would lead to 'militarization' of the US at home, transforming the nature of the US Constitution itself.

the centre of the Spectacle was of course the visual image of the unspeakable horror itself, backed by horrific numbers of the dead: starting with an estimate of 20,000 and only gradually coming down to roughly 8,000. (The estimate came down to 5,000–6,000 over the next couple of days, and it took some weeks to establish that the actual number of the dead was below 3,000 – a terrible toll but much less than what was initially feared.) I noticed that the TV channel of the Canadian Broadcasting Corporation (CBC) that I was watching had virtually ceased to do its own job and had given it all over to CNN, and soon enough, various voices from Europe – Britain, France, Germany – were being heard, saying something like 'in this hour we have all become Americans'. So, one had the distinct sensation of being witness to the ingathering of the Euro-American world into something of a tribal solidarity, against the numerous enemy suspects who were also being named again and again: Iran, Libya, Iraq, the Lebanese Hizbollah, the Afghani Taliban – and with astonishing frequency, in those early hours, the Palestinians. I remember the jolt I felt when three different commentators named – most implausibly – the Popular Front for the Liberation of Palestine (PFLP) as a likely culprit. One simply didn't know which way, and to what lengths, the US would now go.

The World Trade Centre was surely the symbol of imperial trade and finance. Yet, I kept wondering what 'America' it was that was 'Under Attack'. As one who had often visited those Towers, I knew that most of the menial work there was done by undocumented workers and poor immigrants, mainly from Latin America. As a South Asian, I knew that large numbers of the young professionals who worked in those offices were from this region, which inevitably included large numbers of Muslims from Pakistan and Bangladesh, and of course a large number of Indians some of whom were also Muslims. In addition, there were also

6 / Iraq, Afghanistan and the Imperialism of Our Time

Muslim Arabs, Malaysians, Indonesians, and Africans working in various trade offices and financial enterprises in those Towers. Death had been merciless, caring neither for race nor religion as thousands perished. Yet, one was caught between two streams of one's own consciousness. The public, official discourse I was hearing was one of a 'Clash of Civilizations' between barbaric Islamic fundamentalism and the Americo-Occidental democratic societies, unmindful of the demographic variety among the dead. Privately, as a South Asian with some social links with Middle Eastern and Southeast Asian groups in New York, I was viscerally, mournfully aware of how many of *us* had died and that many of those dead were also Muslims. My friend's son who disappeared in that ball of fire was a Muslim, indeed a Pathan (secular, modern, professionally brilliant but no less a Pathan than the Taliban). I soon came to know of a residential community of Pakistanis outside Princeton, in New Jersey, where most parents worked in offices of the Twin Towers and where dozens of children became orphans that morning. Still later, I also came to hear of those undocumented workers from South and Central America who had worked and died in those Towers but whose families could not come forward to claim their dead because, in that case, they would be identifying themselves as illegal aliens subject to deportation. The class complexity which had brought together all these diverse people in the World Trade Centre, from some of the richest white men in America in the top floors to the undocumented menial workers in the basements, was a mirror image of corporate globalization under US hegemony.

There were further complications in one's own affective response. Thousands had been killed in the middle of one of the world's great cities in a matter of minutes, in an act of terrorism that was morally hideous and was likely to be infinitely more dire in its consequences. Yet, I also thought: how lucky, how unique –

and therefore how uniquely incapable of taking the measure of its own tragedy in a historical perspective – America is – that it has had the power to destroy other people's cities but has been so safe from external attack that the destruction of two majestic buildings can be plausibly presented as the greatest attack on mainland America (the comparison with Pearl Harbor was in the literal sense inaccurate, since that was not a part of the mainland but an offshore base). One did not even have to think of the centuries-long colonial history of the destruction of cities across continents. One could only begin with the Second World War: Nagasaki and Hiroshima on the one hand, Dresden and other European cities on the other. And my own generation has of course lived through the bombings of Hanoi, the destruction of Beirut by the Israelis, the American bombings of Baghdad in 1991 well before 2003. Criminality is not a commercial proposition, and the tragedy of that day does not become any less because others, in other cities, have been at the receiving end of far greater barbarity. Even so, modern America's unique privilege of having caused death and destruction in great many cities around the world without its own cities ever having been attacked by an external power makes it uniquely incapable of a response that is restrained and symmetrical. Even retail terror of small groups of zealots must be met with the whole blast of imperial fury and bloodlust, lest the US be seen as 'weak'.

Two days passed, and the US bombed no one. I walked around with a knot in my stomach. I remember saying to a friend on the morning of the 13th that the longer the US takes to start bombing, the more numerous the targets are going to be, and there shall be not pools but rivers of blood.

I had not understood even then what was coming.

II

On 14 September 2001 the Senate of the United States voted 98-0 in favour of a war resolution that said, in part: 'The President is authorized to use all necessary and appropriate force against those nations, organizations, or persons he determines planned, authorized, committed, or aided the terrorist acts that occurred on September 11, 2001, or harboured such organizations or persons, in order to prevent any future acts of international terrorism against the United States by such nations, organizations or persons.'

This resolution was historically unprecedented and its wordings shall therefore bear some scrutiny. First, an attack which was *not* carried out by any 'nation' but by persons who had all died in the course of the attack was nevertheless used to authorize war not only against 'organizations or persons' but also 'nations'. Second, the US Constitution endows the Senate with ultimate war-making powers and therefore the President is required to seek its permission before declaring war upon another country. In this resolution, however, the Senate, voting unanimously, surrendered its own powers, for an indefinite period of time, to the unique determination by the President alone to make war as and when he pleases, and as many wars as he pleases. Second, in an unprecedented move, it was a resolution authorizing war without naming the country upon which war is to be made; indeed, it speaks of 'nations', in the plural – all the nations of the world, if the President so determines. Third, war upon 'nations' was authorized not only in response to attacks that occurred but also to *prevent* any *future* attacks. Now, in the strict interpretation of international law, such as it is, no member of the United Nations is to make war upon another sovereign nation which is also a member of the UN without authorization from the Security Council;

maintenance of peace is a *collective* responsibility. Beyond this, there undoubtedly also is a doctrine of *pre-emptive* war where a nation may make war in self-defence against a palpable, immediate and demonstrable threat of attack by another nation. By contrast, the resolution of the US Senate authorized the President with the perpetual right to make war not to *pre-empt* an immediate and demonstrable threat but even to *prevent* the potential emergence of such a threat at some point in the future. By this logic, Pakistan may invade India any day on the pretext that India *has* the power to attack it and therefore *may* attack it; destruction of Indian military power would thus be, on this view, a priority for the national security of Pakistan whether or not there is any demonstrable evidence that India intends to carry out such an attack. The historically novel doctrine of *preventive war* which the Bush Administration was to unveil with such fanfare a year or so later was in fact already contained in that resolution *and all the Senators from the Democratic Party, without exception, had voted in favour of this resolution*. In other words, this doctrine of preventive wars on a global scale is a bi-partisan, consensual doctrine in contemporary America, and by no means the handiwork of only the neoconservatives, Straussians and the like.

That so sweeping a resolution, so sure of its intent to facilitate a generalized global war, could be presented so quickly (mere three days after the events) and get passed so much without debate or opposition was at least very extraordinary, as if preparations had all been there for an appropriate occasion to arise. George W. Bush's elevation to the US Presidency by the decision of the Supreme Court to stop the re-count of the deeply flawed ballots in the state of Florida (where his brother, Jeb, *happened* to be Governor) and thus award him the White House, had even then felt like a judicially-sanctioned *coup d'etat*. Now, the events of 11 September were deliberately used to generate a mass psychology of permanent fear and to unleash the most hysterical kind of atavistic patriotism. This heady brew of fear and retributive bloodlust was then used to get unanimous consent of the Senate to give to Bush historically unprecedented power of monarchical proportions. Observing all this, one had the distinct feeling that the destruction of the Twin Towers was being used here on the model of the burning of the Reichstag in Germany.[3] That impression was further strengthened by the fact that the US Attorney General Ashcroft, an Evangelical fundamentalist who is given to opening his morning meetings with a Christian prayer, soon started proposing far-reaching legislation to perfect a regime of infinite surveillance and arbitrary incarceration within the United States which would dramatically reduce the scope of the civil liberties traditionally available to the US citizenry, and some of which came to be incorporated in the Patriot Act which too was passed with equally unseemly haste.

That Senate resolution was in any case the first public indication of the scope of war(s) being contemplated. We did not then know that on the morning of 12 September itself, Condoleeza Rice, the National Security Advisor to the President, had assembled her staff to consider how the US could 'take advantage' of this 'opportunity' (strange how the tragedy of so many thousands was in the mind of this upstart billionaire an 'opportunity'!). Nor did

[3] We speak here of the way the events of 11th September were *used,* without any implication that the US government in general or the Bush party in particular *caused* those events to occur. There is reason to believe, though, that Mossad, the Israeli intelligence service, knew something of what was going to happen and some of its agents were found photographing it all from a New Jersey parking lot. What the Mossad knew and whether or not Mossad passed on the information to the appropriate US agencies remains unclear. The Bush Administration has assiduously refused to allow an independent, bi-partisan commission of inquiry – an independent Prosecutor, for example – to look into those events from all aspects. A magnificent collection of articles challenging the US government's account of events can be found at < http://www.globalresearch.ca/articles/NAC304A.html>.

we know that on the same day Donald Rumsfeld, the US Defence Secretary, had argued in a favour of an immediate attack on Iraq, together with Afghanistan, or that the Secretary of State Powell had with difficulty persuaded the President and his cabinet that the two countries should be attacked not simultaneously but in succession, one after the other, because Afghanistan was an easy target while an immediate attack on Iraq would be difficult militarily and hard to justify to allies diplomatically. Only on 12 January 2003, some fifteen months after the fact, did the *Washington Post* report that 'On Sept. 17, 2001, six days after the attacks on the World Trade Center and the Pentagon, President Bush signed a 2½-page document marked "TOP SECRET" that outlined the plan for going to war in Afghanistan as part of a global campaign against terrorism. Almost as a footnote, the document also directed the Pentagon to begin planning military options for an invasion of Iraq.'[4]

By 20th September that Senate Resolution had been translated into a full-scale Presidential policy and a strategic vision of national purpose, as Bush enunciated it on that day in an address to the joint session of the US Congress. 'Every nation in every region has a decision to make', Bush said, 'either you are with us, or you are with the terrorists.' In some respects, this was a re-statement of a long-standing US position, succinctly enunciated by John Foster Dulles, Eisenhower's Secretary of State, during the 1950s: 'non-alignment is immoral.' But the warning was much more extreme: any country that does not actively concede to US demands, whatever they may be, shall be deemed a friend of terrorists and shall meet the same fate: 'regime change', 'dead or alive', and so on. The Afghan government, he said, must 'hand

---

[4] As we point out elsewhere in this book, Niaz Naik, the ranking Pakistani diplomat, was to soon say on BBC that American diplomats had in fact told him in *July* that an attack on Afghanistan was scheduled for October, which is exactly when it came. 11 September was just the peg on which to hang that invasion.

over every terrorist and every person in their support structure'; and 'they will hand over the terrorists or they will share in their fate'. Collective punishment was now an immutable article of policy, and *states* could be objects of invasion in punishment for actions undertaken by *persons* who are not even nationals of that state, while it was the exclusive prerogative of the US to decide who was or was not a 'terrorist' and what constituted their 'support structure'. Moreover, this 'war on international terrorism' was going to be permanent ('a task that never ends '), global (to be waged in 50 or 60 countries) and largely covert and invisible. Incongruously, Afghanistan was immediately declared to be the object of such a war even though the US itself had claimed that the majority of those who had carried out the 11 September attacks were Saudi nationals and none of them was an Afghan; nor was there even a shred of evidence that they had either come from Afghanistan or had acted upon direction of the Taliban government there.[5]

This declaration of permanent, global, largely invisible war *in* and *upon* other sovereign states in retribution for an act of terror carried out by a group of private citizens – coupled with the intent to invade Afghanistan immediately even though none

[5] The excuse was that Osama bin Laden had ordered the attacks while residing in Afghanistan. The Taliban government asked for evidence so that he could be legally extradited. When the US kept refusing to offer any evidence (the US intelligence agencies were to report that there really was no evidence of Osama's personal culpability that could stand up in a court of law), they offered to give Osama over to the custody of the Organization of Islamic Conference (OIC) which is comprised of 52 members of the United Nations. The US refused the offer. A variety of Pakistani political leaders and diplomats then got the Taliban government to agree that Osama would be sent to Pakistan to stand for trial there. President Musharraf of Pakistan turned down the offer under US pressure. The US demand that the whole 'support structure' be surrendered was impossible to grant, since no proportions of that 'structure' were ever specified. That same pattern of refusing peace overtures was then repeated with respect to Iraq as well. According to interviews and documents obtained by James Risen of the

of the perpetrators of that crime was either an Afghan national or known to be acting upon orders from the Afghan government – was so disproportionate that it could not seriously be considered a response to the events of 11 September. What was being announced, rather, was a radical 'Re-Mapping of the Globe' (as the second of my articles on the subject put it) so as to re-define and re-furbish the mode of American imperial dominance. A salient feature of this design was that the '50 or 60' countries where this war was to be waged, and which would thus be considered a threat to US security, were of course never named but did not evidently include any of the past or potential rivals: the EU, China, Russia, Japan. Rather, it envisioned exclusive monopoly over the (expanded) imperial realm itself, i.e. the less powerful countries of the Afro-Asian land mass, with centrality accorded to the Middle East (as usual) and the Caspian Basin countries (a new strategic interest), while a shifting number of countries from the Southern Hemisphere and the Caribbean could doubtless be thrown in, here and there, as need be. Securing the realm, with all its insurgencies but also its critical resources (notably oil, but also markets including the labour market), was an end in itself; neoliberal globalism was to be supplemented and sustained by globalized militarism. But this monopoly over the imperial realm was also designed, indirectly, to checkmate potential rivals: Russia in the

---

New York Times, Imad Hage, a Lebanese-American intermediary with important contacts in the Pentagon and Middle East, met with top Iraqi intelligence officials in Beirut and Baghdad last February, as the US was gearing up for an invasion. Hage said they asked him to communicate to the US that the Saddam Hussein regime, desperate to avoid conflict, was prepared to offer oil concessions to the Americans, assist in the Mideast peace process, open the country to inspection 'by 2,000 FBI agents', hold elections within two years, and hand over a leading suspect in the 1993 bombing of the World Trade Centre. Hage then met with Richard Perle, one of the chief ideologues of the Bush administration and member of the Advisory Board at the Pentagon, in London in early March. Risen says that Perle concedes that it was a 'quite astonishing proposal' which he nevertheless did not pursue – on the advice of the CIA, he says!

Caspian basin for example, or all other potential rivals in terms of their dependence for supplies of oil from precisely the regions that the US was now to set to dominate to an unprecedented degree, as something of a private monopoly.[6] Primary enemies were also chosen from that perspective. Saudi Arabia was neither part of an 'axis of evil' nor a target for 'regime change' precisely because the Saudi monarchy has been rolling around in America's pocket for quite some time and has happily hosted US bases in the kingdom.[7] Nor was Kuwait a candidate for democratic change and human rights expeditions; rather, the dynastic rule of the

[6] China has now become the second largest importer of crude oil, relegating Japan to second position. The US is the largest importer but also controls most of the oil-producing regions and is determined to control the rest. Russia is the only major power which is self-sufficient in oil. An economic alliance between Russia and EU is feasible, in that Russian oil could be exchanged for European technology. However, the existence of a US-dominated NATO which is currently getting expanded up to the Russian border itself pre-empts that possibility, considering that Russia can hardly have such a close *economic* relationship with the EU while the EU cooperates with the US in so aggressive a *military* posture toward it. Russia is likely to favour, instead, the emergence of an independent European military force, as is increasingly advocated by the Franco-German alliance. That day too is a long way away, however. The EU as a whole spends less than half of what the US spends on the military, and its actual military capability amounts to perhaps not more than 10 per cent of the US capability because of equipment duplication, incompatibility of weapon systems among various countries of the EU, over-all much lower technological levels and R&D allocations – not to speak of the fact that Britain, the major European military power alongside France, is and be likely to remain much more integrated into the US military design than the envisioned European one. Meanwhile, the US is ensuring that the ex-Warsaw Pact countries which are joining the EU get integrated much more into NATO, under US umbrella, than into the Franco-German alliance. An independent European military force is envisioned in any case not as alternative to NATO but as autonomous supplement.
[7] Bush the First, George W.'s father, lied to King Saud in 1990 by showing doctored satellite photos which purported to prove that Saddam Hussein had massed 250,000 troops and 1,500 tanks on the Saudi border. Russian satellite photos taken at the same time, however, showed that there were no troops or tanks – only empty desert. Saudis nevertheless agreed to host 500,000 US troops for the so-called 'Operation Desert Storm' during the Gulf War of 1991.

Sheikhs was restored there by the US Armed Forces. Iran and Iraq were nevertheless two-thirds of the 'axis of evil' because their mineral resources were not directly controlled by the US (controlled only through market and currency mechanisms) and because they had diversified their relations among the advanced industrial countries.[8] North Korea was the remaining third of that 'axis' because it was quite capable of giving its nuclear technology know-how to other aspirants of freedom from US domination. And Afghanistan was to be had anyway, as a bridgehead toward the Caspian.

III

Such was my reading of Bush's speech of 20 September 2001 when, two days later, I wrote the first of the seventeen essays which were published in *Frontline* over the next two years. Twelve of those are included in this book, the last one having been drafted in mid-August 2003. Afghanistan was occupied swiftly, in October 2001. Full-scale invasion of Iraq came roughly a year and a half later, in March 2003. The invading forces of the United States and the United Kingdom encountered much heroic resistance in towns on the way but Baghdad itself fell equally swiftly, partly because some key elements in the defence of Baghdad shifted their loyalties but also because the defence of a capital city through conventional means, by an army already battered by eight years of warfare and twelve years of sanctions, and in the face of the kind of military

---

[8] One thinks now of Iran mainly in terms of religion: Islamic revolution, Islamic terrorism, mullahs, fundamentalism, Shi'ites *vs*. Sunnies, and so on. One forgets that it is a key oil-producing country, that its gas reserves are second only to Russia's, and that it claims 20 per cent of oil resources of the Caspian Sea basin where it is in conflict with some other Caspian littoral states, notably Azerbaijan, upon which the US is currently busy establishing its economic and military stranglehold.

technology the US now commands, was simply unfeasible. It is simply a fact that the US today is faced with no credible rival with a remotely comparable economic and military resource; it therefore has no *external* check on the exercise of its power. With a $10 trillion economy at its disposal it can easily allot, let us say, $200 billion dollars to active warfare per year, and use even that sum as a kind of Keynesian injection to boost its own economy. It spends more on its military than the next dozen countries combined, commands over a hundred military bases of its own around the globe as well as active consent of the majority of the governments in the world, and has more sophisticated, more destructive military technology and weapon systems than any imperium in human history has ever known. This power renders obsolete the very modes of warfare that were the norm until recently: large conventional armies, duels in the air, street-fighting in the cities. However much the Iraqi Resistance grows, it is most unlikely, so long as there are 100,000 US troops there, that the Resistance shall undertake the type of battalion and brigade strength attacks that the Vietnamese communists launched during the Tet Offensive of 1968, to occupy and hold dozens of cities and towns, in the face of half a million US troops.[9] Not to understand this is to not face up to how difficult it is for a coherent resistance to emerge, nor to comprehend how very devastating that power can be for its victims, not here or there but routinely. The US has already dropped over two thousand tons of depleted uranium on Iraq, which will result in disease and death on a huge scale over the years and decades to come. Even today, as I write these words, the US is raining down 500- and even 900-pound bombs on little hideouts of the Iraqi Resistance.

However, there are severe limits to this power when it

[9] The US Army has announced that it is preparing to have as many as 100,000 troops in Iraq even in 2006.

comes to fighting on the ground, against decentralized units and individuals equipped with small arms, spread over large expanses of territory, in the midst of populations which are sympathetic to the insurgency so that, in Mao's memorable phrase, the guerrilla lives among the people much as fish swims in water. The US faced such a situation in Vietnam and they set out, in their own inversion of Mao's metaphor, 'to drain the sea so as to catch the fish'; but they eventually failed, even though they had subjected that country to a degree of devastation whose effects are still palpable, a quarter century later, and shall undoubtedly last for decades to come. Something similar is now developing in at least the so-called 'Sunni triangle' in Iraq, though not – at least not yet – in the Shia east and the Kurdish north which remain largely quiescent or are actively pro-American (especially the two main Kurdish forces). If the forty or so disparate organizations which currently make up what we cumulatively call 'the Iraqi Resistance' can coalesce into something of a National Liberation Front, and if they can include substantial elements of the Shia and the Kurds, that same fate awaits the Americans in Iraq which they encountered in Vietnam.

The Iraqi resistance has so far taken a predictable form. In the article I wrote immediately after the fall of Baghdad ('Wars Yet to Come'), I had argued that far from being the end of the war, it was actually the beginning of the real war (until then there had been only an invasion and heroic but hapless defence of outlying towns); that removal of the upper echelons of the regime, military as well as civilian, was a precondition for the emergence of a new form of resistance that would be led by middle and lower levels of the armed forces and the Ba'ath party; that it will have the support of the Iraqi masses among whom hatred of occupation runs deep and who would want revenge for the unspeakable sufferings they have undergone owing to the regime of sanctions and bombardments mandated by the Security Council and enforced by the US for over a decade even prior to the 2003 invasion. All of that has come to pass. Initially, during the first days and weeks after the occupation of Baghdad, effective resistance was largely confined to central Iraq even though there already were sporadic reports of fighting elsewhere as well, notably Mosul and Basra. By now, in early December, some forty per cent of the attacks, including some of the most spectacular ones, are taking place outside this region, even though the US disinformation agencies continue to claim that risistance is confined to Sunnis only. The overall picture remains confused and unstable, however. Most influential elements among the Shia in southern Iraq have so far stayed away from the armed resistance and many have actively cooperated with the client group that the US has foisted upon Iraq as its 'Governing Council', possibly in keeping with advice from Iran, in the hope that the US shall devise some formulae that will eventually pave the way for takeover by them. It would be of course incorrect to say that no substantial numbers of the Shia have participated in the resistance or have welcomed the Americans. The teeming poorer suburbs of Baghdad itself are overwhelmingly Shia and resistance activity there has been intense. Shia-Sunni cooperation in this political as well as military resistance has been in evidence from the beginning, while no sign of serious Shia-Sunni friction has emerged so far, and *hatred* of the occupiers seems common among both religious communities. The alarming fact, however, is that some of the more militant among the Shia clergy whose followers have been part of the resistance are beginning to tone down their rhetoric, cooperate with the Americans and obviously waiting to see if the emerging dispensation shall be satisfactory to them.[10]

[10] Reports in late November suggest that Moqtada al-Sadr, a younger cleric with a large following, especially in the Shia suburbs of Baghdad, who had militantly endorsed the resistance, had now suddenly abandoned the stance and announced

Nor is there much evidence of widespread resistance among the Kurds. Over a decade or more of sanctions and no-fly zones, the Anglo-US forces had sought to create something of a Kurdish protectorate while taking the two major Kurdish parties/militias under their wing. The entry of Turkish troops into Iraq might have led to Kurdish disaffection and even insurrection but that has been effectively circumvented by the decision not to deploy Turkish troops within Iraq's present borders. Resistance in the northern city of Mosul has been substantial since the invasion itself, and recent weeks have seen rapid growth in the number of resistance attacks as well as US casualties there. However, Mosul and its environs have substantial Arab Sunni population and the resistance appears to be concentrated mainly among them; whether or not any substantial number of Kurds are participating in the resistance remains unclear. All over Iraq, the Americans are busy playing the

---

his decision to work cooperatively with the Americans. Pressures that brought this about remain unclear. Nor is it clear whether or not all his followers shall now also make such a stunning about-turn. As regards the very intricate matter of relations between Iraqi Kurds and Shias and Iran's role in that, Iran has been a long-standing supporter of Jalal Talabani's group, Patriotic Union of Kurdistan, in Northern Iraq, which has also enjoyed political and military backing from the US and is now a key component of the US-appointed Iraqi Governing Council. Talabani recently led a 10-member delegation of this bogus Council to Iran. In turn, President Khatami of Iran issued an astonishing statement which said, in part, 'We recognize the Iraqi Governing Council and we believe it is capable, with the Iraqi people, of managing the affairs of the country and taking measures leading toward independence'. Khatami then went on to explicitly endorse the latest US plan to 'transfer power' to a revamped avatar of this Council by June 2004: 'The consecration of this accord will help with the reconstruction and security in Iraq'. One could argue that Iran is conceding on a key issue only to avoid an invasion by the US, which is very much on the neoconservative agenda there. However, it is also the case that the clerical regime in Iran itself has a religio-sectarian view of the realities in Iraq and is hoping that the US would facilitate Shia power in Iraq, at the expense of the Sunni minority. For their own respective and quite divergent reasons, neither Bush nor Khatami seem to have much interest in building a secular Iraq over and above sectarian and communal differences.

ethnic/communal/sectarian card ruthlessly, even though it is not yet clear how far they will succeed.[11] In short, one cannot yet say whether the secular character shall get strengthened in the course of the resistance or shall fall apart owing to US machinations and in the course of the bitter fight over the spoils which is now shaping up as miseries of occupation mount, the welfarist state is dismantled, public services are made to fall apart, public assets are privatized, ruthless marketization pitches each against all, and the social cement that holds together the Iraqi society gets eroded.

Hovering above all of that are the UN, NATO, and that vicious, vacuous thing which is often referred to as 'the international community'. The role of the Security Council has been at best ignominious in imposing the horrific US-mandated sanctions upon Iraq and in acquiescing in the utterly illegal no-fly zones which the Anglo-US alliance maintained over large parts

---

[11] Shias account for roughly 55 per cent of Iraqi population and Arab Sunnis for 30-35 per cent, in addition to Kurds, Turkemens, Christians, Jews and some other minorities. In its political sensibility, however, Iraq remains overwhelmingly secular and non-sectarian, so that the western claims of any unbridgeable Shia-Sunni animosity are vastly exaggerated. Nor is it at all clear how widespread or decisive Irani influence is among the Shia, who remained overwhelmingly loyal to the Saddam regime during eight years of savage Iran-Iraq war. Anglo-US media never tires of referring to the Saddam dictatorship as 'Sunni rule'. It was a ruthless dictatorship but not particularly religious or sectarian; it oppressed Sunnis and Shias with equal fervour. Significantly, it was in cities and towns of predominantly Shia South – Nasseriyah, Basra, Karbala, Najaf – that the invading Anglo-American troops met with the toughest resistance; Baghdad, by contrast, fell fairly quickly. If a serious bid is now made to impose a sectarian or theocratic government on Iraq, and if any bloody conflicts between Shias and Sunnis now surface, this religious fundamentalism and bloodthirsty sectarianism will have been a gift of the Americans themselves. The US-crafted Governing Council itself is organized along these lines, and even Ahmed Chalabi, the convicted criminal, who currently heads the Council, is supposed to represent the Shias. This Council is comprised of 13 Shia members, five Sunni Arabs, five Kurds, one Christian, and one Turkemen. Never in the past has Iraq had a government based on this kind of sectarian/ethnic dispensation.

of Iraqi territory. The former UN Coordinators for Iraq, Dennis Halliday and Hans Von Sponek, both quit and publicly denounced the UN for facilitating genocide through those sanctions. (Brief summary of this UN-sanctioned genocide can be found elsewhere in the book.) It is also common knowledge that Kofi Annan had ordered the UN to begin coordinating for a postwar role with the US and the UK well before the invasion of March this year. On 16 October, in a unanimous vote which even Syria had to join under threat of invasion,[12] the Security Council awarded the Iraqi seat at the UN to the convict, Ahmed Chalabi, and said that it welcomes 'the positive response of the international community . . . to the broadly representative Governing Council . . . [and] supports the Governing Council's efforts to mobilize the people of Iraq . . .' This puppet regime handpicked by the US and UK was nevertheless

---

[12] The place of Syria in all this is complex. The Asad regime there and the Saddam regime in Iraq belonged to rival factions of the once-united Ba'ath party. Unlike all the Arab countries except Libya, Syria sided with Iran in the 8-year long Iran-Iraq war. Then, it sided with the US during the Gulf War of 1991 when the US restored the Sheikhs to Kuwaiti throne and bombed Baghdad itself. However, there is implacable hostility between Syria and Israel which occupies Syrian territory in Golan Heights. For that reason, it dominates Lebanon as a strategic interest, supports the Hizbollah there which fought for some twenty years against Israeli occupation of Southern Lebanon, and hosts a couple of Palestinian factions in Damascus, though not Hamas. For that same reason, the neoconservative cabal which dominates the Pentagon and defines policies and ideology of the Bush administration is bent upon invasion and occupation of Syria as well. After 11 September, Syria provided invaluable information on Al-Qaida to the US and even allowed the US intelligence to operate from the city of Aleppo near the Turkish border, thus earning warm praise and gratitude from the CIA, which infuriated Rumsfeld and his neoconservative cronies. That relationship ended with the US invasion of Iraq which Syria bitterly opposed and saw as a prelude of an invasion and occupation of its own territory. However, Syria is known to have turned down all attempts by elements of the old Saddam regime as well as of the new Iraqi resistance to seek refuge in Syria for fear of that invasion. Even so, in the early days after the fall of Baghdad, Rumsfeld and Co. felt confident enough to start threatening immediate military action against Syria, and the most prestigious newspapers and electronic media in the US and UK began disseminating the most preposterous disinformation about Syria: that

recognized as one that 'embodies the sovereignty of the Iraqi People'.[13] For its part, the Red Cross is the international body charged with ensuring the observance of the Geneva Conventions with regard to prisoners of war. It has said and done nothing about the 10,000 or more Iraqi prisoners being held by the US and UK in gross violation of the Third and Fourth Geneva Conventions, and it even refuses to say whether or not the prisoners are being held under conditions specified in those conventions, declaring it a 'confidential subject'. No wonder that the resistance targeted the head offices of both these organizations in spectacular bombing raids, so that both had to cease operations on Iraqi territory.

NATO has not only taken charge of military operations in Afghanistan, particular NATO countries (notably the UK, Spain and Italy) have a total of 24,000 troops on duty in Iraq, while NATO high command is also guiding the Polish contingent in Iraq itself. The UK has made it known that it envisions an eventual transfer of military responsibility ('peacekeeping' as it is

---

it is harbouring leaders of the fallen Saddam regime, holding 3 billion dollars of Iraqi money to finance resistance there, sheltering Iraqi weapons of mass destruction and developing chemical weapons of its own, etc. When Israel bombed Syrian territory near Damascus in October 2003, Richard Perle, a key neoconservative who is at once a member of the Defence Policy Board at the Pentagon and a member of the board of directors at the Israeli newspaper *Jerusalem Post*, said in a public address that he was 'happy to see the message [that] was delivered to Syria by the Israeli Air Force, and I hope it is the first of many such messages'. In the meanwhile, 'The Syria Accountability and Lebanese Sovereignty Restoration Act of 2003' has been making progress through the US Congress, getting readied for Presidential signature, on the model of the 'Iraq Liberation Act' of 1998 which was passed under Clinton and implemented by Bush.

[13] Interestingly, *Financial Times* reported on 21 November 2003 that two officials of the US-led Coalition Provisional Authority and the Minister of Communication in the Governing Council, Haider al-Abadi, are already being investigated by the Pentagon for taking bribes.

euphemistically called) to NATO there, and in a recent speech to the foreign ministers of NATO countries, Colin Powell thanked them for helping out the Poles and said that he envisioned a much larger role for NATO in Iraq.[14] The EU has explicitly endorsed the most recent US plans for the new political architecture of the puppet regime in Iraq, with the only proviso that the 'international community' be given a larger role, while the UN has announced that it will soon open a 'regional office for Iraq' somewhere in the vicinity, probably Jordan, and return in full force to Iraqi soil later. This new architecture is projected to be in place in June, and the regime which emerges from it is expected to 'invite' the US-UK forces to stay on to 'assist' with 'peacekeeping', as the US-appointed/EU-anointed Karzai regime in Afghanistan did after its appointment. The Security Council is then likely to endorse and legitimize all this, with full European cooperation and with Russia as well as China dragging their feet but coming along; it will probably change the status of the US-UK forces from 'Occupying Authority' to 'Allies' of Iraq and may issue a mandate to assemble an international force under the UN flag that would be 'led' by the US personnel but will open up space for European participation under the aegis of NATO. Bush can then go into the Presidential elections of November 2004 with the claim that his policies have been upheld by the 'international community' and that the burden of war itself shall now be shared with 'allies', with the promise that he will soon be bringing home most of the soldiers currently in Iraq. Re-elected on this platform, he shall then be free to

---

[14] We point out in one of the later articles in this book that NATO's assumption of command in Afghanistan is the first such action it has ever undertaken outside Europe and indicates a widening, globalized future for NATO as an auxiliary of US imperial mission. Since then, Japan and Korea have already resolved to send troops there, in what may be the embryonic formation of a global imperial army which shall routinely draw its personnel from diverse countries of the empire.

escalate within Iraq if need be, and to invade other countries if his gang so desires.[15]

That is the dream scenario that seems to be unfolding now. Whether or not the Iraqi Resistance can puncture it, or at least expose the enormous cynicism of it all, it is yet too soon to tell. All one can say with certainty is that this resistance has certainly halted the forward march of the US imperium. But for this resistance, US troops would now be in Damascus.

IV

In a high-level secret memorandum which was immediately leaked to the Press, the CIA has estimated that the strength of the Iraqi resistance already exceeds 50,000 and may well grow; it pessimistically recommends that the US should prepare for an 'End-game', i.e. a face-saving strategy for exit from an unwinnable war. By contrast, Rumsfeld and his hawks in the Pentagon keep referring to this resistance as 'remnants of the Saddam regime' and 'Saddam loyalists', which shall soon be defeated. They have sought to spread much disinformation about 'foreign fighters' and massive arms supplies being smuggled from Syria. The CIA has countered this by leaking assessments that Syria seems to have played no such role and that there is no evidence of any significant number of 'foreign fighters'; One such document says that 'at least 95 per cent' of these actions are mounted by the Iraqis themselves.

[15] The promise of bringing back the US troops from Iraq shall be a lie even to start with. The US is poised to undertake the largest troop rotation in history, whereby the 130,000 troops stationed in Iraq shall be brought back and replaced with a fresh batch of 110,000 or so. Leaves for large numbers of US military personnel are being cancelled and reservists getting called up from across the land. The US army has announced plans to have 100,000 troops in Iraq well into 2006. All this is creating a crisis of recruitment for the voluntary army as well as the Reserve corps, where far fewer people are coming forward to join as indefinite future wars loom on the horizon.

The killing or arrest of every important figure of that fallen regime is portrayed as yet another step toward the end of that resistance, which is supposed to culminate with the death or arrest of Saddam Hussein; CIA assessments suggest that Saddam, wherever he may be, is much too isolated to provide any command or leadership to the resistance, in which middle-ranking officers and the rank-and-file of the disbanded Iraqi army and the Ba'ath party are the key components.

On the ground, resistance has grown month by month. Bush announced 'victory' on 1 May. By July, the US troops were facing an average of 13 attacks a day, and by October this average had risen to 35 attacks a day. In sum, over four hundred US troops and close to a hundred 'allied troops' have died since the invasion began in March. Roughly a fifth of them, 104, died in November, which ended five days ago as I write this. In all, the US casualties in Iraq, including all those who have been disabled and evacuated, are estimated at roughly 9,000 – or seven per cent of the total US force in the country. The resistance began with small-scale, hit-and-run attacks; by now, the most sophisticated US helicopters have been downed in deadly missile attacks. In no Iraqi city can the US troops move about on foot; they can only move in speeding military vehicles, and some are known to have been lynched by angry crowds when their vehicles were ambushed. All the main symbols of the occupying forces in the heart of Baghdad – including the UN headquarters and the US high command offices – have been hit in spectacular attacks and with numerous casualties. The UN and the Red Cross have been forced to close down offices and flee; Spain, a vocal US ally which has even contributed troops, has had to close down its diplomatic offices in Baghdad. The US has appointed an Iraqi Governing Council which has then tried to appoint its representatives on provincial and district levels; more and more of these local collaborators are getting killed by the resistance. The US had dreamt that it would take hold of the oil wells and start pumping the oil, which would then offset the costs of the war; in reality, pipelines are being hit all over the country and little oil is allowed to flow. The US had undertaken to present the Security Council with a firm date by which an Iraqi constitution would be in place, which the Council accepted gladly without asking what sovereign Iraqi authority was there to give the country its constitution. Normally, a country can give itself a constitution only after the occupation forces have been evacuated and the country liberated; even the Shia clergy demanded that general elections be held and authority transferred to the elected representatives before a constitution can be written. The US rejected the demands of the clergy, reneged on its promise to set a date for the writing of a constitution and has come up with a new plan to 'transfer sovereignty' to a brand new body of 'representatives' without any general elections.[16] In other words,

[16] According to this plan, drawn up by the US and imposed upon a reluctant Governing Council which the US itself had appointed, the US shall supervise this Council in drafting a 'fundamental law' by mid-February which will serve as an interim Iraqi Constitution. This will then be followed by the formation of a 'national assembly' chosen in a series of provincial caucuses whose members shall also be nominated, not elected through a popular ballot. This so-called 'National Assembly' shall then select a 'Provisional Government' and power, such as it is, shall then be shifted from the current 'Council' to that 'Government', by July 2004. All this of course violates international law which forbids an 'occupying force' from altering the structure of the government and the legal structure of the occupied countries, as we explain below. In the meanwhile, constitution-writing, general elections, etc., are promised for 2005, i.e., after the US Presidential elections of November 2004. Considering that the UN Security Council has already recognized the US-appointed 'Council' as 'embodying the sovereignty of the Iraqi people', the so-called 'Provisional Government' which succeeds it shall doubtless be welcomed by the 'international community' as sovereign, democratic, etc.; the EU foreign ministers' meeting in Brussels immediately after the US announced this plan expressed its 'satisfaction' with that plan. Bush can go into the elections with the claim that even those of the allies who did not initially approve of the invasion have approved the 'progress' he has made in the 'democratization of Iraq'.

the resistance has made the country so ungovernable that the stooges who call themselves the Governing Council cannot govern, and the US has got so disenchanted with this set of clients that it is getting ready to replace them with another set of clients, with neither an election nor a constitution, while the US military occupation remains in place. This plan has been welcomed by the Security Council, the EU, President Khatami of Iran and many other components of the global state system which calls itself 'the international community'.

Included in this book is an article on 'Resistance in Iraq, Disarray in the US' which I wrote in August 2003. Over the next three months or so, this disarray has deepened and contradictions of policy can be seen even in the single fact that while the US government issues promise after promise of 'transferring sovereignty' to the Iraqi people in the course of 2004 the US Army is planning to maintain roughly the same size of the occupation army until at least 2006 – which, in effect, means indefinitely. As the casualties mount, the US clamours for troops from everywhere else and now even talks of bringing in NATO officially but cannot bring itself to cut the size of its own occupation force or to share command with its 'allies' because it does not wish to share the spoils of victory if and when victory comes. Meanwhile, it shifts from one set of clients to another and calls them Governing Council, provisional government or whatever, very much as it did in South Vietnam, and Baghdad is increasingly coming to resemble the Saigon of the 1960s and early 70s: huge shipments of consumer goods, truckloads of US dollars for the affluent and the servants of empire, a hostile population beset with fear and anger, resistance hitting from and disappearing into the shadows, an occupation army swaggering around with full battle gear in military vehicles and opening fire at will, the spiralling corruption of the clients tolerated by the imperial authority because clients is all that the empire has.

'Vietnamization' is being re-invented now as 'Iraqization'. This has two aspects. On the one hand is the 'architecture' of 'civilian rule' and 'transfer of sovereignty' to the Iraqis; in this Ahmed Chalabi serves as a resurrected Ngoh Din Diem, a passing crook of no historical significance. Alongside this is what Nixon eloquently called 'changing the colour of the corpses'. Rumsfeld claims that 100,000 Iraqi security personnel have been trained already and many more shall be in place soon, for policing purposes and as a nucleus of the future Iraqi army. Given that unemployment currently runs at 50 per cent or more, that many may well have enlisted and many more well might. But how do you train so many so fast, and how do you test their loyalty? These security forces are likely to be an explosive mix, however, comprised of: desperate innocents needing the money to feed their families and getting caught in the crossfire between 'government forces' (which they have joined) and the resistance (with which they may secretly empathize); macho mercenaries happy to get a uniform and a weapon to lord over whoever is at hand; and, quite possibly, considerable numbers from the resistance itself, to infiltrate the local outfits fronting for the occupiers. Mutual conflicts within these disparate ranks and between the Arab employees and the American overlords are likely. The US forces are already getting very bewildered at how much of their secret intelligence is getting passed on to the resistance; the larger Iraqi security force they assemble, the more often they shall face this situation.

The US is using this occupation to rapidly dismantle the entire institutional and legal structure of Iraq, with its nationalized oil, vast array of state-owned enterprises including most of the key industrial and infrastructural enterprises, extensive welfare systems and workers' rights, heavily subsidized educational and health services, and so on.[17] It is a counterrevolution of private property against state property, and neoliberal privatization against highly popular social ethics of state responsibility for general provision; and this counterrevolution is no less extensive than

[17] This is a subject too extensive to be covered satisfactorily in a brief aside. Just a few details shall indicate the scope of the changes under way. Bush announced 'victory' in May. In June, Paul Bremer, head of the provisional occupation authority, announced plans to sell off the country's state-owned industries and issued CPA order 39 in September announcing that 200 Iraqi state companies would be privatized; allowed foreign investors unrestricted rights to establish businesses in Iraq and/or buy up Iraqi companies, banks, mines and factories, owning them in full; and decreed that these foreign investors shall have the right to move 100 per cent of their profits, dividends, interest and royalties out of Iraq immediately and in full. All this, despite the fact that the Iraqi Constitution outlaws the privatization of key Iraqi state assets and bars foreigners from owning Iraqi firms. The US is signatory to the Geneva Conventions and the 1907 Hague regulations which spell out the obligations of an occupying power. Article 43 of the Hague regulations state that the occupying power must 'ensure, as far as possible, public order and safety, while respecting, unless absolutely prevented, the laws in force in the country' while article 55 describes the occupying power as only an 'administrator' of state property and specifies that 'It must safeguard the capital of these properties'. The UN Security Council's resolution of May 2003 which recognized the US-led 'coalition' as 'occupying powers' stipulated that they must 'comply fully with their obligations under international law, in particular the Geneva conventions of 1949 and the Hague regulations of 1907'. Even before that resolution, the British Attorney General, Lord Goldsmith, had written to Tony Blair as early as March 26, as the occupation was being completed and before any 'restructuring' could have been announced, that 'a further security council resolution is needed to authorize imposing reforms and restructuring of Iraq and its government'. Indeed, the US Army's own Law of Land Warfare says that 'the occupant does not have the right of sale or unqualified use of property'. One of Bremer's first actions was to disband the Iraqi army, a 'restructuring of Iraq and its government' which sent hundreds of thousands of soldiers immediately into unemployment, and all the subsequent orders he has issued in pursuit of privatization of state property and sale of Iraqi assets to foreigners violate the Iraqi constitution, the Geneva conventions and the Hague regulations, the UN Security Council resolution of May 2003 and even the US Army's own Law of Land Warfare. Thus it is that Jeffrey Sachs, the notorious US economist who supervised similar privatizations and sale of state property in Poland and elsewhere in Eastern Europe, himself says that 'We don't even have a legal standing to make the changes we are talking about'.

was the one in Russia after the fall of the Soviet Union. In Iraq, this counterrevoluton is being carried out not by a wing of the ruling party, as happened there, but by an occupation army of the country that has been widely perceived in Iraq for some generations with immense resentment, thanks to the US axis with Israel. In Iraqi eyes, Israel is an occupier of Arab lands and a historical anomaly – a racist settler colony half a century after the end of the colonial era – which would have collapsed long ago but for the enormous injection of weapons and funds from the United States. It is hard to imagine an Iraqi family which has not suffered directly and grievously from the US-imposed sanctions. The dismantling of the entire system of state ownership and widespread social provision by this sponsor of Israeli aggression in the Arab homeland, and one who imposed those sanctions on them directly, is producing an anger of volcanic proportions which the Americans, with their worship of the free market and their self-perception as embodiments of goodness, cannot comprehend. The resistance actually has to do rather little in order to touch the chord in the hearts of millions of people. *Organizing* those millions in a war of national liberation and creating a National Liberation Front which truly represents all segments of Iraqi society is of course an entirely different matter.

As of now, the US is fully committed to the territorial integrity of Iraq. Creation of a sovereign Kurdish state, or even a genuinely autonomous Kurdish republic within a confederated Iraq, would be vetoed by Turkey, one of its key allies in the region and within NATO, which hosts key US military bases on its soil. No one in the Euro-American world can forget that Turkey has the second largest army in NATO, next only to the United States itself, and that this army is not only as modern as any European army but also equipped with the most sophisticated weapons given to it by the US itself, as a frontline state against the USSR and now a strategic ally in the US ambitions in the Turkic zones of the Caspian as well. On the other hand, creating a sovereign Shia state in the east would not only greatly strengthen Iran, of which the US continues to be extremely wary, but would run counter to the ambitions of the Iraqi Shia elite itself; with the Shia solidly in the majority in Iraq, this elite wants to rule from Baghdad and have access to all the Iraqi resources, not be confined to an enclave of its own. However, the US is playing the ethnic/religious/regional card and shall continue to play it, in as extreme a form as necessary, in case it cannot defeat the resistance. Already, as the casualties mount, various formulae for trifurcated division of Iraq – among the Sunni, Shia, and Kurd – are being considered not only within the US administration but even openly, in such prestigious newspapers as the *New York Times*.

The European states shall be deeply unhappy, because being unhappy with American dominance is their existential lot. But they shall not oppose. First, because they do not have the power to oppose; as Mao wisely said 'Power comes out of the barrel of a gun' and the Europeans don't have comparable guns. Second, because they do share with their American cousins across the Atlantic – share in imagination if not in the real world of power politics – what Kipling politely called 'the White Man's burden'. The burden of colonizing and occupying. If the Americans can devise for it something that it can call 'legal' NATO shall be on its way.

V

In closing, a few words about the resistance.

No one quite believed me when I wrote two years ago, at the height of the US invasion, that resistance in Afghanistan shall re-emerge; that the Taliban had provided a level of security for the Afghan people which the earlier set of US clients, the so-called 'mujahideen', had not and which much of the populace cherished; that Afghans have never taken kindly to foreign occupation forces, as the British should have known from their own history of the three Afghan wars they fought; that those regrouped 'mujahideen', now called 'Northern Alliance' and again become favourites of the Americans, are a corrupt lot and the US shall yet live to regret bringing them back to power; and that Hamid Karzai, the so-called President of Afghanistan, is a nobody, a mere former employee of the US firm UNOCAL, who will stay in power only so long as the US Special Forces go on protecting his life and limb. Now, two years later, vast swaths of Afghan territory, virtually three-fourths of it, is too dangerous for the US and its NATO allies to operate in; Kabul is their enclave, and their prison. Nostalgia for the more recent Taliban rule is common among the conservative sections of society, nostalgia for the somewhat earlier phase of communist rule is equally common among the more modernized sections. Resistance is everywhere, and has the occupiers with their backs to the wall. Underneath that, warlordism dominates governance in the regions while poppy cultivation and heroin trade flourishes; warlords give their loyalty to whoever seems powerful in their own vicinity.[18] In the larger frame, one has to consider Pakistan. In strategic terms, Afghanistan is actually much more important for Pakistan than Kashmir. The fall of the

---

[18] Just one set of figures can demonstrate the bogus nature of the central government and, by comparison, the power of the regional strongmen and their militias. The national army being put together by the occupation forces is said to number not much more than 5,000. By contrast, the total number of personnel in the various private militias is estimated at close to 200,000 among whom some 50,000 are controlled by Ismael Khan alone, who finances his own regional setup by collecting customs duties at the Iranian border worth up to $ 800,000 a day. He is said to be in close touch with Hekmetyar, the former prime minister in the mujahideen government who is now collaborating with the Taliban for ousting the US and its allies in a war of slow attrition.

Taliban was a strategic loss, the return of the Northern Alliance a nightmare. Pakistanis acquiesced because they had no power to resist US pressure; Americans promised Musharraf that the Northern Alliance shall not occupy the cities and then swiftly reneged on that promise, allowed that occupation, allotted them the key ministries in the US-appointed Karzai government. Musharraf had taken that promise to his generals to get their consent; they felt insulted and betrayed when the US did not keep it. Pakistan dare not defy the new dispensation overtly; what it does covertly for the Afghan resistance is anybody's guess. In the meanwhile, it does not really matter, historically speaking, how long the Americans, NATO, etc. sit in Kabul; they have already lost the war and will leave sooner or later.

Throughout 2002, as the US got closer and closer to the invasion of Iraq, one kept hearing from Iraqi officials, directly and indirectly, that there would indeed be a defence of Baghdad but also that, in order to prepare for a long-term resistance in case of a full-scale occupation, arms and ammunition were being issued to a million or so Iraqis, with enough rations to last for six months. Since this was being said so openly one could not quite judge how true it was, and where the line was between real preparation and verbose propaganda. The figure of a million was credible, however, given the size of the Ba'ath party, most of which consisted of functionaries with no particular loyalty but which did also have a very large core of dedicated individuals; much of the top was corrupted by power machinations but much of the base was also known to be imbued with old-style patriotism, Iraqi and Arab. One also knew that unlike Afghanistan, much of Iraqi society was modern and capable of putting up a sophisticated resistance. If even a tenth of what one was being told was true – not a million but a hundred thousand, let us say – that was still huge, for a war of *resistance*. That gives us a rough parity between the US conventional forces and the potential guerrilla army. In that case the guerrilla wins, since he operates in a terrain hospitable to him but not to forces of occupation; this numerical equation and the hospitality of terrain, in the environment of a guerrilla war, neutralizes the technological superiority of the occupier. It is only the ideologically induced blindness of the ruling far right in the US which prevented them from understanding this simple arithmetic, even though many of their own professionals in their armed forces and intelligence services kept warning them.

What has the resistance achieved in purely military terms? It has demonstrated to the defeated Iraqi populace that it is possible to fight back. It has demonstrated to everyone its own capacity to hit the main symbols of the occupation army and its allies, in the heart of Baghdad. It has hit the Americans themselves, forcing them to change their tactics, their troops to get disgruntled and demoralized, and their media to constantly question the wisdom of the occupation itself; the kind of troop disaffection and domestic opposition that emerged during the Vietnam War only after about five years has emerged in the US within as many months – and the coffins are going home so regularly that the daily killing of an American soldier or two is now just taken for granted. Everyone knows there is a war: not remnants, but *war*; not 'Saddam loyalists' but *Iraqi resistance*. This resistance has changed even the vocabulary of American reporting, commentary, discussion. The resistance has successfully hit at allied institutions and countries; the UN, with its dastardly collusion with the US, has been forced to withdraw; coffins have been sent back to Britain, Spain, Italy, Poland, Japan, Korea. All the brave statements issued by chancellories of such countries notwithstanding, they are bound to start clamouring for a quick end to occupation; others are forced to reconsider committing their troops, and only just a couple of more months of this resistance is bound to (a) force the EU to reconsider its illusion that quicker transfer of power to a different set of clients will solve the problem, and (b) give a new breath of life to an active anti-war movement on the global scale.

This resistance has saved Syria from invasion and strengthened Iran's bargaining position. The bombing of the Jordanian embassy in Baghdad has put not only Jordan but every other country on notice with respect to their active collusion with the US; Jordan has been after all a significant base for Israeli-US operations against Iraq. The Iraqi resistance, if it continues, is bound to strengthen the anti-monarchical offensive in Saudi Arabia itself, forcing a crisis in relations between the kingdom and the US. The pro-US regimes in the region, notably Egypt, which have been warning the US that long-term occupation of Iraq shall undermine their own rule in their respective countries, can now make that argument with greater force. If the US continues with its remorseless offensive against Russia, as demonstrated recently in Georgia and in countries of the Caspian littoral, and if the Afghan resistance continues, Russia may consider adopting a more actively interventionist role, not just in relation to the resistance in Iraq and Afghanistan but also with respect to Syria and Iran which desperately need more sophisticated missiles which only Russia can provide. In short, a continuing Iraqi resistance is changing and can further change regional and global equations.

How far shall this resistance go? That's hard to tell, mainly because of lack of information about its inner dynamics, and partly because the future is always open and shall undoubtedly bring many surprises, for itself as well as its adversaries, and surely to us, the outsiders, as well. We have already pointed out that the resistance is rather limited among the Shia and especially the Kurds, who make up close to 70 per cent of the Iraqi population. A *national* resistance cannot emerge with so narrow a base. Nor is it clear what the proportions are between its base in the main institutions of the old regime – i.e., the Ba'ath party and the army – and the rest. We do know that there are upward of forty different distinct political groups operating, but this author cannot say with confidence what level and structure of coordination is there among them. Nor is it clear what ideological and organizational cement, other than loyalty to the old order and a very real patriotism, there is to weld so heterogeneous a resistance into a unified force; the passion to defend an independent past is understandable, but what sort of future for Iraq is envisioned? We do not know. That itself can only emerge from continued resistance.

We are living through an interregnum. History's most powerful imperium has committed itself to the occupation of a country it cannot pacify, dominate a population it cannot win over politically or morally. Resistance of historic proportions has surfaced against it, despite all odds, but we do not know what kind of society that resistance wishes to build in the future. The battle is joined, but does this resistance stand for restoration, or revolution? That is too soon to tell, and the nature of the resistance itself shall change with time, for better or worse. What is offered here is a mere book. The world shall change by the time it comes out in print, and the world shall keep changing. What is offered here is not a prediction about the future but an attempt to somewhat illuminate the past – and the present. As I said in the preface, this book is the record of how an observer, living mostly in Delhi, understood these momentous events as they unfolded – and an attempt, in the closing long essay at the end of the book, to understand the larger motion of the imperial history of our times in a more theoretical manner.

II

12 OCTOBER 2001
'A Task That Never Ends'
BUSH PROPOSES PERPETUAL WAR

The date of 11 September has a powerful resonance in the annals of modern history. Twenty-eight years ago on this date, in 1973, the CIA-sponsored coup of General Pinochet overthrew the democratically elected socialist government of President Allende and established a regime of terror which killed an estimated thirty-five thousand people in the first few weeks and continued to brutalize Chilean society for some two decades. 11 September was also the date of the Camp David Accords which signalled Egypt's final surrender to American imperialism and Israeli Zionism, putting the Palestinians at the mercy of the latter and leaving them without the backing of the one Arab country that could have posed a credible military and diplomatic challenge to Israel. And, 11 September was the day when George Bush, father of the current President of the United States, made his fateful speech to the US Congress announcing the war, the so-called Gulf War, against Iraq – that supreme act of terror which killed an estimated 200,000 people in the course of that brief assault and which has led to the death of at least half a million Iraqi children over the next decade, thanks to the US-dictated sanctions against their country.

Betrayal of the Palestinians, the destruction of Iraq! One can reasonably assume that these two great devastations of the Arabo-Muslim world were vivid in the memory of those hijackers on this year's 11 September, when they commandeered four civilian aircraft owned by two major US airlines, and smashed three of them into the World Trade Centre (WTC) and the Pentagon – famous nerve centres of US financial and military power – while committing a collective suicide in the process.[1] The White House – the seat of America's political power – was probably to be struck by the fourth aircraft but something in the hijackers' plan went awry.[2] Over 6,000 innocent civilians from 60 countries – some five hundred of them from South Asia alone, including the son of a close friend of the present writer – died within a couple of hours in an act of calculated, hideous act of terrorism carried out with stunning technical precision.[3]

Hiroshima and Nagasaki, with their 220,000 dead, are of course the most famous of the numerous cities that the United

---

[1] When this article was first published, some progressive US intellectuals took exception to this sentence, and to the paragraph as whole, claiming that I had simply taken American claims at face value. Since then, the Bush administration has indeed blocked all attempts to institute an impartial inquiry into the events of 11 September, so that what we know about those events still comes from claims of US intelligence agencies. My main assumption that this attack was carried out by the same forces which had been periodically attacking US targets elsewhere proved correct, however. I proceeded from that assumption from the beginning because no *political explanation* of September 11 was possible without seeing the cruelty of that act as a response – albeit a humanly intolerable and politically irrational response – to the accumulated cruelties perpetrated by the United States and Israel in the Arab world.

[2] The fact that the fourth aircraft crashed – probably shot down by the US – as far away as Pennsylvania makes it unlikely that the White House was to be the other target. The story was put out by the US administration to deflect attention from the cowardice of its President who was at that time in Florida, refused to return to the White House, flew to a military air base in Louisiana, and went from there to hide in the underground bunker of the Strategic Air Command in Nebraska, which was built half a century ago as a place to which the US leadership would retreat in case of a nuclear attack. He stayed in that bunker until the next day, leaving the government of his country to other people.

[3] Figures of the dead in the beginning were so imprecise that Robert Fisk, the magnificent (and anti-imperialist) British correspondent, put the figure at 20,000 in his first published reflections after the attack. The final figure was close to 3,000.

States has destroyed around the world in the course of the 20th century with the deliberate, terroristic intent of targeting innocent civilians, just as civilians were targeted in their towns and hamlets alike throughout Indochina during the Vietnam War. The spectacular terror which destroyed the World Trade Centre and killed so many so callously pales by comparison; as one journalist has calculated, the death of 6,000 civilians means that this same level of violence would have to be carried out every day for several months for the resulting death toll to match the death toll in Iraq over the past decade. Even so, this was the first time that Americans came to experience what it means for cities to be at the receiving end of such destructive force. It is an indication of America's privilege in modern history that this hijacking operation, carried out by less than two dozen individuals, was the largest attack on mainland United States in its history, larger than Pearl Harbor, while American armies, assassins and covert operators of all kinds have been active around the globe for well over a century.[4]

And, because being at the receiving end of violence on their own soil was such a novel experience for the US centres of power, this attack on a couple of buildings at the heart of the imperial centre produced effects that no amount of terror and destruction in the outposts – or even the secondary and tertiary centres – of the empire could have produced. An economy that was already slowing down went into a full-fledged downturn, and

---

[4] This is inaccurate. Pearl Harbor was an off-shore colony of the United States, away from the mainland. In retrospect, one can see that memories of the attack on Pearl Harbor were invoked by the US media in order to suggest, subliminally as it were, that the carnage of 11 September was not due to just an act of a small number of terrorists but an act of war – 'War on America' was the phrase that adorned the CNN screens for the next week – comparable to the attack on Pearl Harbor, which indeed was the first attack in a war initiated by Japan. This idea of a 'War on America' is what then legitimized the idea of a 'war on terrorism' that was to be waged, permanently, not just against specific groups of terrorists but against any number of *countries*, as Bush was to soon announce.

the week following the hijackers' attack proved to be the worst in the history of US finance since July 1933, with Dow Jones and Nasdaq posting 2-digit losses virtually every day and liquid assets losing $1.4 trillion of their value over the week. The 30-year Treasury bonds continued to decline day by day, amid speculation that further issues of long-term federal debt shall be required to fund the war-without-end that is now envisaged, not to speak of the reconstruction costs and coping with the expected recession.

Not just fresh investment but also consumer spending dried up and the working people paid the price. 116,000 jobs were lost in the airline industry alone during that week, and the twin fears of war and economic recession led to plummeting of sales across North America. An emergency $15 billion assistance package was quickly put together for the airlines while Boeing, the lynchpin of American aerospace industry, threatened to fire 31,000 of its employees unless federal aid and subsidy came in. Insurance companies were in similar turmoil, with insurance claims arising from the World Trade Centre tragedy alone expected to exceed $73 billion. The companies hit back by notifying airports across North America and Western Europe that wartime coverage would be withdrawn as of 24 September, calculating that governments would be forced to step in with subsidies to renew that coverage while airports would be forced to beef up their security systems, requiring more outlays and more subsidies.

What happened was unspeakably hideous, cruel, senseless. The loss of thousands of precious lives, many of them cut down in the flower of their youth, has neither a moral nor a political justification. For once, the speechwriter of President Bush was right: those who carry out such acts in the name of Allah blaspheme the name of Allah; they hijack Islam in the name of Islam; in the larger, largely humane world of Islam they are a dangerous, fringe element. And a danger to their own people, I would add. In their fit of fundamentalist psychosis they might have believed that they were serving the Palestinian cause. Their actual act was a gift to the Zionists, however, and it was just as well that Yasser Arafat was quick to denounce the act even though Saddam Hussein, true to form, did not have the decency to do so. (Interestingly enough, the Taliban denounced it too, and begged the United States to act sensibly and not use the tragedy as justification for further destruction of Afghanistan.)[5]

Taking advantage of the anger and human anguish arising from the tragedy, and exploiting the fears and frustrations arising from the prospect of massive economic recession, the US administration moved quickly to plan a new, globalized, permanent war; to expound what amounts to a new doctrine of America's right to use its might as it pleases; to expand the war-making powers of the Presidency; to put in place a new regime of infinite surveillance; and to demolish whatever restraints had been introduced after the Vietnam War on America's right to undertake assassinations and covert actions across the globe. All this was accompanied with hair-raising rhetoric which tended at times to portray the coming war as a clash between Judeo-Christian and Muslim civilizations.

Bush called his so-called 'war on terrorism' a 'crusade' early on, with no sense of the historical meaning of that word. Only expressions of outrage from a wide spectrum of opinion in the Muslim world made him retract that stance and start saying that the war was not against Islam as such but only against certain Muslims. Not to be outdone, Pentagon named its planned operation

---

[5] Afghanistan was to be invaded and occupied less than a month later, as punishment for events of 11 September. Two years later, no evidence has yet been produced to show that the Taliban had anything at all to do with those events. On the other hand, they did offer to hand over Osama to the government of Pakistan under the supervision of the Organization of the Islamic Conference (OIC, involving 52 countries), as we explain elsewhere in this book.

'Infinite Justice', a phrase not even from the Bible but from the lexicon of Christian fundamentalism. Not only Muslims but even liberal Christians were outraged, and Protestant pastors themselves pointed out that 'Infinite Justice' referred to God's own divine justice, an attribute that no human power ought to claim for itself, America's vision of its own omnipotence notwithstanding. Pentagon sheepishly promised to reconsider the code name. The US Congress swiftly passed a resolution authorizing Bush to use wide powers in pursuance of this war on terrorism, asserting that 'all necessary and appropriate force' could be used against nations, organizations and individuals.[6] No nations were named, nor were any organizations, let alone individuals; the President could determine which one was to be attacked as he went along. Nor was there a time limit; he was authorized to act against present danger as well as in anticipation of 'future attacks'. The powers were in some ways wider than a mere declaration of war could have bestowed, since such a declaration would name the country against whom the war was to be waged.

Meanwhile, the Justice Department started putting together a package of proposed legislation giving the US

---

[6] On 14 September, the Senate of the United States voted 98-0 for a resolution which said, in part, that 'The President is authorized to use all necessary and appropriate force against those nations, organizations, or persons he determines planned, authorized, committed, or aided the terrorist attacks that occurred on September 11, 2001, or harboured such organizations or persons, in order to prevent any future acts of international terrorism against the United States by such nations, organizations and persons'. This is unprecedented in US history in three respects. First, the wording goes beyond any war resolution of the past in that it names no country that is to be the object of war. Second, it surrenders to the sole discretion of the President, in advance of any identification of enemies, the power to make war against as many as he chooses, thus abrogating the senate's own war-making powers in favour of an imperial, indeed dictatorial, presidency. Third, the President is to enjoy such powers indefinitely, without any time-frame and without any need to ever come back to the legislature for renewal of war-making authority.

intelligence agencies much wider powers to wiretap telephones, enter into people's internet accounts, deport suspected immigrants, seize evidence from suspects, including DNA samples, and obtain information from educational institutions, taxation records and a whole range of public and private agencies without prior court order or subsequent court review of the evidence. Attorney General John Ashcroft is said to be actively considering permanent video surveillance in public places and issuing 'smart cards' to all Americans which the surveillance devices can read electronically so as to distinguish citizen from non-citizen, keep a record of the movements of citizens themselves in public places and to have quick access to personal data linked to each of the 'smart cards'. It is also being contemplated that certain immigrants, chosen by intelligence at will, be required to report their activities regularly, like ordinary criminals on bail, and that airport security personnel be authorized to interrogate particular passengers at will and do on-the-spot check of their private baggage without having to explain why and what they are being suspected of.[7]

In his address to the joint session of Congress on 20 September, Bush was blunt. The war is against a network of hundreds of thousands of people spread across some sixty countries, he said, and this war was, in his considered phrase, 'a task that never ends'; Echoing John Foster Dulless, the rabid Foreign Secretary of the Eisenhower years who said that non-alignment was 'immoral', Bush too has put the whole world on notice: 'Every

---

[7] For a fuller treatment of these domestic changes, see my 'Growing Authoritarianism', in *Frontline*, 30 August 2002. In a more recent article, 'Imperialism of Our Time', included in this volume, I argue that the current Bush administration wants to roll back not only what Americans call 'the Vietnam syndrome' (the reluctance of the US public to get involved in full-scale wars abroad) but also certain fundamental liberties that are inherent in the US constitution and a level of welfare policies and social security that have been customary in that country since the New Deal of the 1930s.

nation in every region has a decision to make. Either you are with us or you are with the terrorists'. Enemies are lurking in thousands of little corners, in dozens of countries across the globe, and America will choose its targets as well as its methods and timing for dealing with them as it goes along, according to its own convenience; every country must join up each time, or else it too becomes an enemy and perhaps the next target. This war – 'unlike any we have ever seen', he said – shall be perpetual but largely secret. Some of it shall be seen on television, he said, but much shall go unrevealed – even in success, he emphasized. Congressional leaders in Washington are now talking of putting the CIA 'on a war footing' and cite with admiration the Israeli example of an open policy of assassinations without regard to legal niceties.

It is quite astonishing, though predictable, how quickly one government after another has fallen in line. India of course joined the crusade and offered its airspace and naval facilities with shameless alacrity, putting the lives of Indians at risk of retaliation from those against whom India has offered its facilities. Musharraf then cited India's pre-emptive oath of allegiance as his reason for offering the same to the US; India would otherwise have a strategic edge, he reasoned. Competitive servilities, one might say. Tony Blair, a veritable lapdog of Washington who doubles as the British Prime Minster, flew across the Atlantic to register his presence at the moment of birth of this new era of perpetual war. The European Commission has been scurrying around formulating new policies of cooperation over the question of terrorism, urging individual members of the EU to allocate more funds and build new systems of surveillance. The Russian parliament has passed a bill to create an international body to fight terrorism and, aping the US President, calls for elimination of terrorists as well as the governments which are said to finance them. China has been somewhat more shrewd, somewhat more independent; it urges a policy that involves presentation of concrete evidence, does not involve sacrifice of innocent civilians and is within the bounds of international law, but it also promises cooperation if the US were more receptive to its interests in Tibet, Taiwan and Xinjiang – and on the issue of NMD; the US has in turn moved quickly to put in place a new deal facilitating China's entry into the WTO.

The less powerful, many of whom also happens to be directly involved – even in some cases directly targeted – are of course treated differently. On 14 September, William F. Burns, Assistant Secretary of State for Near Eastern Affairs, called in ambassadors of fifteen Arab countries, including Syria which is otherwise one of the 'target' states as well as the PLO, and imperiously read out to them a list of actions they were to undertake, including arrest and prosecution of those on their soil whom the United States designates as 'terrorists'. Everyone seems to have fallen in line, including Yasser Arafat who has extended 'full cooperation', with the implicit and possibly misplaced hope that the US would press Israel for an immediate and durable ceasefire. Even President Khatami of Iran has made sympathetic noises and wishes to use the occasion for drawing closer to the United States which he has been wanting to do for some time. Iran has sealed its borders with Afghanistan, as have Pakistan and Tajikistan. China has gone so far as to seal its own borders with Pakistan itself, blocking the Korrakuram highway in the process.

Specially heavy burden has fallen on Pakistan, which was given the blunt choice of either getting treated in the same category as the Taliban or meet US demands: air space, naval facilities, stationing facilities for troops and covert operatives, full revelation of what the Pakistan intelligence services know about Afghanistan, Osama bin Laden and allied elements. Pakistanis tried to plead that such far-reaching cooperation with the US war designs in the region would rip apart the fabric of Pakistani society itself, but to no avail. Since then, a Gallup poll has revealed that 62 per cent of Pakistanis oppose any kind of cooperation with the US against another Muslim country; whether this opinion can be mobilized for effective political opposition is yet to be determined. In the midst of great fear of Taliban retaliation on the one hand, uncontrollable civic unrest on the other, foreign companies have pulled out of Pakistan and the US embassy itself is functioning with a skeletal staff. In these conditions, it remains unclear how all those foreign funds would pour in to solve Pakistan's economic problem, as the Pakistan Finance Minister Shaukat Aziz is promising.

As of now, however, the only concession the US has made to Pakistan – aside from offering some economic benefits, most notably the lifting of sanctions – is that it will not call upon Pakistan to lend its own troops for operations in Afghanistan.[8] Musharraf of course yielded, but it is far from clear just where substantial elements among the corps commanders stand on this issue and where the violent protests that have erupted already might lead. It will probably all depend upon the nature, intensity and longevity of the projected US military operations in the region. Nor is it yet clear just what Musharraf's offer of 'full cooperation' would imply for such US demands as that it immediately cut-off fuel supplies to Afghanistan, but we do know that the Afghan clerics' invitation to bin Laden to leave voluntarily was obtained on Pakistan's insistence.

Soon after the hijacked civilian planes smashed into the

---

[8] Two years into this 'war on terrorism', the US is now asking Pakistan, as well as India and any other country that can be pressed into service, to contribute troops to its war on Iraq.

World Trade Centre, the dominant electronic media set out to identify all sorts of people as the culprits. PLO and the Popular Front for the Liberation of Palestine were the early favourites. By noon, the focus shifted to Osama bin Laden. By the afternoon the channels were abuzz with the idea that bin Laden could not have done it without the diabolical expertise of Saddam Hussein. The focus on Iraq soon became so alarming that Secretary of State Colin Powell as well as Vice President Dick Cheney and others were eventually forced to say on record that Iraq had nothing to do with it.[9] Indeed, Powell has been the cool head in Washington, arguing that the US ought not go around shooting all over the Middle East and should judiciously concentrate on one major target at a time, and that Afghanistan should be the first. He is also the one arguing that too much of an escalation against Iraq at this time, when the US wants Arab governments to join it in a coalition against the Taliban, would be counterproductive.

Niaz Naik, the senior Pakistani statesman, has revealed on BBC a personal conversation with high US officials in July this year, well before the recent events, in which these officials had spelled out the set of US demands which have now been presented to the spellbound TV-watching world as non-negotiable and a retaliation against the 'attack on America': hand over the Taliban and, in Bush's words, 'deliver to the United States authorities all the leaders of Al Qaida. . . . Give to the United States full access to terrorist training camps' and so on – demands which the Taliban

---

[9] We now know that on 12 September itself, Rumsfeld had argued in favour of attacking Iraq immediately while Powell has argued persuasively that the focus should be retained on Afghanistan and Iraq be invaded later. This early policy of *not* identifying Iraq with 11 September was reversed later and the connection, entirely fictitious, was made so often by sundry US officials and the media that by the time the invasion of Iraq began, polls showed that forty per cent of the Americans believed that Saddam Hussein was personally responsible for that attack.

would find it impossible to accede to, even if they so wanted. The emphasis is significant: it is the United States, not some international tribunal or UN forces, which shall take custody of these people and places. The tactic too is obvious: present non-negotiable and impossible demands, issue a short notice, and invade. That there shall be an invasion is clear, but there is still a far-reaching debate within the US government as to what kind of invasion it would be.

A decade of the most brutal military and economic warfare without committing ground troops or trying to occupy large chunks of Iraq has not succeeded in toppling Saddam Hussein. Chances of success of that sort of warfare in Afghanistan are even fewer; as one of the Taliban put it, 'we don't even have a factory which could be a reasonable military target'. Direct landing in Kabul or Kandahar would only turn the Taliban into phantoms scurrying around in the hinterlands, bleeding the US militarily and financially, and winning new allies in the face of a foreign occupation force. Bin Laden's numerous camps are perfectly well known to the Americans since he initially built them with their money and assistance. But he is a moving target, with a widespread following, and with numerous camps many of which are dug deep under the mountains.[10]

One of the likely scenarios is a round of massive bombings and well orchestrated commando operations to disorganize and soften up the targets, killing great many and hoping that many of those killed would be the Taliban and members of Al Qaida. This could then be followed by actual landing and taking over ghost cities from which the surviving civilians would have fled, as a

---

[10] See 'Afghanistan: The Forgotten War' in this volume for analysis of the situation as it stands after almost two years after the invasion. The US has not been bled financially or militarily, as the hyperbolic formulation here predicted. All the rest of our prediction has been proven correct.

prelude to establishing a UN-sponsored Afghan administration drawn from among the enemies of the Taliban, and settling down to a long-term scorched earth policy, from some bases inside Afghanistan but mainly from the outside. Hence two emphases in American pronouncements thus far. Bush emphasized to the US public time and again that there shall be casualties this time and that the campaign shall be prolonged. And, there is an enormous pressure on Pakistan, Azerbaijan and Tajikistan to provide basing facilities, and upon Russia to use its influence in this regard. The information obtained from Pakistan's Inter-Services Intelligence Agency (ISI) would be crucial for even moderate success of the American design. Pakistan's historic involvement in Afghanistan on the side of the Americans and its enduring geo-political location may yet come to haunt Jaswant Singh's dream of turning India into America's 'most allied ally', as Pakistan was once called.

What does all this portend for Afghanistan? It is a country devastated by some two decades of the most brutal warfare and, since the fall of the People's Democratic Party of Afghanistan (PDPA) government, equally brutal forms of rule.[11] For a population of roughly 26 million, there are six million land mines dug into its earth which kill or maim 100 people per week. There are 3.6 million Afghan refugees in Pakistan and Iran, and another one million or so internal refugees, hungry and homeless, who roam around the country hoping to survive another day. It has suffered three consecutive years of drought, and the combined effects of war, misrule and the drought has meant that until only a few days ago the UN World Food Programme was feeding three million Afghans in the countryside and some 300,000 in Kabul itself. Virtually the whole of that institutional infrastructure has now collapsed under

---

[11] The forces which are now aligned with the US are estimated to have slaughtered 50,000 people in Kabul between 1992 and 1996.

the threat of US invasion, and those who are now deprived even of that meagre ration are facing imminent death without the US firing even a shot – just like the Iraqi children who die not of bullets but for lack of the food and medicine which the US-imposed embargo denies them. Afghanistan is in this state in consequence of the anti-communist, Islamized crusade that the US cynically waged there before abandoning it to its own miseries. This is the country that the mightiest empire in human history has now set out to subjugate with all its technological and financial might, but with little chance of success.

America cannot win but it shall not suffer substantially either. The Afghans shall not be subjugated but they shall suffer and perhaps even a majority of them might perish or become homeless and get consigned to a subhuman existence. That is the asymmetry of power in our time: those who rule the universe shall not be victorious against the poorest and the most wretched of this earth; those who refuse subjugation shall be made to suffer miseries that no military power in the past had the capacity to inflict. War shall be permanent because the war cannot end without justice and justice is what the US has set out to deny, permanently. The war shall be globalized because the era of 'globalization' requires that wars of repression be fought across the globe. And much of this war shall be secret, like much of the movements of finance capital, because finance capital is what this war serves and therefore imitates. Bush is right: this is truly 'a task that has no end' – until someone rises to end it.

Will there be organized opposition to these imperial designs? That's still hard to tell. *Haaretz*, the Israeli newspaper, mentions a poll taken in 30 countries in which only the US and Israel are shown to be the two countries where majorities are in favour of war; 77 per cent in Israel, an overwhelmingly war-mongering society in any case, but only a bare majority in the US itself, with 54 per cent. Will even this majority hold once the immediate shock and grief have been absorbed and put in some perspective? Will the majority shrink or expand if Americans begin to die in faraway places? It is too soon to tell. What is already heartening is that there is great opposition to the type of military operations which involve large numbers of civilian deaths, and a student movement of anti-war activists is beginning to emerge on many campuses. According to the same poll, 80 per cent in Europe and 90 per cent in Latin America want the action restricted to application of law and judicial process. The grand coalition of governments choreographs its dance of death on TV channels, but among the masses of people the ideology does not hold.

A brief word about this particular form of fighting which is called 'terrorism'. Bush was careful enough to say that America's enemy was that particular 'terrorism' which 'has global reach'. In other words, he is not particularly concerned with the great many varieties of terrorism which include the IRA in Ireland, the LTTE in Sri Lanka, the RSS fraternity in India. Nor is 'fundamentalism' the issue: Taliban fundamentalism is bad but Saudi fundamentalism is good, and Bush himself of course speaks the language of that Christian fundamentalism which defines the far right in the contemporary United States. 'Terrorism with global reach', the designated enemy, is the one that challenges American power.

This is a complex and important subject and we shall return to this some other day. Briefly put, the 'terrorism' that torments the US is what comes when the communist left and secular anti-colonial nationalism have both been defeated while the issue of imperialism remains unresolved and more important than ever. Hatred takes the place of revolutionary ideology. Privatized, retail violence takes the place of revolutionary warfare and national liberation struggles. Millenarian and freelance seekers of religious martyrdom replace the defeated phalanx of disciplined revolutionaries. Un-Reason arises where Reason is appropriated by imperialism and is eliminated in its revolutionary form. There were no Islamic terrorists in Afghanistan before Americans created them as a counterweight against the secular left. Islamism arose to fill that space in Iran which had been left vacant with the elimination of secular anti-imperialist nationalism and the revolutionary left by the CIA-sponsored regime of the Shah. Islamic secret societies arose in Egypt after imperialism and Zionism combined to defeat Nasser's secular nationalist project. Hamas arose in Palestine because the cosmopolitan Palestinian nationalism was denied its dream of a secular state in the historic land of Palestine where Jew and Arab could live as co-equals. What gets called 'terrorism with global reach' today is a mirror of our own defeat but also the monster that imperialism's faustian success made possible and which now haunts its own creator. The loss of over 6,000 lives in the blaze and collapse of the World Trade Centre is the price the victims and their families paid for our defeat and imperialism's victory.

America can never defeat 'terrorism with a global reach' because for all its barbarity and irrationality, that religiously motivated 'terrorism' is also a 'sigh of the oppressed': misguided, suicidal, barbaric, but a *response* to the much greater cruelties of imperialism itself. The only way to end this 'terrorism' is to rebuild that revolutionary movement of the left whose place it occupies and with whose mantle it masquerades.

The author wishes to register that he has written this essay with the memory of Taimur in his heart, a lovely young man who was last seen on the 92nd floor of the World Trade Centre.

9 NOVEMBER 2001
Re-mapping the Globe

As I begin drafting this essay on 18 October 2001, on the twelfth day of the war on Afghanistan, it has become quite clear that the real strategic aim is not so much a change of regime in Afghanistan but to obtain re-alignments of power across the globe. The destruction of the World Trade Centre was by any reckoning an act of a group of desperados with so few resources that even after twelve days of bombings which have brought the main cities of Afghanistan – Mazaar-e-Sharif, Herat and even Kabul and Kandahar – close to collapse, the so-called 'terror with a global reach' has not been able to retaliate even in one place in the entire world. Yet, the event has been cited by the US time and again as the one that authorizes it to make overt and covert wars wherever and whenever it so desires, in all corners of the globe.

In his televised address to the joint session of the US Congress a few days after the hijackers' attack, on 20 September, President Bush claimed that there were tens of thousands of terrorists lurking in some sixty countries and the US was going to wage a global, permanent war to weed them out from every nook and corner of the earth. As the pounding of Afghanistan began, John Negroponte, chief US envoy to the United Nations, wrote a letter to the Security Council stating 'We may find that our self-defence requires further action with respect to other organizations and other states'. This was undoubtedly the first communication in the history of the UN in which a member state notified the Security Council of its intent to make war against other member states without naming them, nor even revealing how many of the member states were to be targeted. At about the same time, Canadian media revealed that a Seattle-based company that makes maps had received instructions from the US government to supply all existing maps of all parts of Afghanistan soon after the World Trade Centre attack, and that by the end of the month it had received a similar instruction to forward all possible maps of Sudan and Yemen as well. Were they also to be targeted?

A week into the war on Afghanistan, the International Herald Tribune reported that an influential group in the Pentagon which possibly includes Defence Secretary Donald Rumsfeld was arguing that the next step in the war should be the ouster of Saddam Hussein by American forces in an operation which might include occupation of a part of Iraq so as to install a 'government' comprised of Iraqi exiles close to the US and even the capture of oil fields near Basra in southern Iraq so as to sell the oil from there to pay the expenses of this puppet regime. This, despite the fact that a whole host of intelligence agencies, from the Israeli to the Jordanian – not to speak of Colin Powell, the American Secretary of State – have said that Saddam had nothing to do with the 11 September attacks. The Defence Policy Board, a prestigious bipartisan board of national security experts that advises the Pentagon was reported to have met for nineteen hours to consider this option, with Henry Kissinger (Nixon's Secretary of State), Harold Brown (Carter's Defence Secretary), James Woolsey (Clinton's CIA director) Admiral David Jeremiah (a former deputy chairman of the joint Chiefs of Staff), Newt Gingrich (the infamous Republican Congressman and former Speaker of the House of Representatives) and other such luminaries in attendance. In light of his career as a chief spook, Woolsey was assigned the task of assembling 'evidence' that would show Saddam's links to 'terror with a global reach' and would then be used to prepare a 'legal case' to justify such an operation. By now, the US has even invented a name for this new global policy: 'regime replacement'. Any regime that is not to the liking of the US may face such 'replacement'.

In the strict sense of course, this is not a new policy. The US has a long history of overt and covert interventions around the globe with the explicit aim of overthrowing existing governments. The Islamicist jihad in Afghanistan which eventually gave rise to the Taliban was itself product of such a policy, to overthrow the government of the People's Democratic Party of Afghanistan (PDPA), and the policy had come into force well before the Soviet Union had intervened to defend that government. In more recent years, such a policy was implemented successfully in Yugoslavia and unsuccessfully in Somalia. What is new is a certain globalization of this policy, a declaration that the US has the unique right to make war against any and all governments that it considers inimical to its interests, and the notice that has been served upon the world to either support this policy or face retribution. Kofi Annan, who does the US bidding in such matters, has even been awarded a Nobel Prize for his efforts.

What are the costs and prospects of success for this policy in Afghanistan? Estimates suggest that even before the bombings began many more Afghans had died than the total number killed in the World Trade Centre attack, owing to the chaos and devastation caused by just the threat of US strikes, generating new internal refugees and leading to the collapse of the food aid programmes upon which some half a million Afghans had until then relied. Pakistan now expects a million new refugees; all the other neighbouring states are bracing for unpredictable levels of influx. British commanders have already warned that the campaign against the Taliban shall last 'at least into next Summer'. The attendant and inevitable human suffering that such a campaign promises to bring about is strictly unimaginable.

Afghanistan is now in the midst of the scenario we had predicted. The first phase of this scenario involves a round of massive bombings and well-orchestrated operations by 'special forces' to disorganize the Taliban resistance and destroy what little infrastructure the devastated and drought-ridden country still had. At the time of this writing, British Prime Minister Tony Blair has already promised a new phase soon and all indications seem to be that the landing of ground forces is imminent, first to occupy some outlying areas to establish bases of operation and then to occupy ghost cities from where the population will be made to flee through saturation bombings. Regardless of what the US says about its intent to avoid civilian casualties, population centres shall be bombed precisely because it is into the general population that the Taliban and their allies shall melt away.[1] The US would prefer to not occupy Afghanistan for long. Domestic support for this operation is likely to evaporate if any significant number of Americans start dying in the battlefields. They would like to hand over the occupied country to the United Nations which would be required to finish the job that the US itself cannot.[2]

There are problems, however. Whether the spectacular

---

[1] In the event, Kandahar, the second largest city in Afghanistan, was bombed so mercilessly that 85 per cent of the population fled and much of the city was reduced to rubble, becoming precisely the 'ghost city' we had predicted.
[2] At the end, the US imposed its own hand-picked 'Interim Authority' which then 'invited' the UN to authorize an international security force, which was duly done. In August 2003, NATO itself assumed the command of this force. See 'Afghanistan: the Forgotten War' in this volume for an overview of these later developments.

strikes end in weeks or in months, they will not be followed by peace. Afghans do not take to foreign occupation kindly, and there is bound to be a long period of low-intensity warfare, hit-and-run skirmishes and so on, which would involve many more than just the remaining Taliban. This would then be complicated by regional, ethnic and tribal conflicts and shifting alliances, among the larger nationalities but also even among the Pashtuns themselves who comprise some 40 per cent of the population. The US has thought up four responses to these difficulties. First, much hope is pinned on Zahir Shah, the 86-year old former king who has been cooling his heels in Rome since 1973 and whom Richard Haas, a senior State Department official, went to visit before the bombing began, with the offer of a long-forgotten throne. Second, this fraudulent monarchical restoration is to be buttressed by a UN-sponsored *loya jirga* (grand gathering of the elders and notables from different ethnic groups) so as to prop up the pretence of a broad-based, indigenously constituted government.[3] Third, a 'green force' authorized by the Security Council and comprised of troops drawn from some Muslim countries is being mooted as a peacekeeping force to oversee a post-Taliban transition and the dawn of a new order. Turkey, a Muslim country that commands NATO's second largest army, is being proposed to lead such a multilateral force. Finally, the US hopes to win the loyalty of the vanquished Afghans with huge amounts of

---

[3] The *loya jirga* (literally, big gathering) is, strictly speaking, a specifically Pashtun custom that brings together tribal chiefs. The Uzbeks or Turkemans have no such tradition, and Tajiks are in any case a largely urban group and have no tribal chiefs to offer. The so-called *loya jirga* that was held in the wake of the US occupation and for which the Germans provided most of the security personnel was a gathering of notables from various ethnicities hand-picked by the US authorities, which then annointed Hamid Karzai as the new ruler of Afghanistan under pressure from Zalmay Khalilzad, the special US envoy.

humanitarian aid for the populace and development aid for the well-healed.[4]

Each of these proposals is beset with difficulties, however. A quick end to the operations is unlikely not only because the cessation of large-scale bombings would be followed by long-drawn low-intensity warfare but also because the US does want the Taliban government to collapse but does not want to have the Northern Alliance occupy the cities on its own. The Alliance is supported by not only India, which makes it impossible for Pakistan to allow it to triumph, but also Russia and Iran, whom the US itself will not like to give so prominent a role in the final settlement. Musharraf claims that he has 'iron-clad' guarantees from the US that the Northern Alliance will not be allowed to gain much advantage in case of a Taliban collapse. Indeed, Pakistan is reported to have threatened to close its airspace to US aircraft and cancel other kinds of support if the US allows the Northern Alliance to occupy Kabul. Internally, the Alliance is comprised mainly of Tajiks and Uzbeks, so that its victory is likely to unite most of the Pashtuns behind the Taliban. On the ground, therefore, the present situation is ambiguous.[5]

---

[4] Turkey dutifully contributed troops but other Muslim countries declined and, instead, Germany came to dominate the security forces that came to function alongside troops from the US and UK. These were, in essence, NATO troops and it is only logical that NATO eventually assumed command of them directly. The so-called 'humanitarian aid' has been paltry and majority of Afghans appear not to have been won over, as we explain elsewhere in the book.

[5] Given the history of shifting alliances and internecine warfare among factions, the genesis and composition of the Northern Alliance, sometimes called National Alliance, is hard to summarize. In sum, it consists of many but not all of the groups – the so-called *mujahideen* – that the US had sponsored against the PDPA government and the soviet troops and which ruled Afghanistan between the collapse of that government and the rise of the Taliban. Some of those groups – most notably the group led by Hekmetyar, the main Pashtun leader of that time – are not a part of the Alliance. The US did allow the Northern Alliance to march on Kabul, then assimilated most of its leaders into the new 'Interim Authority' but foisted its own candidate, Hamid Karzai, upon them, as chief

The fighting front between the Taliban and the Northern Alliance lies some fifty-five kilometers from Kabul, and instead of disintegrating the Taliban are reported to have sent reinforcement to the front, assuming that the US will not bomb them for fear of letting the Northern Alliance march on Kabul. The US is indeed faced with a hard choice. It can either bomb the Taliban positions, let the Northern Alliance enter Kabul, allow the coalition around Pakistan unravel and accept enduring Russian influence in the country; or, it can leave the nucleus of the Taliban forces intact and send its own occupation force into the cities before taking on those forces, facing the possibility of guerrilla attacks on its operating units. Sketchy reports seem to suggest that the US has started bombing the Taliban forces and that units of the Northern Alliance led by Rashid Dostum, an Uzbek, are closing in on Mazaar-e-Sharif, a largely Uzbek city, while units of Ismael Khan, a Tajik, are likewise closing in on Herat. Significantly, both Dostum and Ismael Khan are supported by Iran while Dostum in particular has also received aid from Russia and India. The US thinking on all this remains unclear.

Thanks to the prospect of continuing low-intensity warfare in which the indigenous guerrillas would have great advantage, the US and UK are keen to disengage as soon as possible but the UN itself is not keen to step in, for fear of unsustainable level of casualties. Nor is it at all clear that many Muslim countries would volunteer troops for such an engagement. On paper at least, Iran has not even allowed its air space to be used for US operations. It

---

client. On 6 October 2001, the day before the US invasion of Afghanistan began, Human Rights Watch issued a detailed account of the composition of this Alliance and its record of massive atrocities, naming particular leaders who have been directly responsible for those atrocities. The most important of those leaders occupy leading positions in the current Karzai dispensation. This report can be easily accessed from the website of Human Rights Watch.

is also well-known that before agreeing to offer all the support to the US even Pakistan got the latter to agree that its own troops shall not be available for operations in Afghanistan. Turkey is complaining that its compliance with the US-imposed blockade of Iraq, previously its largest trading partner, has already cost it $30 billion. Nor can the government there ignore the fact that in a recent poll only 29 per cent of the Turks supported the US action at all, let alone the deployment of their own troops. Arab governments are so fearful that Saudi Arabia itself, the arch enemy of Osama bin Laden, has refused to freeze bank account of companies and charities associated with him, despite US pressure, for fear of reprisals. Impressive anti-American protests have already taken place in every Muslim country, from Indonesia to Kenya, Iran to Morocco, not to speak of Pakistan where protests have broken out not only in the larger cities like Karachi or Peshawar or Quetta but even in the small town of Jacobabad in the interior of Sindh where thousands rampaged through the town and two were killed.

American difficulties regarding the projected post-Taliban setup are equally formidable. It is doubtful that Zahir Shah has much following beyond the circle of exiled notables or that any of the contenders for power inside Afghanistan want to be subjected to his titular authority. The Irani regime, heir to an anti-monarchical revolution, has made known its great displeasure, and Pakistan was not enthusiastic about any such dispensation even in the 1980s when both the Soviets and the Americans had considered it at one time or another. Negotiations to bring back the king are reported to have stalled already. Nor would a *loya jirga* called by the Americans to install a government favoured by them be acceptable to any of the Islamicist groups, and it is yet to be seen if many of the Muslim countries that could carry conviction in Afghanistan would be forthcoming to take over the responsibility to clean up the mess Americans are making.

Given all these factors, it would appear from currently available evidence that the US would either be unable to extricate itself speedily from the engagement it has taken upon itself and would continue to bomb and kill in the name of what its ideologists and philosophers would sell to the world as a 'just war'; or, the US would at some point declare its war on Al Qaida won and would then withdraw, leaving Afghanistan with a human tragedy even worse than what it currently faces. The one great asset the US does have is money, in unimaginably large quantities, which it can use to buy clients among the elite or to feed some of the millions whom its policies of the past twenty years have rendered hungry and hopeless. So, they are likely to throw money at the corpses and call it 'humanitarian aid'.

The compulsion to withdraw may come also from the shape of the US economy which declined in September for the twelfth consecutive month, experiencing the longest decline since 1975. The WTC attack only worsened the state of the investors' confidence which had been plummeting for a whole year, despite nine interest cuts by the Federal Reserve which brought the lending rate from close to 6 per cent down to 2.5 per cent within that year. This absence of investor confidence despite great incentives and inducements mirrors the loss of consumer confidence in an economy where hundreds of thousands of jobs have been lost during these months and millions of families are fearful of losing stable incomes and therefore reluctant to spend. This fear is fed further by the fear of war and terror, not to speak of warnings by the Federal Reserve itself that the economy shall decline further before any recovery can be firmly predicted.

It would be extremely foolish, however, to imagine that

the US is headed for a policy failure. The retreat, if it comes, shall be an orderly one, with gains already made. For, the internal settlement in Afghanistan, or the well being of its inhabitants, is an insignificant part of US objectives. More crucial is the project to re-draw the geo-strategic and political maps of the world. If the relentless destruction of Iraq has been a project to consolidate the Western alliance and silence the Third World through a decade-long demonstration of what the 'sole superpower' can do to a Third World country after the 'other superpower' – the Soviet Union – has been dismantled, this so-called 'war on terrorism', starting with one of the poorest and long-suffering countries on this earth, is designed to draw the OECD countries actively into junior partnership in warmongering and to tell the Third World that is not only to be silenced but to actively serve in the imperial project, much as native armies used to be activated for colonial conquest.

Under Blair's stewardship, Britain has been drawn actively into a military action which, for that wretched country of colonial nostalgia, serves something resembling the fourth Afghan War, with success guaranteed by the US this time around. In Germany where the postwar settlement had restricted the country's military might at home and military operations abroad, Gerhard Schröder, at the head of the Socialist-led government, announced 'unlimited solidarity' with the US 'war on terrorism', won 71 per cent of public support in the polls, and went on to announce the possibility of German troop involvement abroad, while his coalition partners, the supposedly pacificst Greens who supported the US in the Kosovo invasion, sit gaping. In Japan, equally constrained after the Second World War, a parliamentary panel has already drafted a new law that would enable Japan to despatch troops for war operations abroad. China, the most powerful country in the Third World, has abandoned its long-standing policy of opposition to any UN role in the internal affairs of member states, calling upon the UN to play an active role in putting together the ruling coalition in Afghanistan after the Americans have succeeded in overthrowing the Taliban regime.

The case of Russia is the most pathetic. Afghanistan is the land where countless Russian soldiers died in defence of the secular and progressive government of the PDPA in a war after which the US succeeded in foisting a bunch of Islamicist murderers on that devastated country. Yet, the current Russian Duma simply passed a resolution echoing the words of Bush to the effect that not only terrorist organizations but also governments that support terrorism must be punished. Putin briefly balked at the idea that member states of the Commonwealth of Independent States (CIS) would offer any facilities for the Americans, but then fell in line as other states simply ignored him. Tajikistan, a member of the CIS Collective Security Treaty, offered its airspace; Uzbekistan went further and offered its military bases; Kazakhstan offered air corridors for access to Afghanistan, as did Kyrgyzstan; and Turkemanistan, eyeing the possibility for a pipeline for its gas through Afghanistan and thus re-aligning its oil economy with the US instead of Russia, opened up its airspace as well as territory for military operations. In the process, Uzbekistan became almost as important as Pakistan for the American war on Afghanistan. At length Russia too offered airspace for so-called 'humanitarian aid'.

These items of piecemeal news in fact signify a historic re-alignment in maps of global power. For, America's Afghan War which began in the Soviet period and has now lasted for over two decades has always had the key dimension of a fight for control over the immense and largely untapped economic resources of the Asian republics of the former USSR. The competition for pre-eminence in the region has been fierce between Russia and the US even after the dissolution of the USSR. Even the Taliban were brought in, by the Pakistanis but with American backing, with the calculation that their dependence on Pakistan would facilitate the American and Pakistani economic interests in the region, notably the oil and gas interests in Turkemanistan. Turkey itself was once encouraged to play a forward role in the region on America's behalf, thanks to its historic ties with the region, harking back to the Ottoman period, and if Turkey now agrees to play the gendarme in Afghanistan, it would be with an eye to that role in a region for which Afghanistan is something of an underbelly. What this current phase of the war on Afghanistan has brought about is this re-alignment of the resource-rich Central Asian states with the US at the expense of Russia, in a time when Russia itself has no alternatives.

Iran presents us with an equally important and complex case. Khamenai, heir to the authority of the chief jurisconsult in Iran after the death of Ayatullah Khomeini, has denounced American attack on Afghanistan and the government of President Khatami has dutifully denied the US the use of Irani airspace for those operations. However, that same government has offered cooperation in rescuing and safeguarding any personnel if it were shot down in that airspace and is urging the Northern Alliance to cooperate with the US. This paradoxical policy framework is related to the fact that Iran almost went to war with the Taliban in 1998, has always feared for the plight of the Shia sectarian minority under the rabidly Sunni rule of the Taliban, is host to over a million Afghan refugees, and is fearful of the influx of more refugees, narcotics and weapons. It also fears that the war may lead to a North-South division of Afghanistan and a continued civil war as a consequence; or that Pakistan would engineer a government out of its clients, past and present; or that the monarchy would be re-established in Afghanistan. Its official position is that Burhanuddin Rabbani's government which is recognized by the UN, should take power after the Taliban have been routed, as an interim step before a broad-based government is assembled. In this context, then, Iran is reported to have intelligence-sharing arrangements with the US and is in active dialogue over the question of the post-Taliban dispensation in Kabul. The US has returned the favour by carrying out a comprehensive policy review so as to prepare a 'tilt' toward Iran against Iraq. Enemies of the recent past are fast becoming strategic allies.

Tests of loyalty have been required globally. Most of the bombing missions have been carried out from offshore aircraft-carriers but troops have been stationed in 'countries within striking distance', such as Saudi Arabia, Kuwait, Oman, Tajikistan, Pakistan, as well as Diego Garcia. NATO was reminded early that the US had treaty rights to seek cooperation. Australia has been pressed to promise active military support while Canada is pressed to alter even its own regulations for immigration and border checking. Indonesia has had to pledge support in the face of a popular opposition so threatening that US operatives are already stationed in the country to pick out the more militant elements. Even North Korea has issued a statement that could be construed, and has been so construed in Washington, as a declaration of support for the US.

For us, undoubtedly, the most important is the re-alignment of forces in South Asia itself. US interests in India remain as before but in relation to Afghanistan India is, in the view of the US, a peripheral element. The shameless alacrity with which the Vajpayee government offered Indian airspace and naval facilities was at best abject. Actually, the US dos not even need Indian airspace, given Pakistan's availability, but India is a significant force in Asian affairs and it should have required from the US guarantees that Pakistan would cease sponsorship of militancy in Kashmir. In actual fact, India got as little out of this unilateral concession as it did from the earlier, equally abject support for the American National Missile Defence programmes.

Musharraf, by contrast, has been the main beneficiary and has played his cards well. Sensing the extent of the US dependence on him, he has extended his own term as army chief for an indefinite period and got rid of the senior generals who had helped him come to power in the first place. The network of Pakistan's Inter-Services Intelligence agency (ISI) operatives in Afghanistan and the information they possess is invaluable for America's regional aims. The US also knows well how intimately the Afghan situation is connected with the refugee camps, the Afghan settlers, the religious seminaries, the Islamicist establishment, the military-bureaucratic elite in Pakistan, and that the Pakistani and US interests coincide not only in the Gulf region but also in Central Asia. Knowing that he has suddenly gained almost as much leverage as did General Zia when the Afghan War began in 1978, Musharraf has bargained for major concessions across the board.

On the economic front, Musharraf has already obtained an estimated $1 billion in aid, debt re-scheduling and indirect benefits arising from Washington's decision to lift the nuclear-related sanctions. In a parallel move, the European Commission rushed through trade concessions worth $ 1.35 billion, removing all tariffs on textile exports which account for 60 per cent of Pakistan's exports to the EU, so as to compensate for the expected decline in export earnings owing to the global recession and sharp rise in insurance costs. As America's military and strategic involvement in Pakistan gets revived, large sums of money are likely to pour in, forcing much of the upper class and the military to fall in line.

On the matter of Afghanistan itself, Musharraf has won the key concession that the Northern Alliance shall be cut to size, that some sections of the Taliban be accommodated in the new dispensation. In the joint press conference with Powell, Musharraf emerged as the more vocal partner and outlined the overall strategy of the successive phases of military destruction, political re-alignment and economic reconstruction as a long-term solution for the Afghan problem. 'We agreed', he said, 'that durable peace in Afghanistan would only be possible through the establishment of a broad-based multi-ethnic government representing the demographic contours of Afghanistan'. Translated into plain language, the formulation implies that the Tajiks, Uzbeks, Hazaras and other ethnic minorities shall receive their due share but Pushtun dominance shall continue. This should reassure not only the Pashtun population in Afghanistan and the refugee camps but the 20 million Pakistan Pashtuns as well, including that 25 per cent of the Armed Forces which are drawn from among them. Pakistan will undoubtedly seek a prominent role in any post-Taliban settlement and one can fairly well assume that just as US troops have arrived at bases in Sindh and Baluchistan, Pakistani operatives are active within Afghanistan even more than the American or the British.[6]

By far the most important concession was that Musharraf got Colin Powell to speak of Kashmir in the language that Pakistan prefers: that the Kashmir dispute 'be resolved in accord with the wishes of the Kashmiri people'. This, along with the continued operations of the Pakistan-sponsored militants in J&K, is what he

[6] In the latter phase of the war and in the dispensation that emerged thereafter, the US reneged on both these promises. It allowed the Northern Alliance to take over Kabul and the ensuing 'interim Authority' was dominated by figures and nominees of that Alliance. We commented on the ensuing political disarray in Pakistan in 'Pakistan's Time of Reckoning', *Frontline*, 19 January 2002. Karzai is a Pashtun but has no standing among them, and all the major ministries are occupied by non-Pashtuns. Ethnic rivalries have intensified and, having been thus re-buffed, Pakistan did comply with all the main US demands but is now again finding its room of manoeuvre widening as the Taliban stage a comeback.

will take to the people as he launches his attack on the domestic Islamicist groups, as evidence that he has not compromised Pakistan's interests in Kashmir by offering support to the American designs in Afghanistan. Nor is it likely that the US shall now press Pakistan to cease its meddling in J&K, however much it may be displeased by particular terrorist acts there. The US-Pakistan alliance has been revived for good and is here to stay, unless a full-scale Islamicist uprising undoes it.

That sort of uprising seems unlikely in the short run. Musharraf has re-shuffled the command structure and has gone on the offensive against the Islamicist groupings, even to the extent that Maulana Fazlur Rehman of the Jami'at-ul-Ulema-e-Islam (JUI), the most illustrious of the pro-Taliban clerics in Pakistan, has become the first leader to be charged with treason, for inciting the armed forces. This long-awaited offensive, on the part of a soldier who once declared himself a Kemalist, is the only good thing that has come out of the global re-alignment of forces. So far the offensive is succeeding because the Islamicists in Pakistan represent a vocal, well organized, partially armed but still a very small minority. However, public outrage at America's crusade in the region is very much on the rise and can only increase as long as the war continues. And if the US does settle down to a perpetual war, as Bush has proposed, we may yet see a Pakistan in which the elite gets regrouped behind America, in pursuit of wealth and economic benefit, while the masses of people move into a settled opposition and resentment which gets to be represented by a new generation of populist Islam. That is all the more likely in the absence of a strong enough secular force harnessing that anti-imperialist sentiment for rational purposes. What effect all that may have for the Armed Forces themselves, especially among the junior ranks and the common soldiery, it is too soon to tell. That is so because we are witnessing only the first few skirmishes of a war that imperialism itself foresees as being globalized and perpetual. Much shall change over the next few weeks, months, years. India seems ill-prepared to cope with the uncertainties of that future.[7]

---

[7] Pakistan's Islamicist parties at the time of this writing about two years ago undoubtedly were minority groupings, as they have been since the very inception of the country. The Musharraf government's subservience to the US in matters of war against neighbouring Muslim countries without getting much in return has, combined with two years of American atrocities in Afghanistan and Iraq and Israeli atrocities against the Palestinians, has helped them widen their base greatly. After the recent elections, they formed government in Baluchistan and NWFP, the two Pakistani provinces bordering Afghanistan, and emerged as the largest bloc in the National Assembly. The same Maulana Fazlur Rehman whom Musharraf had charged with treason came close to becoming Prime Minister. Ideologically, he represents precisely the populist Islam which is emerging as the main contender for power in Pakistan, thanks to the American pursuit of a 'Clash of Civilizations'.

28 SEPTEMBER 2002
In the Shadow of Permanent War

Even to ask ourselves whether or not the United States shall invade Iraq in the near future is an obscenity. Anglo-American bombardment of Iraq has now lasted longer than did the American invasion of Vietnam – longer than the combined duration of the two world wars. Four years ago, in 1998, the UN Humanitarian Coordinator for Iraq, Dennis Halliday, resigned his post in disgust, claiming that the blockade alone, aside from the direct bombardment, had caused upward of a million deaths. Asked whether the death of half a million children was worth the price of throttling Saddam Hussain's regime, Madeline Albright, the then US Secretary of State, did not deny the deaths and merely said that 'the price was worth it'.[1]

Iraqi society has been under siege during this whole period militarily, economically and politically. Per capita income has been cut to about a fifth of what it was a decade ago, more than a quarter of the population suffers from malnutrition, schools and hospitals have decayed and 60 per cent or more of the population has no more access to clean water – this, in a country that had

[1] Continuity between the Clinton and Bush administrations is worth recalling. In 1993 Clinton informed the UN that the US will act 'multilaterally when possible but unilaterally when necessary'. Six years later, in 1999, Clinton's Secretary of Defence William Cohen declared that the US is committed to 'unilateral use of military power' to defend vital interests which include 'ensuring uninhibited access to key markets, energy supplies, and strategic resources'.

the most developed welfare state among the more populous of the Arab countries.[2] Large parts of northern Iraq have been put outside the sovereign jurisdiction of the Iraqi government to the extent that even its aircraft are not allowed in those zones while American and British planes patrol the whole area freely. There are reports of foreign as well as mercenary troops having already arrived in the region around Mosul.[3] The question, therefore, is not whether Iraq shall be invaded or not – it is already under prolonged invasion – but the likely timing, scale and consequences of the vastly escalated destruction that the US is intent on inflicting on the suffering people of that country.

The speech of President Bush to the UN General Assembly on 12 September 2002, which was hailed in the western media as a deft invitation for multilateralism, was in fact a virtual ultimatum of war, threatening, yet again, a 'regime change' and putting forth nine conditions that Iraq must meet in order to avoid an invasion – in a manner remarkably similar to the way the US had couched its ultimatum to the Taliban on the eve of the invasion of Afghanistan. 'Regime change' is of course the euphemism the US uses for its plan to replace an existing government with a client outfit, as it did in the case of Afghanistan, forcing out the Taliban and foisting the Karzai dispensation. There is obviously nothing Saddam can offer in return. Even the other conditions – total disarmament, for example – far exceed the UN focus on weapons

[2] Documentation regarding the devastation of Iraq through war and subsequent UN-imposed sanctions is vast. A fine collection of articles soon after the Gulf War of 1991 can be found in Phyllis Bennis and Michel Moushabeck (eds), *Beyond the Storm: A Gulf Crisis Reader*, New York: Olive Branch Press, 1991. The best single collection of articles on the havoc caused by the sanctions is Anthony Arnove (ed.), *Iraq Under Siege: The Deadly Impact of Sanctions and War*, London: Pluto Press, 2002, updated edition; Indian reprint from New Delhi: Viva Books.
[3] By early 2003, evidence of this kind of covert intervention had mounted to such a degree that even *Time* magazine ran a cover story entitled 'The CIA's Secret Army' on 3 February 2003.

inspectors to ensure that no facilities for production of weapons of mass destruction are operative. In short, Bush was deliberately going far beyond the Security Council Resolutions, demanding from Saddam what the latter cannot give and saying to the world, in effect, that the US would act with others if others accept the US policy, or it would act alone.[4]

When the combined diplomatic efforts of the Arab League and some European states succeeded in getting Iraq to agree unconditionally to the re-entry of the weapons inspectors in a peace initiative that was hailed by everyone from Kofi Annan to Nelson Mandela, the swift rejection of the initiative by the US was not very surprising, since the larger US design could hardly be deflected by resolving the issue that has been foremost for everyone else. Indeed, the last few weeks have witnessed an extraordinary effort by a wide variety of forces in the world to stave off what appears to be inevitable. President Chirac of France and Chancellor Schröder of Germany have openly opposed the idea of a full-scale invasion, going out of their way to say so in the most prestigious sections of the US press. Russia has said that it would veto any such resolution if one is presented to the Security Council. Kofi Annan has expressed horror at the idea of a war of that kind. Nelson Mandela, perhaps the most revered world leader alive today, has declared that the current US policies are 'a threat

---

[4] This unilateralism in waging illegal wars in pursuit of its own interests has of course been a punctual feature of US policy since at least the Second World War, and the US is the only country in the world that has been condemned by the World Court for international terrorism (in a case brought against it by the Sandinista government of Nicaragua on the question of US sponsorship of the Contra terrorists). Just about the time that Bush addressed the UN he also sent to the US Congress a lengthy document, National Security Strategy of the United States, in which a novel doctrine of 'preventive war' (as distinguished from 'preemptive war') which violates several articles of the UN Charter and in which the US reserves for itself the right to invade a country even when there is no evidence of imminent threat from that country.

to world peace' and has described US Vice President Dick Cheney, the current leader of the war lobby, as a 'dinosaur' – harsh language indeed from a man whose soft-spoken manner is legendary. From Qatar and Saudi Arabia to Turkey, most of Iraq's neighbours have demurred at the idea of permitting the US the use of military bases on their territory for the contemplated invasion.[5] All this has been done in the most visible way possible, precisely because the US move seemed imminent. *Financial Times* has even reported the withdrawal of as much as $ 200 billion of Saudi investments from the US banks and, at the very height of these tensions, a high-level Saudi delegation visited Baghdad to discuss expanded economic ties, even perhaps a free trade zone with Iraq, in the future.

Intentions of the US have actually been an open secret for some time. A typical story in the *Observer* of 4 August 2002 thus began with the following words: 'President George W. Bush will announce within weeks that he intends to depose Iraq's ruler, Saddam Hussein, by force, setting the stage for a war in the Gulf this winter. "The expectation is that President Bush will make a final decision on the timing of a war over the course of August. That would be followed by British-led efforts to get a mandate for action at the UN, either under existing resolutions or a new UN resolution", said one senior source. The disclosure came as US Secretary of State Colin Powell dismissed an offer by Iraq to talk to the chief weapons inspector of the United Nations. "Inspection is not the issue, disarmament is, making sure that the Iraqis have

---

[5] Later, as the invasion became imminent, most of these countries succumbed and the US indeed used bases in Qatar, Kuwait, etc. Only mass public demonstration prevented Turkey from joining in the war at the time. By now, in August 2003, the Turkish President has agreed in principle to contribute substantial troops to the 'allied' armies in Iraq under US command, although final decision by parliament is still awaited.

no weapons of mass destruction", said Powell during a visit to Manila.'

John Bolton, US Under Secretary for Arms Control, was quoted in the same story as saying 'Let there be no mistake – while we also insist on the reintroduction of the weapons inspectors, our policy at the same time insists on regime change in Baghdad and that policy will not be altered, whether inspectors go in or not'. The story then went on to say 'In a further indication of preparations for war on both sides of the Atlantic, Tony Blair is expected to begin a campaign of softening up public opinion for war in the autumn'.

An analysis of troop deployments in the region that this author saw just about that time in early August estimated that 'the US already has well over 100,000 military personnel in as many as 11 countries around Iraq. Additional analysis shows that another 100,000 or more crack assault and support personnel have just completed a major training exercise for a hypothetical conflict that bears a strong resemblance to Iraq. These troops can be ready to fight in the region on 96-hour notice. "Stealth" mobilizations of Reserve and National Guard units, begun after September 11, also indicate that as many as another 150,000 military personnel can be deployed within days or weeks of an initial surprise attack. . . . All told, including foreign troops, there are potentially 400,000 military personnel that are either in the theatre of operations, ready to go, or deployable on very short notice. There are many other units that have gone into stealth mode and cannot be located.'

Similar predictions had come some ten days earlier in a public speech by Scott Ritter, former UN weapons inspector in Iraq for seven years, who had previously been part of the US Marine Corps for twelve years, had fought against Iraq during the

Gulf War and introduced himself on the occasion of the speech as 'a card-carrying Republican in the conservative-moderate range who voted for George W. Bush for President'. At the time when he was serving as a weapons inspector in Iraq he was widely known to fly frequently to Tel Aviv and coordinate his policies closely with the Israel military intelligence. Over time, however, he had come to believe, and to say openly, that 90 to 95 of the facilities in Iraq that could possibly be used for production of chemical and biological weapons or for nuclear weapons had been destroyed so thoroughly that continuation of the blockade made no sense. He was dismissed from the UN team under pressure of his own government for holding such views. On the occasion of the Boston speech, this is what he had to say: 'The Third Marine Expeditionary Force in California is preparing to have 20,000 Marines deployed in the (Iraq) region for ground combat operations by mid-October. . . . The Air Force used the vast majority of its precision-guided munitions blowing up caves in Afghanistan. Congress just passed emergency appropriations money and told Boeing Company to accelerate their production of the GPS satellite kits . . . by September 30, 2002. Why? Because the Air Force has been told to have three air expeditionary wings ready for combat operations in Iraq by mid-October. . .You got 20,000 Marines forward deployed in October, you better expect war in October.'

Ritter also had an explanation for all this war-mongering: 'The national security of the United States of America has been hijacked by a handful of neo-conservatives who are using their position of authority to pursue their own ideologically-driven political ambitions'. Not bad for a Republican and a former Marine officer! Ritter has elsewhere testified that Iraq was justified in complaining that the United States had sought to use the inspectors in the UN Special Commission (UNSCOM) for spying purposes and for gathering information unrelated to any nuclear facilities or to any plants for production of weapons of mass destruction.

Ritter offered those remarks in Boston on 24 July. Five days later, on the 29th, *Financial Times* (*FT*) reported on an interview that the distinguished Swedish diplomat Rolf Ekeus, who had formerly headed UNSCOM for seven years, had given Swedish radio in which he was reported as saying that there was no doubt that countries, especially the US, attempted to increase their influence over the inspections to favour their own interests. 'As time went on, some countries, especially the US, wanted to learn more about other parts of Iraq's capacity'. According to *FT*, Mr Ekeus said the US tried to find information about the whereabouts of Saddam Hussein, Iraq's President, and that the US and other members of the Security Council pressed the teams to inspect sensitive areas, such as Iraq's ministry of defence when it was politically favourable for them to create a crisis situation. In a separate interview with Svenska Dagbladet, the Swedish newspaper, Mr Ekeus also said that he had learnt after he left his position that the US had placed two of its own agents in the group of inspectors.[6]

That Iraq has offered to let such inspectors return without

---

[6] The case of Rolf Ekues is most curious. He has the reputation of being a liberal, suave, impartial diplomat and civil servant. However, in an article entitled 'Meet the Real WMD Fabricator: A Swede called Rolf Ekeus', in *Counterpunch* of 2 August 2003, Alexander Cockburn revealed that when Ekeus was heading UNSCOM he was briefed, as indeed the CIA and other western intelligence agencies and foreign offices were also briefed, by high-ranking Iraqi officials who had defected to the West, including Saddam's brother-in-law, who testified that Iraq had indeed destroyed its stock of chemical and biological weapons in 1995, and that Iraq had no ongoing nuclear weapons production program. Ekeus did not reveal this information and continued with his inspections as if such information did not exist. Had he revealed the information, the very basis for the UN sanctions would have collapsed, tens of thousands of Iraqi lives would have been saved, and the subsequent invasion itself may have been avoided. The collusion of such 'liberal' people is part of the story of the destruction of Iraq.

any preconditions certainly shows that it is trying to avoid a war at all costs. Considering that the US has committed itself unilaterally to toppling him ('regime change'), the move is obviously meant to address other Arab regimes, the European Union, the UN and world opinion at large so that the world does not rally behind the United States as happened in the case of Afghanistan. The hopeful sign here is that both France and Germany have said that no new UN resolution is needed for speedy despatch of inspectors to Iraq, for which preparations have begun already, and that public opinion across Europe, including Britain, is overwhelmingly against the US design for full-scale invasion even as opinion across the Arab world is solidly against such a move. The European mood is well reflected in the remark that Germany's current Justice Minister, Herta Daeubler-Gmelin, is reported to have made to a gathering of trade union leaders in which she said that Bush was comparable to Hitler in that both used war to deflect attention from domestic problems (*International Herald Tribune*, 20 September 2002).[7]

The real danger lies in the extensive US commitment to unilateral action, the solidity and sweeping scale of the US strategic design, and the propensity of the other major powers, including Russia and China, to eventually accept US unilateralism, in some puported larger interest. What, then, is that inflexible strategic design which the events of 11 September 2001 have allowed the US to pursue with dramatic vigour? And where does Iraq fit into it? We shall take up these two questions in sequence.

As for the strategic design, we could begin with a commentary that appeared in *Pravda* on 19 September 2001, eight days after the attack on the World Trade Centre but one day before

---

[7] In the event, the said Justice Minister was removed from her post soon after her remark, made in a private meeting with some trade union leaders, came to light.

Bush made his famous speech announcing a 'global war against terrorism'. The commentary was significantly titled 'America to Wage War for USSR Inheritance' and it said, in part: 'the ruling Republican Party is going to correct America's domestic and foreign policies due to the grand terrorist attack. The Democrats' remnants are going to be completely removed from the military and reconnaissance structures and the control over the private and public life of the American people is going to be toughened. . . . The US will shift its emphasis from hi-tech constituents over to the raw materials companies – the ones which deal with oil and gas fuel first and foremost . . . and the national ABM program will certainly be launched. . . . The USA will use those priority procedures when fortifying the armed forces in the Persian Gulf area, modernizing the bases there, and delivering additional arms and defence technology. . . . America will increase its military presence along the entire 40th parallel, which is what we can see now in Bosnia, Kosovo, and Macedonia; soon we will also see it in the republics of Georgia, Azerbaijan, Turkmenia, and Uzbekistan. The Injirlik military base, which is deployed in Turkey, will surely be modernized, and this base will become one of the key points of the American presence. The establishment of reserve points on the territory of several countries of the Commonwealth of Independent States will be performed under different forms. However, the mid-Caspian area and Turkmenia's deposits will be taken under the control of the United States. It should be mentioned that the authorities of Azerbaijan and Georgia republics are in willing contact with NATO and the United States. . . . The USA will make the republics of Middle Asia to reconsider the Collective Security Treaty of the CIS and Russian troops will be called back to Russian territory. The United States will gain total control over Central Asia, over the Indian Ocean, and the country will be able to efficiently control the processes in Indo-China and

Indonesia. This will actually bring about the total control of the United States of America over the Islamic world, since the moves of Iran, Pakistan, and Iraq will depend upon the military presence of the United States.'

We have quoted at length because what the US has done over the past one year, in the name of 'war against terrorism', is very close to what this remarkably prescient commentary had predicted, in virtually every detail. By January 2002, barely four months after the 11 September events of last year, US military tent cities had sprung up in 13 new bases around Afghanistan and in proximity of Iraq, including all five of the Central Asian countries that have arisen out of the territorial collapse of the former USSR. From Bulgaria to Uzbekistan and Kuwait to Turkey, some 60,000 US troops were living in these forward bases. And what had formerly been tiny bases were quickly expanded and modernized, as for example the one at Al Adid in Qatar, where some modest expansion had begun in April 2,000 but which has now received a billion-dollar investment and built a 15,000-foot runway to take the largest of US planes in good numbers. A large contingent of US troops is now due to arrive in Georgia. As regards Iraq itself, *Washington Post* of 27 August quoted Gen. Tommy R. Franks, commander of the US Central Command, as saying that American soldiers shall be there for 'a long, long time', somewhat on the model of Korea where there still are a good number of US troops roughly half a century after the end of the war.

These more recent developments can also be seen in terms of more long-term strategic perspectives that have been developing over some years, as illustrated by two documents reported recently, one from an American think-tank and the other from an Israeli one. Thus, *The Guardian* of 3 September 2002 referred to a paper published in 1996 by an Israeli think-tank, the Institute for Advanced Strategic and Political Studies, written for the former

Israeli Prime Minister, Binyamin Netanyahu, and entitled 'A Clean Break: A New Strategy for Securing the Realm'. It advocates that the Oslo Accords with the Palestinians be scrapped and that Israel refuse to vacate any of the occupied territories, concentrating instead on re-shaping the region. This re-shaping is supposed to start with the toppling of Saddam and establishing a Hashemite monarchy there, in conjunction with Jordan which would also be expected to help contain the Palestinian problem. Together with Turkey, this revamped Israeli-Jordanian-Iraqi axis would then roll back Syria and reorganize Lebanon by linking the Shia population there with that of the newly re-monarchized Iraq.

The most striking feature of this amazing document was that its chief author was Richard Perle, now chairman of the Defence Policy Board at the Pentagon,[8] assisted by a team of seven others which included such luminaries as Douglas Feith, Washington lawyer who now holds one of the four top posts at the Pentagon as Under Secretary of Policy. Several of these authors are connected, in one way or another, with the current US Vice President, Dick Cheney. No wonder that some of the anti-Zionist Israeli critics of Sharon and Cheney refer to the current US strategic design as in fact a US-Israeli design.

The other such document was reported in *Sunday Herald* of 15 September 2002. Entitled 'Rebuilding America's Defences: Strategies, Forces and Resources for a New Century', it was written before Bush was actually elected, in September 2000, by the neoconservative think-tank Project for the New American Century (PNAC), for Dick Cheney (now Vice President), Rumsfeld (now Defence Secretary), Paul Wolfowitz (Rumsfeld's deputy), Lewis Libby

[8] Perle subsequently resigned his post as chairman, even though he continued to be a member, of the Defence Policy Board at the Pentagon after his connections with arms dealers and smugglers such as Adnan Khashogi were revealed. He continues to appear around the world as an authoritative spokesman for US policy.

(Cheney's Chief of Staff) and Bush's brother Jeb. It says, among other things, that 'while the unresolved conflict with Iraq provides the immediate justification, the need for a substantial American force presence in the Gulf transcends the issue of the regime of Saddam Hussein' and calls upon the US to 'fight and decisively win multiple, simultaneous major theatre wars' as a 'core mission'. The document warns against the growing strength and potential for rivalry from Europe and designates China as a country where 'regime change' would be desirable, while also saying that countries like North Korea, Libya, Syria and Iran pose a threat that requires the creation of a 'world-wide command-and-control system'. It advocates the creation of `US Space Forces' and even recommends 'biological warfare' as a 'politically useful tool'.[9]

Documents of this kind abound in the United States but we have illustrated our argument here with these particular ones because (a) they state in blunt and extreme terms what has roughly been US policy at any rate, especially since the breakup of the Soviet Union; (b) because these two reports were actually drafted by, and for, the key policy-making group in the current administration; and (c) they also show the US-Israeli nexus in sharp outline. One may write a report for an Israeli think-tank one day and occupy a key position in the Pentagon the next day. On this point, Uri Avnery, the Israeli writer, has emphasized that what the Bush administration envisions today is something Sharon has been advocating since the 1980s.

Why does Iraq occupy such a central position in the current designs? For one thing, the US has had a strange love/hate

[9] Completed about a year before the attack on the World Trade Centre, the document went on to say that the proposed changes were so far-reaching that it would take a long time to implement them *unless an 'apocalyptic event' such as a 'new Pearl Harbor' were to occur and buttress the American will.* Events of 11 September were then indeed portrayed by the US administration and the servile media as a 'new Pearl Harbor' and the occasion to announce a US policy closely modelled upon the PNAC document.

relationship with the Ba'athist regime in Iraq. It helped the Ba'ath come to power, as an alternative to the then very powerful Iraqi communist party and to Nasserism on the pan-Arab scale. However, the Ba'ath's claims to leadership of Arab nationalism – comprised of certain kind of economic nationalism on the question of oil, and its implacable hostility toward Israel – has also been a great source of tension between the US and the Iraqi regime. Of the three major Arab oil-producing countries – along with Saudi Arabia and Kuwait – Iraq has been the only defiant one. It overthrew the kind of monarchy that survived in the other two countries as well as Jordan and the Emirates, all abject clients of the US Then Iraq was, along with Egypt and Syria, among the three Arab countries that sided with the Soviet Union during the Cold war. With the passing of Nasser and Sadat's reconciliation with both US and Israel, Iraq staked its claim for leadership of secular Arab nationalism, in whatever distorted form, and fancied itself relatively independent thanks to its oil resources.

These tensions between the US and Iraq were then dissolved after the Islamic Revolution in Iran and both viewed the Khomeini regime as a threat to their respective interests. It was upon US instigation that Saddam then invaded Iran, inaugurating a war that lasted for almost a decade, ruined Iraq economically, and cost roughly a million lives in each of the two countries. It was during the war against Iran that the US and UK supplied the Saddam regime with capacity to manufacture chemical and biological weapons, helping Saddam in other ways as well. After that war, however, Saddam made a fatal miscalculation when he planned to occupy Kuwait, partly in the light of the historic Iraqi territorial claim that Kuwait was a part of the country that had been separated from it forcibly by British colonialism, and partly to obtain massive economic resources to re-build the Iraqi economy which lay in shambles after the war with Iran. He thought that his alliance with the US was strong enough to get away with this scheme, and the US ambassador to Iraq at the time seems to have reassured him that the US would not take any great exception to it; whether the ambassador's assurances had been cleared with Washington or not still remains unclear. From the long-term perspective of the US/Israeli nexus, in any case, Saddam's invasion of Kuwait was unforgivable because Kuwait was a secure US client whereas a successful Iraqi occupation of Kuwait – a principality that had often been administered from Baghdad or Basra until the British bestowed upon it a monarchy of its own – would have united a fifth of the world's known oil resources under a government that was hostile to the Saudi monarchy and saw itself as an adversary of Israel as well as an emerging giant in the region. That was the political side of why, since the Gulf War, Iraq has been the singular country where exemplary punishment had to be administered for defying America's will, even though the Ba'athists were brought to power by the CIA and Saddam had fought a war against Iran on America's behalf.

The economic side has been, if anything, even more compelling. The National Energy Policy Report, named after Dick Cheney and known as the 'Cheney Report', which was released by the US administration in May 2001, showed that half of the US oil consumption already came from imports and that the share of imports could rise to two-thirds by 2020. The war over Afghanistan was in an important sense a war for oil of the Caspian basin, aside from 'a war over Soviet inheritance', as *Pravda* put it, and the build-up of US military presence in Southeast Asia, notably the Philippines, is designed as much for control over the Malacca Straits and sea-routes to east Asia as it is about stationing troops close to Indonesian oil.[10] However, with its proven reserves of

---

[10] On the question of the Philippines, see my 'The Philippines as the next US target', *Frontline*, 19 July 2002.

112 billion barrels Iraq is in quite a different league than, say, the Caspian Basin where the proven reserves still stand at barely 15 billion and even speculative estimates of 95 billions still fall short of what Iraq is known to have; as for estimates, some suggest that it may have the largest amount of hydrocarbon deposits in the world, exceeding those of Saudi Arabia. It is on the strength of these expectations that Saddam Hussein has been awarding exploration rights to European, Russian and Chinese companies – not to speak of the much lesser ones from India, Vietnam or Algeria – while seeking their political support in curbing the US threat. The flip side of course is that the US itself is luring those same countries with promises of a share in the loot after the war if they would support the US in installing its clients there – and threatening with denial of share in the loot if they don't. Considering that the US surely has the military capability, and apparently abundant political will as well, to seize Iraqi oil unilaterally, these non-US corporations are wondering whether it would not be more prudent to try and win favour with the US in hopes of future accommodations, while the US is still looking for some international backing. Reports suggest that national governments of these non-US corporations are currently discussing the future of Iraqi oil both with US officials as well as the various puppets the US is considering for a post-Saddam dispensation. Ahmed Chalabi is in fact only one of these various puppets under consideration. The kind of pressures and temptations – carrots and sticks – that the US is holding out is well illustrated, for example, by the following statement by the former CIA director James Woolsey as he was quoted in *The Washington Post* on 15 September 2002: 'France and Russia have oil companies and interests in Iraq. They should be told that if they are of assistance in moving Iraq towards decent government, we'll do the best we can to ensure that the new government and American companies

will work with them. If they throw their lot with Saddam, it will be difficult to the point of impossible to persuade the new Iraq government to work with them.'

Bush and Cheney have both worked in the oil business and have close ties with the major corporations in the field. They have already installed Karzai, formerly an employee of the UNOCAL corporation, in Afghanistan. Plans are afoot for the formation of a consortium of US corporations to manage Iraqi oil after the war, in coordination with the Iraqi National Congress (INC), an umbrella organization of groups floated and kept afloat by the United States. The group is headed by Ahmed Chalabi, a scion of a family very prominent in the monarchist period, who merrily says that 'American companies will have a big shot at Iraqi oil'. For one thing, a revival of Iraq's petroleum production to its full potential under US control could pave the way for the break-up of OPEC and steep fall for prices of oil from Russia, Venezuela or Iran, with disastrous consequences for the economies of such countries. All this could also put to rest the growing nervousness in Washington about Saudi Arabia.

Majority of those who plotted and carried out the 11 September actions were middle class Saudi youth. Key members of Al Qaida came from wealthy Saudi families, including Osama bin Laden who came not from the royal family but a very prominent one close to it. Osama was so popular among the Saudi youth that the kingdom refused to freeze his assets despite US pressure, fearing a rebellion. It is said that he was even financed by some elements of the royal family which feel that unquestioned Saudi loyalty to the US is harmful to their own interests. The international channels of Osama's finances were so deeply connected with those of many a prominent Saudi financiers that the US could not isolate his accounts and starting thinking of freezing a good number of Saudi accounts in US banks, which is said to have precipitated a surge of Saudi withdrawals, which in turn is said to have contributed to recent fall in value of the dollar. Meanwhile, the royal family has warned that Sharon's policies in Palestine are creating such distress among Arabs that it cannot forever support all US policies. Many an expert believe that Saudi Arabia is on the brink of an anti-monarchist revolution.

In other words, the situation is unstable. Grabbing Iraqi oil is important for the US both as alternative source in case of possible Saudi collapse but also as a point of pressure upon the Saudis in case they have some rebellious thoughts in their head. With the Caspian basin already captured, the fall of Iraq could give the US unprecedented superiority in the resource war against not only Russia or China but also its friendly rivals in Western Europe and Japan, especially since the US could then control not only the production but also the directions of flow of most of the oil in the world; pipelines would go in one direction rather than another.

The case in favour of a full conquest of Iraq is thus overwhelming. That virtually the whole world is ranged against such a move, especially now that Iraq has agreed to give the inspectors full and unconditional access, is certainly a deterrent but by no means an insurmountable one if the US does decide to act unilaterally. However, there are obstacles. The kind of occupation which may yield the desired results will require a much larger land army than was necessary in Afghanistan, considerable loss of life and a much longer presence for a considerable number of Americans even after victory of some sort is obtained. It is not at all clear that the US public, pliant and stupidly patriotic as it is, would be ready for that kind of prolonged war situation for its own boys. And if the US simply comes in, destroys and leaves, the outcome is even less clear. Will Iraq break up into three entities – Kurdish, Shia and Sunni – while all sorts of gangs fight among themselves for grabbing slices of resources? That is the most likely outcome but that kind of chaos is hardly conducive to long-term exploitation of resources. Sharon has been killing Palestinians with unspeakable savagery and complete impunity, and yet there has been no perceptible convulsion in the Arab world; will the same calm prevail even after the destruction and occupation of Iraq? One cannot predict with any precision. Yet, we may be sliding into a situation where the US may have already gone too far to now retreat, and the Iraqis may yet give the US more trouble than it has prepared for. What then?

When will the war come, if it does come? Probably not before the mid-term US elections in early November this year, but not very much later either, since Bush will then have about 18 months in which to finish his campaign for the capture of Iraq before his own re-election campaign begins. But, then, no one really knows.

31 JANUARY 2003
US Design and Global Complicity

With 120,000 US troops already stationed in the Gulf region, reservists being called up across the country, and the US gripped by war hysteria, all the way from its leaders to its media networks to the overwhelming majority of the population, it now seems beyond doubt that the full-scale invasion – and possible occupation – of Iraq by the US shall come sooner rather than later, even though the UN-appointed inspectors, who are doing the US bidding, have so far failed to produce any evidence of Iraq's having in its possession or having the capacity to produce any weapons of mass destruction, be they nuclear or biological or chemical weapons.[1] The US seems determined to proceed with its plans, however, regardless of any evidence proving or disproving its claims, while it is also possible that some sort of evidence may well be manufactured in the foreseeable future. In any case, the invasion shall come because it is part of a much larger, inflexible global design which we shall detail below. Before proceeding with that wider analysis, though, it is important to recall some salient

[1] In a report oddly entitled 'US Decision On Iraq Has Puzzling Past', *Washington Post* of 12 January 2003 revealed that 'On September 17, 2001, six days after the attacks on the World Trade Centre and the Pentagon, President Bush signed a 2½-page document marked "TOP SECRET" that outlined the plan for going to war in Afghanistan as part of a global campaign against terrorism. Almost as a footnote, the document also directed the Pentagon to begin planning military options for an invasion of Iraq, senior administration officials said'.

features of the situation as it has prevailed in the immediate past.

In an article that was published some months ago ('In the Shadow of Permanent War' in this volume) I had pointed out that the Anglo-American bombardment of Iraq had lasted longer than the US war on Vietnam, indeed longer than the combined duration of the two world wars. This began with the Gulf War of 1991 which, in a very important sense, has never ended. It was then, some twelve years ago, that Bush Senior, the father of the current US President, first determined that the overthrow of Saddam Hussein and full mastery over Iraq was a key objective, and the US has never swerved away from that objective. The only reason why the full-scale invasion which is now impending did not come sooner is that while the objective of overthrowing Saddam and defeating the Iraqi army could be achieved very quickly, thanks to overwhelming US military superiority, the US has never been quite sure what would follow that victory and has therefore toyed with various more or less dubious scenarios while its unremitting warmongering has held a nation of 22 million suffering people to ransom.

In an opinion piece that Victor Marshall contributed to *Los Angeles Times* on 5 January 2003, he reminds us of some of that suffering: 'A United Nations mission in March 1991 described the allied bombing of Iraq as "near apocalyptic" and said it threatened to reduce "a rather highly urbanized and mechanized society to a pre-industrial age". . . . A subsequent demographic study by the US Census Bureau concluded that Iraq probably suffered 145,000 dead – 40,000 military and 5,000 civilian deaths during the war and 100,000 postwar deaths because of violence and health conditions. The war also produced more than 5 million refugees. Subsequent sanctions were estimated to have killed more than half a million Iraqi children, according to the UN Food and

Agriculture Organization and other international bodies'. Meanwhile, air power was used to destroy or cripple Iraqi infrastructure and industry. This included destruction of electric power stations and refineries which deprived Iraq of 92 per cent of installed power capacity as well as 80 per cent of its oil production capacity, not to speak of the destroyed petrochemical complexes, telecommunications centres (including 135 telephone networks), bridges (more than 100), roads, highways, railroads, hundreds of locomotives and boxcars full of goods, radio and television broadcasting stations, cement plants, and factories producing aluminium, textiles, electric cables, and medical supplies. The losses were estimated by the Arab Monetary Fund to be $ 190 billion.

Having done all that about a decade ago, the Anglo-American axis has kept up its pressure in numerous ways. US officials have owned up to seven coup attempts that they have instigated; how many more there were, we do not know. The failure of those coup attempts is sometimes cited as a reason why nothing short of a full-scale invasion is likely to work. All of Iraq initially, and much of it subsequently, has been declared a 'no-fly zone' where the Anglo-American axis powers do not allow the government of the country to fly its own aircraft, in flagrant violation of Iraq's sovereignty and without any basis in international law or a Security Council Resolution; they have bombed most of the country at will, again without any sanction from the Security Council. Indeed, the conversion of the Security Council into a tool to implement its own designs has been a singular achievement of the United States and its supine allies during this period, with respect to Iraq and Palestine as much as the various parts of the former Yugoslavia. It is purely on the insistence of the US that the Security Council imposed upon Iraq the most draconian sanctions that any country has ever had to face, and it has done absolutely nothing to punish the US-UK which has imposed those 'no-fly zones' without any basis in international law. Writing in *Foreign Affairs* ('Sanctions of Mass Destruction', May/June 1999), Karl and John Mueller pointed out that those have killed more Iraqis than had been killed by 'all the weapons of mass destruction in human history'. As Denis Halliday, former Assistant Secretary General of the United Nations and UN Humanitarian Coordinator in Iraq 1997–98, put it in his recent speech in Cairo 'We have a UN Security Council out of control. A Council corrupted by the USA, the sole hyper-power, and undermined by the veto power of the five permanent members'. He then goes on to point out that the claim that Iraq possesses weapons of mass destruction is a 'Washington fiction' and that the sanctions against Iraq, which have been in place for twelve years and have caused unspeakable sufferings for millions of people, 'are built on US war crimes' and constitute an 'ongoing collective punishment of Iraqi people'.[2]

Under cover of this 'no-fly zone' and incessant bombardment, the US has tried to install a parallel government of its choosing, stationed in the US-protected Kurdish territory in Northern Iraq and comprised of the Iraqi National Council (INC), which it has spawned under the shadowy leadership of Chalabi, a scion of a monarchist Iraqi family who was sentenced in absentia some years ago to a total of thirty-four years of hard labour by the Central Court of Amman for embezzlement of funds from the Petra Bank of Jordan. This Chalabi is a great favourite of the far-right super-hawks in power at the Pentagon who are generally known as the 'Wolfowitz cabal' – named after the deputy secretary of state Paul Wolfowitz – and may yet be imposed on Iraq pretty much the way Karzai, a former employee of UNOCAL corporation, was imposed on Afghanistan. The CIA is said to have invested $

---

[2] See Appendix: 'Report to UN Security Council: re Iraq' by the former US Attorney-General Ramsey Clarke.

100 million in propping up that puppet entity and its base in northern Iraq, which was then routed by the Iraqi army in 1997, with Chalabi fleeing to the UK, thousands of his followers fleeing to Turkey and perhaps an equal number losing their lives to the Iraqi troops. One of the consequences of that misadventure has been that the CIA has lost faith in Chalabi while the Pentagon hawks, with little experience, continue to believe in him, so that the CIA continues to rely on its own professional operatives for information-gathering while the Pentagon hawks, not getting from the CIA the information they want, have created a parallel agency of their own, which listens more to Chalabi and his 'dissidents'. The prompted testimony of these hired 'dissidents' shall soon be used to justify full-scale invasion. The US has also instructed the UN inspectors to get Iraqi scientists to defect. Once in US custody, these captive scientists be required to corroborate the 'evidence' provided by those US-manufactured dissidents.

This focus on Iraq has taken remarkable turns. We now know that on the morning of 12 September 2001, the day after the World Trade Centre events, the US Defence Secretary Rumsfeld argued vigorously in favour of invading Iraq as the first target and was only dissuaded by Secretary of State Colin Powell's argument that Al Qaida was more clearly connected with Afghanistan, that Afghanistan was an easier country to invade and conquer, and that the US should not be engaged in two theatres of war simultaneously. A month later, on 13 October 2001, *The International Herald Tribune (IHT)* revealed that the Pentagon-based Defence Policy Board, a powerful bipartisan group of national security experts, met for nineteen hours on 19 and 20 September, and members of the board agreed 'on the need to turn to Iraq as soon as *the initial phase* of the war against Afghanistan and Mr bin Laden's organization was over'. (Emphasis added) The dates of the meeting (19/20 September) are significant: this was concurrent with the televised address to the joint session of the US Congress in which Bush famously declared his 'global war on terrorism'. If anything, the membership of the 18-member bipartisan board is even more significant, as it includes Harold Brown, President Jimmy Carter's Defence Secretary; former Secretary of State Henry Kissinger; James Woolsey, director of central intelligence in the Clinton administration; Admiral David Jeremiah, the former Deputy Chairman of the Joint Chiefs of Staff; former Vice President Dan Quayle; and James Schlesinger, a former defence and energy secretary.

It was at this meeting that Woolsey, the former CIA chief, was directed to proceed to Europe to (a) 'find' information that would link Iraq with the 11 September events and (b) consult with the London-based Iraqi 'dissidents' (Chalabi and company) regarding the feasibility of instigating uprisings within the country. That same report in *IHT* quoted Newt Gingrich, the notorious former speaker of the US House of Representatives and a member of the group, as saying, 'If we don't use this as the moment to replace Mr. Saddam after we replace the Taliban, we are setting the stage for disaster'. The report also went on to say that the group was 'laying the groundwork for a strategy that envisions the use of air support and the occupation of southern Iraq with American ground troops to install an Iraqi opposition group based in London at the helm of a new government. . . . Under this notion, American troops would also seize the oil fields around Basra, in southeastern Iraq, and sell the oil to finance the Iraqi opposition in the south and the Kurds in the north'.

We shall return to the matter of this rather incredible 'strategy' but the matter of this group, and especially of its leading lights such as Wolfowitz himself as well as Richard Perle who chairs it, should detains us somewhat longer. These two, along with the current Vice President Cheney, were prominent figures at the Pentagon during Bush Senior's administration and were then – along with Rumsfeld, Lewis Libby (Cheney's chief of staff), William Bennet (Reagan's Education Secretary) and Zalmay Khalilzad (Bush's ambassador to Afghanistan) – founders of the key think-tank called 'Project for the New American Century' (PNAC), which was itself one of the chain of right-wing think-tanks, such as the American Enterprise Institute, the Hudson Institute, the Institute for Democracy and so on. Jason Vest of *The Village Voice* (21-27 November 2001), Neil Mackey of *Sunday Herald* (15 September 2002) and John Pilger in *New Statesman* (16 December 2002) are among journalists who have drawn our attention to the PNAC's seminal report, 'Rebuilding America's Defences: Strategy, Forces and Resources for a New Century', drafted as a blueprint of American aims for Bush Junior before he actually won – rather, stole – the Presidential election. As Pilger phrases it, 'Two years ago it recommended an increase in arms-spending by $ 48bn so that Washington could "fight and win multiple, simultaneous major theatre wars". This has happened. It said the United States should develop "bunker-buster" nuclear weapons and make "star wars" a national priority. This is happening. It said that, in the event of Bush taking power, Iraq should be a target. And so it is.'

That report had described the global spread of the US military forces as 'the cavalry on the new American frontier'. It recommends that the US replace the United Nations in 'peacekeeping' projects; that bases in Saudi Arabia, Kuwait and elsewhere in the Gulf be maintained even after Saddam's overthrow; that the US encourage 'regime change' in China and undertake 'increase of American forces in Southeast Asia'; that 'US Space Forces' be created to ensure supremacy in space and total control of cyberspace; that the US consider developing 'advanced forms of biological warfare'; and identifies North Korea, Libya, Syria and Iran as among the states that require the US to establish a 'worldwide command-and-control system'. As Neil Mackay points out, 'The PNAC blueprint supports an earlier document written by Wolfowitz and Libby that said the US must "discourage advanced industrial nations from challenging our leadership or even aspiring to a larger regional or global role".' This aspect of the recommendation is clearly directed against Japan and Western Europe.

It is now, after 11 September 2001, rather eerie and astonishing that this report, drafted a year before those events, actually suggested that what America needed as justification for putting in place its global design for the 21st century was 'some catastrophic and catalysing event - like a new Pearl Harbor'. As images of the World Trade Centre tragedy were flashed across the world, incessantly, day in and day out, dozens of commentators indeed compared that event to Pearl Harbor again and again and again, until the analogy - the two great and evil attacks on America - were indelibly inscribed in the minds of viewers, especially within the United States. And, the tragedy of thousands of grieving families was soon turned into the empire's golden opportunity. Nicholas Lemann revealed in the *New Yorker* of April 2002 that Condoleeza Rice, Bush's National Security Advisor, told him she had called her senior officers and asked them 'to think about "how do you capitalize on these opportunities"'.

As regards the military design, that thinking has centred essentially on one question: should the US fight several wars at the same time (a view held by many in the Pentagon) or should it go after its designated little enemies around the globe one by one (the Powell view)? According to James Webb, a former Assistant Secretary of Defence and Secretary of Navy in the Reagan administration, this debate as well as the unwavering focus on Iraq has been going on for over a decade. As he puts it, it is 'a rift that goes back to the Gulf War itself, when neoconservatives were vocal in their calls for "a MacArthurian regency in Baghdad"'. (*Washington Post*, 4 September 2002) In other words, they have been arguing for all these years in favour of a full-scale US occupation which would last long enough to re-make the Iraqi state much as the US re-made the Japanese state after the Second World War. Webb himself, who confesses to being a former Marine officer and an abiding Republican, offers unanswerable arguments as to why this is pure fantasy. However, that kind of argument gained great momentum after 11 September, especially because those who represented that view were now fully in control of the US military policy at the Pentagon. Thus, Jason Vest was already reporting in November 2001: 'According to both Pentagon and intelligence sources, in mid-September the Project for the New American Century – a hawkish private policy group whose membership overlaps with the official Defence Policy Board – sent President Bush a letter after a two-day conference, declaring that failure to promptly remove Saddam would constitute a "decisive surrender in the war against terrorism". Ominously, it also held that if Syria and Iran refused to drop all support for Hezbollah, "the administration should consider appropriate measures of retaliation against these known state sponsors of terrorism". . . . Perle's Defence Policy Board also sent Bush a letter recommending all measures be taken to install the heretofore dubious and ineffectual Iraqi National Congress of Ahmed Chalabi as new leadership in Baghdad, backed by the deployment of American troops to secure Iraqi oil fields.'

By 2 December 2001, *The Observer* was reporting that 'America intends to depose Saddam Hussein by giving armed support to Iraqi opposition forces across the country. . . . President George W. Bush has ordered the CIA and his senior military commanders to draw up detailed plans for a military operation that could begin within months . . . the planning is being undertaken under the auspices of a the US Central Command at McDill air force base in Tampa, Florida, commanded by General Tommy Franks, who is leading the war against Afghanistan'. This same Tommy Franks was to later go on record as saying that the post-war settlement in Iraq will require the stationing of substantial US forces there for a long time, on the model of South Korea (where US troops have been stationed for half a century). This of course goes far beyond the earlier idea of a short-term 'MacArthrian regency'. General Tommy obviously fancies himself a proconsul for life, and then to be succeeded by similar proconsuls, into infinity.

By February 2002, Colin Powell, the Jamaican-born US Secretary of State who is generally credited to be the moderate and prudent voice in the Bush administration, was declaring that the question of the UN inspections of Iraqi facilities had become irrelevant and that the US was in any case committed to the removal of Saddam Hussein. Afghanistan had been captured by then and the US felt more confident of concentrating on this other, larger prize. Since then, a new generation of weapons are being churned out by the military-industrial complex; the US has established new military bases and upgraded the existing ones in the whole region; prepared its own corporations and negotiated with other countries the parameters for sharing out the Iraqi oil bonanza; cajoled the more powerful countries and intimidated the weaker ones into giving it a Security Council Resolution which can be easily interpreted as permission to wage war in case Iraq fails to meet any of the impossible demands that the US keeps making, including a 'regime change', i.e., imposition of a regime comprised of US clients. By now, of course, virtually all of Iraq's neighbours, from Qatar to Turkey, have fallen in line; as have, in the world of great powers, France, Germany and Russia.

I have traced this earlier history to illustrate how predictable the more recent events have been, and how much Iraq has been at the centre of an unfolding strategic design of a global scope. This design is rooted in the fact that we are living through an extremely dangerous phase of history, in which (a) the United States commands more power than any imperial centre ever has in entire human history, with no competitors worth the name; (b) the United States is ruled by not just the usual Republican right-wing but a regime so much of the Far Right that some of the more notorious US presidents of this century, from Teddy Roosevelt to Richard Nixon, seem positively more civilized; (a) the core of these far-right zealots have taken hold of the US military establishment in so complete a fashion that the Pentagon is emerging as something of an autonomous centre of power which treats even the CIA with contempt as being too liberal and cautious. (Perle is reported to have said that the information they are getting from the CIA is 'not worth the paper it is written on' and has helped Rumsfeld create parallel agencies more loyal to this far right cabal.)

Writing in the *The London Review of Books*, Anatol Lievan, a Senior Associate at the Carnegie Endowment for Peace in Washington D.C., has quite correctly described this far right cabal as 'the dominant neoconservative nationalists' and, more pointedly, as representatives of 'anti-Muslim American nationalism'. Every member of this cabal has had and continues to have extremely close relations with leaders of the Likud, Sharon's ruling party in Israel, in whose own policy formations Perle and Wolfowitz have featured prominently, so that in addition to the historic alignment of the US and Israeli policies, we are also witnessing a new and extremely dangerous convergence between the politically organized far right in the two countries as well as a historically unprecedented convergence between Zionism's expansionist militarism and the American Christian fundamentalist messianism. Aside from the key question of oil, Iraq is so central in their thinking because, if left to peace and prosperity, Iraq would be the last remaining Arab country that could effectively oppose Israel as part of its own ambition to emerge as a leader of secular Arab nationalism, which is the only ideology that is capable of harnessing the immense anti-imperialist sentiment that prevails in the Arab world.[3]

Conversely, in case of a full-scale invasion of Iraq, Israel is likely not only to accelerate its destruction of the Palestine Authority and impose upon the Palestinians a new regime comprised of its collaborators. It will look for opportunities to precipitate the exodus of maximum number of Palestinians of the West Bank and Gaza into such neighbouring states as Jordan and Egypt, and in the worst case scenario an Israeli military excursion into Syria and Lebanon cannot be ruled out. If this design succeeds, Iran would be the next target. Some 12 per cent of the Israeli air force is already in Southeastern Turkey and parts of it are routinely flying around the Irani border for gathering of intelligence, provocation, and so on. The US and Israel are also encouraging Azari separatism in Iran, with possible collusion from Turkey, and aggression against Iran can be prepared any day, on the pretext of its own nuclear programme.[4] Similarly, if Saudi Arabia finds it

[3] US policies in the Gulf region are closely coordinated with the policies and interests of Israel, and the Zionist element is virtually dominant among the neoconservatives who now control US military strategy. It is therefore not really possible to fully grasp US designs in this region without simultaneously understanding the nature of Israeli state, polity and strategy. See my 'Israel's Colonial War', *Frontline*, 1 March 2002; 'The Nazification of Israel', *Frontline*, 26 April 2002; and 'West Asia – the War that Never Ends', *Frontline*, 20 July 2002.
[4] In the *New York Times* of 16 February 2002, US Vice President Dick Cheney was quoted as saying, 'There is a great yearning on the part of the Iranian people to restore and re-establish relationships with the US and the West. By the same token, the government appears to be committed, for example, to trying to destroy the peace process as it relates to the Israeli-Palestinian conflict. And we've seen all too many examples of their active support of terrorism and their, as the President said the other night in the State of the Union speech, unstinting efforts to develop weapons of mass destruction'.

in its own interest to be less pliant or if there are radical, anti-monarchical developments there, the US may well move to create a separate entity there in the Shia-dominated eastern zone where much of the oil resources are located. And it is of course unclear what future awaits Iraq itself.

The US can dislodge Saddam easily and it is very likely that the Iraqi army shall disintegrate under unbearable military pressure; some commanders may even defect to the United States. However, it is very unlikely that men like Chalabi can provide a stable, even remotely popular government there. Massive disorder, with various ethnicities getting played out against each other, in an unending fight over spoils of war, is much more likely. The ongoing tussle among Kurdish, Turkmen and Arab groups in the oil-rich region around Kirkuk, thanks to the disintegration of the central Iraqi authority under Anglo-American pressure, is perahps a foretaste of things yet to come, after the full-scale invasion. As Lieven puts it in the article to which we have referred already, 'The planned war against Iraq is not after all intended only to remove Saddam Hussein, but to destroy the structure of the Sunni-dominated Arab nationalist Iraqi state as it has existed since that country's inception. The 'democracy' which replaces it will presumably resemble that of Afghanistan – a ramshackle coalition of ethnic groups and warlords, utterly dependent on US military power and utterly subservient to US (and Israeli) wishes'. Meanwhile, it is also possible that the level of the strife on the one hand, and the high stakes in establishing its own oil monopoly on the other, shall force the United States to station substantial number of its own troops in garrisons across Iraq and establish something of an 'indirect rule', in the style of colonialism's heyday, above the ethnic clients.

In a much broader geo-political perspective, complete monopoly over oil, the world's most strategic commodity, not only in the Gulf region and the Caspian Sea basin but also all the way from Venezuela to Indonesia, is also seen by these 'neoconservative American nationalists' as a major weapon for coercion and manipulation in their relations with secondary powers in the advanced industrialized world itself, Western Europe and Japan surely but also, increasingly, China. This, however, is a large and complex matter to which we shall return in a subsequent piece when we shall also detail some of the salient features of the new weapons systems as well as the weapondollar-petrodollar connection in the US military-industrial complex which is the driving force impelling the imperial authority toward permanent war.

14 FEBRUARY 2003
World Peace in the Balance

This article is being drafted on the afternoon of 25 January, the day before the UN inspectors are to deliver their preliminary report to the Security Council. Estimates of the Iraqi dead during a decade of a lawless siege by the US-UK alliance range between one million and a million and a half. It is not at all clear how many thousands, or hundreds of thousands, shall die in the course of the impending invasion and the subsequent war, chaos and misery that will inevitably drag on for months and years thereafter. Pretending to perpetrate this crime against a whole people in the name of the lofty purpose of getting rid of a dictator and making the world safe against 'international terrorism', this lawless alliance has tried to pass off its designs as something of a benevolent genocide; millions must die so that the US may gift to the remaining Iraqis the gift of a 'democracy' assembled by its clients which are at present headed by Chalabi, a convicted criminal.

Under duress, of course, these benevolent genocidists are quite willing to drop even this pretence. 'If it can't be solved peacefully and if the UN should fail to act, and I hope that is not the case, then the United States reserves the right to do what it thinks is appropriate to defend its interests', BBC News of 23 January has reported Mr Powell, the famed 'dove' of the Bush administration as saying.[1] The formulation is worth repeating: 'the

[1] This reputation of Colin Powell as a 'dove' and a 'moderate' is puzzling. Powell

United States reserves the right to do what it thinks is appropriate to defend its interests', and international law be damned! The latest twist, however, is that the UN is now quite likely to 'fail to act', the extraordinary brinksmanship of the unreliable Mr Blix notwithstanding. France, Russia and China – three of the five countries who command the veto power in the Security Council – have taken the position that (a) the Council must pass a fresh resolution authorizing military action if such action is to be taken; (b) the US has so far failed to establish and the inspectors have not so far produced any evidence that Iraq has any weapons of mass destruction; (c) if and when such evidence is produced, military action may emerge as a possible option but political solution must be first sought even then.

Germany, which does not have a veto but is clearly the most powerful European state, has said that it will simply not vote in favour of a resolution calling for full-scale military invasion of Iraq. 'War is proof of failure, everything must be done to avoid it', French President Jacques Chirac is reported to have said. Indicating that there was enough support across the EU – minus Britain – the French foreign minister Dominique de Villepin announced: 'It is important that Europe speak on this issue with a single voice. We are mobilized, we believe war can be avoided'. Belgium from within Europe and China from across the seas announced immediately that they held positions similar to that of France – 'on the same wavelength' was the Belgian foreign minister's phrase while the Chinese Foreign Ministry Spokeswoman Zhang Qiyue said that China would 'advocate solving the Iraq

---

first shot to fame during the Vietnam War when he authored a report justifying the My Lai massacre which had otherwise shaken the liberal conscience in the US, as something of a Jallianwalla Bagh of the Vietnam War. He has consistently argued that the US must maintain a military superiority so overwhelming that no rival or competitor ever arises to challenge its pursuit of the national interest, regionally or globally.

question through political and diplomatic means'. Not to be left behind, Russia has also said that there is no evidence that would justify a full-scale war in Iraq and Putin told President Bush in a telephone conversation that 'the main criterion' in assessing the situation in Iraq should be the weapons inspectors' findings. Meanwhile, *Globe and Mail*, the Canadian newspaper, reported on 24 January 2003: 'Prime Minister Jean Chrétien says the United States has not yet made the case for war with Iraq, and that he has told US President George W. Bush that Canada does not want the United States to attack without a UN mandate. Arguing that United Nations weapons inspectors should be given more time, a skeptical Mr. Chrétien said yesterday he is not afraid to part company with Canada's closest ally'. Galvanized by this strong position taken in unexpected quarters, a meeting of six Muslim countries which met in Turkey and included Saudi Arabia and Egypt as well as Iran – though, significantly, not Pakistan – declared themselves opposed to full-scale invasion of Iraq at this time and recommended diplomatic solutions.

We shall return to the causes and likely outcomes of this sudden erosion in the global complicity with the US, at least for the present. The extraordinary fact is that the unbridled belligerence of the US-UK alliance continues in the teeth of this erosion. 'Germany has been a problem, and France has been a problem', US Defence Secretary Donald Rumsfeld said loftily and then dismissed them, with contempt, as just 'old Europe' – as if only the statelets of Eastern Europe were the 'new' Europe. As for loss of support from Canada, which has had a relationship with the US even more slavish than that of Britain, he was equally nonchalant: 'it's up to Canada to decide what it wishes to do'. Richard Perle, a former Assistant Secretary of Defence (under Ronald Reagan) who now heads the powerful Defence Policy Board at the Pentagon, said with equal nonchalance that the US shall proceed with military action regardless of what the UN inspectors find or do not find. Meanwhile, the extraordinary US military mobilization continues, with troops pouring into the region around Iraq and reservists being called back to duty across the United States. Not to be outdone, and in sharp opposition to the other major EU states, the dim-witted Tony Blair has ordered another 26,000 British troops into the war theatre, promising the largest British military action since the equally mindless Suez adventure of 1956, forgetting that that adventure was the one that sent Anthony Eden, the then British Prime Minister, into oblivion. Time may yet come when Blair shall have to choose not only between the US and the EU but also between his loyalty to Bush and his own political survival in a country where anti-war sentiment is running at over eighty per cent, as it is in France and Germany as well.

This issue of the anti-war sentiment brings us back, then, to why dissent has grown so much and so suddenly in the world state system outside the US and UK. By far the most important is a virtually global rebellion, from below, against the prospect of the genocide under preparation. Second, the upsurge in the anti-war sentiment across the globe is then supplemented by the very impressive showing of the anti-globalization forces symbolized by the mass congregations of the Social Forums across the globe. The nightmare in the European capitals is that the anti-war movement shall converge fully with the anti-globalization movement and may bring about a worldwide anti-capitalist, anti-imperialist rebellion of an unprecedented scale and in historically novel political forms. Third, there is now a new upsurge of the left in the political field as such, quite aside from the anti-war demonstrations and the anti-globalization congregations but converging with them, as is symbolized by the government of Chavez in Venezuela and the election of Lula to the presidency of Brazil.

Fourth, Iraq has cooperated with the UN inspectors so thoroughly, throwing open the entire country, that no one who is not already committed to making war at all costs and against all evidence can claim that the failure of the inspectors to produce any credible evidence is owed to the Iraqi regime's intransigence; if they can't produce hard evidence of weapons of mass destruction, then it is most probable that the capacity to produce such weapons does not – at least, does not *any longer* – exist. Fifth, and inadvertently or not, North Korea has offered Iraq a reprieve. As the US threatens full destruction of Iraq on the flimsy grounds that the Saddam Hussein's regime has (yet unproven) weapons of mass destruction, North Korea has defiantly repudiated the Non-Proliferation Treaty and has been at best ambiguous in clarifying whether or not it has the capacity and/or the intention to produce nuclear weapons; this, on top of the fact that the US has been accusing North Korea of supplying nuclear missile technology to Pakistan and Iran. However, the US dare not move against North Korea because South Korea itself will not allow it, let alone Japan or China or Russia. So, the contemplated destruction of Iraq is clearly shown to be possible only because it is so very vulnerable and has only imperialism's clients for its neighbours – and clients far more supine than even South Korea which still has 37,000 US troops stationed on its soil but has calmly offered to 'mediate' in the dispute between the US and North Korea.

Finally, even the prospect of war has sent shock waves through the financial markets of the core countries, including Britain, and no one can quite tell how far the fall may go in case the US-UK crazies actually do what they are promising. These realities were palpable in the contrast between the two world economic forums that were held simultaneously, that of the managers of globalization in Davos, which sank into pessimism and irrelevance, and that of the anti-globalization forces in Porto

Alegre, which shimmered with enthusiasm and excitement at the level of strength the movement has achieved in a matter of five years or so. Significantly, President Lula, the son of an agricultural worker and himself a legendary trade union leader, was the chief guest at both events, celebrating the expansion of the anti-globalization forces in Porto Alegre and then telling assembled magnates of global capitalism at Davos that corporate globalization has little chances of survival and that capitalism would have to reform itself if it is to survive at all.

Some of these factors deserve further comment. When this author was last in North America, in December 2002, the scale of the anti-war movement was already impressive – indeed, exhilarating. Washington, San Francisco and New York had already witnessed the largest anti-war rallies since the Vietnam war and sizeable demonstrations had taken place by then in over 400 lesser cities and small towns of the US This author was then impressed by three facts. One, anti-war demonstrations of that size had first occurred in the US during the Vietnam period three years after Kennedy had first despatched US troops to fight there; now, it was happening even before a full-scale invasion had begun. Second, these demonstrations were not a matter only of the larger, more cosmopolitan cities; they enveloped the country as a whole and were taking place in surprising places, some of which had been bastions of right-wing republicanism. Third, and by the same token, these demonstrations were not affairs limited to college and university campuses – though those too were stirring – nor led by or confined to those who had been active against the Vietnam war – though seeing old friends who were again on the move was undoubtedly exciting. What was even more exciting was the palpable fact that the movement was already reaching into what in America is called 'middle America' – that is to say, the general citizenry, not only the college rebels, not only the leftists or left-leaning radicals but just the person across the street who saw no reason why any of her compatriots should go and risk their lives in a war that made no sense. One also felt (and others felt), however, that most of the anti-globalization elements in North America were still not part of this growing anti-war movement.

The more recent anti-war demonstration in Florence, which coincided with the European Social Forum and which brought out 400,000 people, coming after the earlier demonstration in London itself which is said to have brought out roughly quarter of a million, laid to rest the fear that anti-war movement and anti-globalization movement may remain separate and may even compete with each other. The two had by then converged very substantially, in Europe at least. It is in this perspective that the demonstration of 18 January in Washington D.C. which is said to have brought out close to half a million people – along with demonstrations in the rest of the US and the world – gains its historic meaning. By now, Washington alone has seen close to a million people, travelling from as far as New Mexico and Alaska, telling their rulers to back off from a war that is both senseless and immoral. Meanwhile, an anti-war movement of the veterans of America's former wars is also developing. An open letter, signed by 100 war veterans and addressed to the soldiers currently on duty, is now doing the rounds, asking them to obey not their commanders but their own conscience; it is bound to gather thousands of signatures, and the idea of the heroes of previous wars opposing a war-on-the-horizon has historically had great resonance and sympathy among the American people. Even the *New York Times* was constrained to notice editorially that the anti-war movement had reached what it called 'mainstream America'. Refusing to recognise the actual size of the demonstrations, the newspaper nevertheless entitled its editorial 'A Stirring in the Nation' and acknowledged that 'it was impressive for the obvious mainstream roots of the marchers'. Never in history had so many citizens of a country that was about to wage war come out into the street to shout their protest against a war that was yet to happen. (This should, by the way, put us Indians to shame, considering that the streets of our cities witnessed no anti-war demonstrations when our rulers amassed 750,000 troops on the Indo-Pakistan border and squandered 100,000 crore rupees merely to build the image of the BJP as a party that will give us a 'strong' India.)

It was under this pressure that the broader support for the war in America plummeted rapidly and we again saw the phenomenon of the masses on the move pulling along masses who had not been on the move. Two days after the demonstration, an ABC poll which asked 'Do you believe there is a case for war in Iraq' showed that 82 per cent thought that there was no such case, only 18 per cent thought that there was. Another poll, conducted January 16-20, also found that Bush's own approval ratings had dropped to its lowest level since before 11 September 2001. For the first time, the poll also found approval levels on his handling of the economy coming down to as low as 43 per cent while support for his handling of the Iraq crisis was 'down by 6 to 8 percentage points in just six weeks'. This mass dissent has forced even the Democratic party to stop playing chicken and start expressing at least some reservation against at least the more extremist plans of their far right government.

Possibly under this pressure, but also for professional grounds alone, the dissension between the professionals of the armed forces and the CIA on the one hand, and the ideologues led by Rumsfeld and Wolfowitz on the other, seems to be growing to the point where there are strong rumours of a split among even the Chiefs of Staff, some of whom are said to be arguing that America is 'unprepared' for facing the consequences of its 'excessive' plans for military action.[2] 'I think all the chiefs stood shoulder-to-shoulder on this', said one officer tracking the debate, which has been intense at times. Advice of this kind may yet fall on deaf ears, since the civilian core at the highest levels of US government that wants to make war represents the far right politically and the petrodollar-weapondollar complex economically. However, Europe is not ruled by similar forces, and over 80 per cent of the public opinion against the war has had its consequences. Schröder, the German Chancellor, for example, won the elections on anti-war platform, then tried to wriggle out of it but was then pulled back by the sheer force of public opinion not only in his own party, nor only the Greens who are his coalition partners but also the German conservatives who too are overwhelmingly against following the US lead into a war that may well shake up the planet. For example, in response to Rumsfeld's attack on Germany and France as 'Old Europe', the conservative daily *Frankfurter Allgemeine Zeitung* lined up an array of European intellectuals including Habermas, Derrida and Debray to defend 'Europe'.

However, this European opposition, combined with that of China and Russia, may have other dimensions as well. It has been a matter of much amazement for this author that this opposition has not come earlier, more consistently and more vigorously. Limitations of space require that we again postpone any extended discussion of the oil interests, which is what this

[2] *The Washington Post* of 24 May 2002 reported: 'The Joint Chiefs of Staff have waged a determined behind-the-scenes campaign to persuade the Bush administration to reconsider an aggressive posture toward Iraq in which war was regarded as all but inevitable. . . In a series of meetings this spring, the six members of the Joint Chiefs – the chairman, Air Force Gen. Richard B. Myers; the vice chairman, Marine Gen. Peter Pace; and the chiefs of the Army, Navy, Air Force and Marine Corps – hammered out a position that emphasizes the difficulties of any Iraq campaign while also quietly questioning the wisdom of a military confrontation with Hussein'.

war, like the earlier war on Afghanistan, is all about. Even so, I have been convinced for some time that this US race to establish complete monopoly over the combined oil resources of the Middle East and the Caspian Sea – as well as the oil resources in such far-flung areas as Venezuela, Nigeria and Indonesia – is directed, at least in part, against its main competitors in the advanced capitalist world itself: the EU, Japan, China and Russia (in the singular case of China, one would have to say 'advancing' rather than already 'advanced'). Consequently, I have never understood why these countries do not oppose this US bid more forthrightly. It may well be the case that corporate and governmental experts in these respective countries are beginning to understand that their own economic future is at stake, that complete US monopoly over the strategic resource of oil shall relegate them to a second-rate status for any foreseeable future, and that the time to mount the challenge is now, when they have even the masses of the Middle East raging against this prospect of US monopoly and even the Gulf regimes seem to be afraid of the consequences for themselves of the genocidal blitz being planned by the Anglo-American axis. Furthermore, since these other countries are not driven by the tie between Christian fundamentalist messianism and Zionist expansionism, they might not wish to face the likely terrorism of the terrorized that American state terrorism is likely to bring about among sections of the Arab youth.

And then, there is the simple fact that money speaks. It speaks to the bankers of Europe more loudly than do the voices of people. And the noise it makes becomes all the more persuasive when the message it sends is the same that the bankers get from the street. They are the most responsive when the demands of the multitude and demands of money seem to converge. *The Independent*, a British newspaper, noted for 24 Januray that 'the stock market notched up the longest losing streak in its history yesterday'. The FTSE 100 Index of leading shares had by then seen 80 billion pound sterling wiped off its value since 13 January, closing at the perilously low level of 3622.2. At an earlier stage of this slide, The Financial Services Authority, which serves as a watchdog for the City, had warned that if the Index ever falls below the 3500 mark, the decline may well pose problems for a variety of pension funds in which large sections of the salaried strata have their savings and retirement prospects tied up. By all counts, the decline was owed to investor anxiety in face of war and its possible consequences. Other stock markets, including the US market, also experienced declines though not always to the same extent. No one quite knows what will happen in case the war actually breaks out. If the US does not win quickly, financial markets slip dramatically and even pension funds get effected, dissent is likely to grow widely among the articulate middle classes and perhaps even those sectors of the big bourgeoisie which are not invested much in the petrodollar-weapondollar complex. The political future of the Bushes and the Blairs, and of the US far right generally, will then be at stake.[3]

This far right has been projecting its own wet dreams as the likely scenario for the war itself as well as what comes after it. In the process, it is also minimizing the financial costs of the

---

[3] With the benefit of hindsight, one can now say that three things happened. One, practical demonstration of the anti-war sentiment was infinitely stronger *before* the invasion when it seemed preventable; once the invasion began and Baghdad fell so quickly, populations in the US and UK converged behind their leaders and armies as usually happens in time of war, while most others who had opposed to war felt helpless. Second, the overwhelming economic and military power of the US was eventually irresistible for the would-be competitors and, one by one, they too fell in line. Third, instability of the markets in fact buttressed the resolve to mount a devastating attack and get it over quickly so that investor confidence came back. It is only now, some months after the grand invasion, with resistance emerging and the costs of war mounting by the week, that anti-war sentiment as well as anxiety of markets are again on the rise.

war. It is certainly the case that a controlled dose of military Keynesianism – let us say, $ 200 billion ploughed into the war economy – may well boost the investment climate in the sagging US economy. It is also the case that if the US achieves all its war aims, it will monopolise the world's oil resources, will eventually push down oil prices sufficiently to wreck not just OPEC but also the Russian economy, and will control the production levels, prices and even access to the world's central raw material resource, of which some 70 per cent seems to be located in the Gulf region and the Caspian Sea Basin. In the process, vast profits shall accrue not just to the various US corporations but also personally to Bush, Cheney, Condoleeza Rice, etc. all of whom are deeply involved with the oil and weapon-producing corporations.

There is no certainty, however, that the war will necessarily go that way. The American Academy of Arts and Sciences, an international society of scientists, scholars, business people and political figures, released in December a report assembled by its researchers which argued that there really is no reliable way of estimating the costs of the coming war, which may go as far up as $ 2 trillion over a decade. Nor is it at all clear what may happen to Iraqi oil in the foreseeable future. Iraqi oil fields were so intensely aflame in consequence of the much more limited Gulf War that it took more than eight months to restore a reasonable level of production. With the whole world put on notice that the US-UK forces will seek to seize Iraqi oil permanently and even the territorial unity of the country to be destroyed in the process, it is far from clear just what kind of defence the Iraqis have prepared, not just in the cities but also around the oil fields. British press is rife with rumours that seizure of the fields has been assigned to British troops, purportedly to refute the claim that it is the US that seeks to take over these resources. It is just as likely that this is the area where casualties are expected to be high and

British troops are being called in to do the dirty and dangerous work for the Americans so as to reduce the number of the American dead.[4]

Nor is it at all clear what the political fallout in the region shall be. In Pakistan where the populace has never given the fundamentalists any sizeable representation in parliament, repercussions of the American invasion of Afghanistan were such that these fundamentalists came close to forming government despite General Musharraf's best efforts to keep them out; a full-scale invasion of Iraq and the mounting conflict in Afghanistan is likely to deliver the country to them altogether, sooner rather than later. This is complicated by the fact that Pakistan not only has nuclear weapons but is also said to have considerable reserves of oil and gas. 'Massive untapped gas reserves are believed to be lying beneath Pakistan's remotest deserts, but they are being held hostage by armed tribal groups demanding a better deal from the central government', Agence France Presse had written just days before 11 September. Will the US then invade Pakistan as well, on the pretext of keeping nuclear weapons out of the hands of the fundamentalists but in fact to monopolise those untapped gas and oil reserves? Is this part of what Musharraf meant when he warned a few days ago that Pakistan may be the next target after Iraq? And, at what point does the empire overstretch itself, as opposition to its diabolical designs grows across the globe, including sizeable sections of its own population?

It is said that the Israeli atrocities in Jenin alone have driven thousands of youth, many of them perfectly secular, into the looser networks of the Al Qaida because it is perceived as actually taking up arms against the Americans. Jordan is said to

---

[4] The Iraqis decided not to blow up their country's oil resources but the subsequent resistance has made it impossible for the occupation forces to even repair the facilities, let alone exploit them on any appreciable scale.

be already very much on the boil, Saudi monarchy is fearful for its survival, and Hosni Mubarak of Egypt has not only warned of a 'firestorm' enveloping the Middle East in case of the expected invasion but also allowed an internationally publicised anti-war conference to take place in Cairo. In the midst of all this, Sharon is being returned to power in Israel with even a broader mandate, with his own plans to revamp the maps of the entire region which overlap with the plans of the American far right. Under the tutelage of these overlapping power centres, America may well be preparing not for a short excursus with the limited aim of a 'regime change' in Baghdad but for something resembling a 30-year war.

It is within this climate of dire danger, as world peace hangs in the balance, that Mr. Hans Blix is to submit his interim report to the Security Council tomorrow. Teams of UN inspectors have routinely included US and Israeli agents in the past and Blix himself has been known to work within a framework set by the United States. More recently, however, the ideologues of the American far right, such as Richard Perle have said harsh things about him. As sharp divisions now emerge between the EU and the US, Blix may find that he is himself a man of divided loyalties. It is too early to say whether his impending report – and his future actions – will reflect the emerging Franco-German agenda or the settled US agenda. That will depend in part on how firm the EU leaders are in what they are currently saying.

14 MARCH 2003
Imperial Overreach and the Resisting Multitude

Close to a million people marched in Rome on February 15th, to protest their government's collusion with the US on the question of the forthcoming imperial blitzkrieg against Iraq; over a million had marched in London that same day, in the largest public demonstration in British history. On the 20th, Tony Blair arrived at the Vatican for an audience with the Pope, in an absurd show of piety and with his Catholic wife in tow; the Vatican, in turn, took care to publicize widely the fact that Pope had advised him not to go to war. In between, 90,000 protesters had gathered in Glasgow outside the hall where he was addressing a Labour Party conference. Meanwhile, a poll showed that a staggering 90 per cent disapprove of his will to make war on Iraq. On the 21st, fresh from his embarrassing audience with the Pope, he participated in a four-way telephonic conference with Bush and Prime Ministers Silvio Berlusconi of Italy and Jose Maria Aznar of Spain to back Bush's statement that the US was going to table a fresh resolution at the Security Council seeking authority to make war. All this, in the teeth of the largest anti-war demonstration that his country – indeed, the world – has ever witnessed.

And, the protesting multitude – estimated at anywhere between eight and fifteen million people – who poured into the streets of the world in something of a global chain really was vast and unprecedented. It began in Auckland, on the southeastern tip of the empire and gave to New Zealand easily the largest anti-war demonstration in its history. Next was Melbourne with 200,000 in the streets, and the centre of gravity in this human wave kept shifting as the sun itself moved westward. The epicentre was in Western Europe, especially the three countries of 'Old Europe' – UK, Italy and Spain – whose governments are identified with the US; Barcelona had seen nothing like this since the fall of Franco three decades ago. 150,000 in Paris and close to half a million in Berlin were a fraction of what the multitudes would have been if their governments had not broken with Washington.

North America was in the next time zone and 400,000 gathered in New York even though the city government, backed by an extraordinary ruling by a judge, had banned a march. This was synchronized with protest marches in roughly 300 small and medium-sized towns across the US. 100,000 came out in Montreal and 80,000 in Toronto, in the largest peace demonstrations in the history of the two cities. What had begun in Auckland then ended 48 hours later in neighbouring Australia, with a quarter million marching in Sydney. The sun had gone full circle, and it was dawn of another day. War against the planet had brought forth the first planetary rebellion against it.

This outpouring of humanity against an imperial war which has not even begun on the scale at which it is being planned is of course deeply connected with the anti-globalization movements which have also become global in scale over the years, doing their work in a thousand locales across continents and periodically holding the various Social Forums which then culminate in the World Social Forum. Indeed, it was at the time of the European Social Forum (ESF) in Florence that the first of the really vast anti-war rallies had taken place; 40,000 attended the ESF but ten times that many marched against the war. This convergence of movements against corporate globalization with movements opposed to imperialist war may well prove to be the forerunner for the making of an authentically anti-imperialist movement of the 21st century. A notable feature of these anti-war mobilizations, as in the anti-globalization movement, is that these consist overwhelmingly of young people, or of older people who have never marched before in their lives. The other, equally important feature is the sheer breadth of the anti-war sentiment.

This is reflected in public opinion polls where anti-war sentiment across Europe ranges between 80 per cent or above in most countries and 60 per cent or so in some. In Germany, the Forsa poll found 57 per cent of Germans held the opinion that 'the United States is a nation of warmongers' while only 6 per cent said they thought President George W. Bush was concerned with 'preserving peace'. Public opinion in eastern Europe, where most governments have lined up behind the US, is even more hostile to war than in the west. A Gallup International poll found low support in the region for war, even if sanctioned by the UN – just 38 per cent in Romania, 28 per cent in Bulgaria and 20 per cent in Estonia. The figure for Russia was 23 per cent. In Turkey, some polls are suggesting a figure of as much as 94 per cent opposed to the war.

What may prove decisive in building a truly anti-imperialist movement is the massive unrest and dissidence in the working class. In Britain, for example, five of the biggest unions, with a membership of 750,000 – including the rail union Aslef; Rail, Maritime and Transport Union; and the Communication Workers' Union – have threatened widespread industrial action, boycotts and strikes if Blair goes to war without explicit Security Council authorization. At the other end of the globe, the Korean Confederation of Trade Unions campaigned actively for mass mobilization on the issue of war and issued a statement which said, in part: 'The US should stop immediately the war against Iraq and the military threat imposed on Korea peninsula. . . . The

US had attacked Afghanistan using the excuse of "war against terrorism" after September 11. . . . After the invasion of Afghanistan, the US has shifted its military target into Iraq . . . and the US is now even touting the possibility of using nuclear weapons. . . . The US is driving another war in the Korean peninsula addressing the North Korea nuclear issue. . . . Regardless of the demands of the Korean people to solve the issue in a peaceful manner, the US has increased military tension over the Korean peninsula by pushing ahead with additional military deployment'.

The really surprising development – a potentially historic shift – has actually occurred in the United States itself. According to the current issue of *Village Voice*, leaders of more than 400 labour organizations, representing 4.5 million union members (roughly 30 per cent of all unionized labour in the US), have signed on to a tough resolution condemning the Bush administration's push toward war. 'There is no convincing link between Iraq and Al Qaida or the attacks on September 11', it states. 'Neither the Bush administration nor the UN inspections have demonstrated that Iraq poses a real threat to Americans'. The principal victims of a war, says the resolution, 'will be the sons and daughters of working class families serving in the military' and 'innocent Iraqi civilians'. The billions of dollars needed for the action will come from 'schools, hospitals, housing, and social security', it states. The war push, the resolution proclaims, is already serving as a 'pretext for attacks on labour, civil, immigrant and human rights at home' as well as a 'distraction for the sinking economy, corporate corruption, and layoffs'.

The resolution was initially adopted at a conference in Chicago last month, and among the signers are the national leaders of the communications workers, postal workers, state and municipal employees, as well as the central labour councils of Los Angeles; Philadelphia; Washington, D.C.; Cleveland; Sacramento; Albany;

and northwest Indiana – in short, across the US. Separately, several large labour bodies, including the giant Service Employees International Union, have sent their own messages of concern to the White House. In New York, more than two dozen unions have signed on, led by health and hospitals workers union 1199/SEIU, now the state's largest union, which has given office space to anti-war protest organizers and bought radio time to advertise the latest rally near the UN. This is by all counts an extraordinary development, indicating that anti-war sentiment is running higher among American workers today than in almost a hundred years, since World War 1. More broadly, 90 cities and towns – including Chicago and San Francisco – had gone on record by 13 February opposing the impending war and dozens of others were considering anti-war resolutions.

This remarkable shift in the US toward a fairly generalized anti-war sentiment in labour unions, city councils and the populace at large – not just in the larger and more cosmopolitan cities but deep into what Americans call 'middle America' – is taking place in the context of great skepticism among intellectuals, opinion-makers and professionals of various kinds. On the religious side, we have spoken already of the Pope's highly publicized advice to Blair, which has worldwide repercussions. Within the UK, the Archbishop-designate of Canterbury and the head of the Catholic Church there have combined their forces to oppose the impending war. Similar voices have been raised in the US by a variety of religious figures, all the way to the Presiding Bishop of the United Catholic Church. One hundred American law professors have written to Bush saying that if he goes through with his war plans he is liable to be prosecuted for war crimes, and the fact that the US has not signed on to the International Criminal Court offers him no more immunity than had the Nazis who were tried at Nuremberg. The legal case against the war has been laid out in painstaking terms in the current issue of *London Review of Books* by Michael Byers who teaches international law at Duke University.

Some of this spills over among former and serving military personnel. A group of US soldiers, parents of soldiers and Members of Congress have filed a lawsuit challenging Bush's authority to make war without a specific declaration of war from Congress. A letter signed by a large number of war veterans is doing the rounds, opposing the war. And with good reason, since many of them have had gruesome recent experience of the Gulf War of 1991. On the surface, US casualties were very low – 148 killed and 467 wounded – compared to the scores of thousands of Iraqis who died within a couple of weeks. However, what never gets said – but is well known to these veterans – is that nearly two of every five of the approximately 540,000 Gulf War veterans are on disability as a result of illnesses they believe they sustained during that conflict. About 161,000 Gulf War veterans are receiving disability payments from the US government, and about 209,000 have filed VA claims and are still waiting. They, their fellow-veterans and an indeterminate number of serving soldiers and officers are not convinced that a much larger war which is now getting planned is in their interest or is even wholly legal.

Forty-one American Nobel laureates in science and economics issued a declaration on 27 January opposing a preventive war against Iraq without wide international support. These are by no means people who would otherwise be identified with a peace movement. Among them are Hans A. Bethe, an architect of the atom bomb; Walter Kohn, a former adviser to the Defence Advanced Research Projects Agency at the Pentagon; Norman F. Ramsey, a Manhattan Project scientist who readied the Hiroshima bomb and later advised NATO, and others of their kind. At the other end of the spectrum, when Laura Bush, the President's wife, tried to organize a poetry reading at the White House, so many, including former Poet Laureates, refused that the event had to be cancelled. When Sam Hamill, one of those who refused, sent out a message to invite anti-war poems, he expected to receive perhaps fifty; he got 2,000.

This generalized disaffection in the core capitalist countries is then supplemented by fears in Iraq's immediate vicinity. Among the six states bordering Iraq – Turkey, Syria, Jordan, Saudi Arabia, Kuwait and Iran – only Kuwait is wholly with the United States. Turkey, which is now coming on board is extracting such a high price (close to $ 30 billion in aid) and such an extensive role for itself in Northern Iraq that it makes a mockery of the US plans to arm some 40,000 Kurds as foot soldiers in its own largely aerial assault. For the rest, Iran knows that it is likely to be the next target in case the US succeeds easily in Iraq; indeed, some 12 per cent of the Israeli air force is known to be operating already against it in the border zones. As for Syria, it fears that Israel may well use the US-led war to move its own armies into more of Syrian and Lebanese territories, aside from attempting to push as many Palestinians as possible into Jordan, Syria and Lebanon; Jordan shares the same fears. The Saudi monarchy, meanwhile, has two different nightmares to contend with. First, it is already facing massive domestic unrest, so much so that CIA compares its domestic situation to that of Iran just before the revolution. In case of Saudi acquiescence in an American occupation of Iraq, the monarchy faces the possibility of getting overthrown by internal forces, sooner rather than later. Second, even if the US achieves all its war aims and the monarchy survives, prices of Saudi oil are likely to collapse, Organization of Petroleum Exporting Countries (OPEC) itself shall be wrecked and the centrality of Saudi Arabia in world oil trade shall be a thing of the past.

All this was reflected in an extraordinary two-hour lecture

that was delivered at the Cairo Book Fair earlier this month by Sheikh Ahmed Zaki Yamani, the first Secretary General of OPEC and Saudi Arabia's Minister of Petroleum and Mineral resources from 1962 to 1986 who became famous when he masterminded the oil embargo – and the dramatic rise in petroleum prices – in 1973. He described Arab leaders as 'their highnesses, excellencies . . . who do not derive their power from the people' and as 'lackeys who are working faithfully to satisfy the Godfather'. Now, when a man of Sheikh Yamani's eminence utters such words publicly in Cairo, defying the Egyptian government as well as his own; and when, in addition, he receives a standing ovation and the words then get published in Egypt's leading newspaper despite official displeasure, one knows how high the disaffection runs among sections of the highest echelons of even Saudi and Egyptian societies.

Yamani then went on to outline three possible scenarios. One is that there would be no war, the US would succeed in ousting Saddam through other means, sponsor a government of its favourite henchmen and absorb most of the Ba'ath party into the new regime; all else would remain the same except that the US would now determine the future of Iraqi oil. The second, more grim scenario would be that the US shall invade and Saddam would put Iraq's own oil wells aflame. 'If that happens', he said, 'there would be an expected shortfall of more than 10 million oil barrels on the [international] market, a gap which no country could fill – not even in part. In this case, oil prices would reach $ 80 to $ 100 per barrel. None of the world's industrial countries' oil supplies would help out of this devastating situation. Many factories across the globe would be forced to shut down, which would result in a massive wave of unemployment with no historical precedent. Not to mention, of course, what would happen to innocent children, women, elderly and other people. I hope this scenario does not happen, but we shouldn't ignore it either. This scenario would mean the end for the US, Europe and the West'.

The third possible scenario he offered was only a little less grim: that Iraq would be quickly occupied and partitioned. Oil production could resume and keep increasing after a brief interlude, reaching as much as 10,000 barrels a day within the decade and shipped to the west through pipelines reaching into the eastern Mediterranean. Oil prices shall collapse, Saudi production and revenues would fall drastically, Jordan would lose the enormous subsidies it gets from Saddam Hussein and will have to cope with the influx of Palestinians pushed out by Israel. 'Then it's Iran's turn and Syria will fall. The end result is that Israel will be the strongest and most powerful country in the region', he said and concluded with a warning that has been staring the world in the face for some time: 'The horrifying repercussions of an attack on Iraq are frightening. There will be hundreds of Osama bin Ladens'.

So, will there still be war? The short answer is: very likely. As I write this, the US has announced that it will table a new resolution in the Security Council (SC) and will defy any permanent member to veto it. As if on cue, Hans Blix, the chief UN inspector, has ordered Iraq to start destroying its Al-Samoud missiles within the week, or get ready for consequences. (Iraq has offered to let him pick any of its missiles and test-fire it, to see for himself that they all have a range well within limits prescribed by the UN itself, but Blix is unwilling to exercise that sensible option.) He can come to the UN any day and report that Iraq is defying his orders, which will give the US the excuse it needs. Meanwhile, every country in the world even outside the Anglo-American axis, and of course the world media, has been issuing pronouncement to the effect that full-scale invasion would be fine if the UN endorses it. In the process, the SC itself has been endowed with utterly undeserved but a virtually mystical halo, as if it had some great history of rectitude in making fair judgements, enforcing its supposedly binding resolutions and preventing wars.

Fact of the matter is that the UN has never prevented any major war, and certainly none that has been waged by the US or Israel, be it the Vietnam War or the Israeli attack on its neighbours in 1967. These same permanent members of the SC have sat around twiddling their thumbs as Israel has defied scores of its resolutions; has continued its occupation of territories it captured illegally in 1967, including Syrian territories; has built up a nuclear arsenal of over two hundred nuclear warheads complete with advanced delivery systems; and is daily committing in the Occupied Territories what everyone knows are crimes against humanity, and so on. The obstruction to the US designs in the SC is so precarious that Germany itself never tires of pointing out that it has contributed 35,000 military personnel to the US build-up – it just doesn't think the time is right.

So, it's really up to the US, and the factors that are driving it toward war are various. The US now has 180,000 troops in the vicinity of Iraq and more are scheduled to arrive; a third of the British military is either already positioned there or on the way. These forces are not there to play war games or simply to impress Saddam Hussein. Nor are they there to put pressure while the inspectors do their work. Everyone worth the name in the administration, from the 'extremist' Wolfowitz to the 'moderate' Powell, has been saying for over a year that the US wants to oust the legally constituted regime of Iraq regardless of what the inspectors do or do not find (this alone violates the UN Charter and international law generally).

We are in fact living in perhaps the most dangerous time in imperial history. Never in history has there been an imperial power without a rival somewhere or the other; the US military superiority is so overwhelming that its military budget is larger than the combined military budgets of the next 25 countries. Thanks to this vast military superiority, and thanks also to the intoxication caused by its victory over the communist states (USSR in particular), it fancies itself invincible. At precisely this time, the US is ruled by a faction of the far right so extremist that no previous US administration in recent memory can compare with it, not even Nixon or Reagan. To understand the danger Bush and cronies represent, one would have to imagine Narendra Modi with US military and economic power at his disposal. At the core of this ruling group are individuals – the Bush father-son duo, Dick Cheney, Condoleeza Rice, and others – whose careers and personal wealth have been deeply tied to the oil corporations. So, the world is facing a macabre situation in which grabbing Iraq oil, at any cost, is crucial for US hegemony *per se*, the US oil corporations in general, and the key members of the administration personally, starting with the President himself who stands to amass much wealth in consequence, thanks to his father's business deals. This is quite additional to the fact that Bush and his ruling group owe even their political fortunes to the petrodollar-weapondollar complex.

As for oil and gas resources, a fuller analysis shall have to be presented in the future. Some salient facts are as follows. Numerous studies, reports and plans were developed in the US during the 1990s with the objective of securing its hold over the world's resources of these strategic raw materials, and Cheney, among others, was closely associated with them. The long-standing US interest in Afghanistan has always been connected with these resources in the Caspian Sea Basin, estimated at $ 5 trillion; the heretofore undeveloped resources are said to comprise of 6.6 trillion cubic metres of natural gas and 10 billion barrels of oil. The recent invasion of Afghanistan, and the building of 13 new US military bases in the Caspian region leading up to that invasion, had to do with those resources, not with the Taliban with whom the US was in cosy negotiations for many years, right into the summer of 2001.[1] The US itself has only 3 per cent of the world's known oil resources, which is at any rate far more expensive to produce and bring to the market than is the Gulf oil. Meanwhile, the US accounts for a quarter of the world's oil consumption and imports 60 per cent of its daily consumption, 16 per cent of it from the Gulf region which alone has close to 20 per cent of the world's resources. Iraq has the second largest reserves, next only to Saudi Arabia, and the US has not been able to dominate its oil in some thirty-five years, as it does in Saudi Arabia and Kuwait. This is now the target, after securing control over the Caspian Basin.

The US is now talking of an initial period of 2-3 years in which Iraq shall be under direct US administration, with perhaps a token Muslim international civil servant formally occupying a key position. They expect to have a permanent military presence there for an indefinite period; Gen. Tommy Franks, who is likely to lead the assault, has spoken of the 'Korean model', where US troops have been stationed for half a century. This presence is to

---

[1] The US awarded $ 43 million to the Taliban government as late as May 2001 even as Osama and his colleagues were living happily in Afghanistan and even as Afghanistan continued to suffer under the sanctions the UN had imposed under pressure from the US. *La Figaro* the prestigious French newspaper also reported that the CIA station chief in Dubai met with Osama in a hospital there in July that year, three months before the US invaded Afghanistan ostensibly to capture him, dead or alive.

ensure control not only over Iraq but also over the region as a whole, including Saudi Arabia which is fast becoming unpredictable. Sheikh Yamani is right: with Iraq already secured as a staging-post for military action elsewhere, ouster of regimes in Syria and Iran shall be easier.

Then, there is the US economy itself, which is suffering from a crisis of stagnation, overproduction and great under-utilization of productive facilities and liquid assets. Funnelling some $ 200 billion or so into the war economy – what some of us have been calling 'military Keynesianism' – is expected to boost the economy as a whole. Second, the re-building and breakneck expansion of Iraq's ailing oil industry under US control is expected to stimulate US investment; this is in addition to the Caspian basin where all the US oil giants are already at work. Third, complete US control over resources of the Gulf and Caspian regions will greatly contribute to building a superior competitive edge against its rivals in Western Europe and Japan. It will then control not only production and flow of oil from these regions but it will ensure that the dollar becomes the exclusive currency for transacting oil trade. Indeed, ensuring the continued supremacy of the dollar as the world's primary currency is crucial to the US economic position in the world. Not the least of Saddam's recent sins has been that he has increasingly traded Iraq's oil in Euros, which has arisen as a competing currency. The war on Iraq is, among other things, a currency war between the dollar and Euro.

Will the US succeed? There are too many imponderables. What one gets in the world media is an unreliable mix of fine investigative reporting, sheer speculation passed off as news, and disinformation dressed up as revelation of secret documents. We do not know how loyal or battle-worthy the armed forces of Iraq shall be under America's genocidal firepower. It is perfectly possible that much of the top military brass shall defect, leaving their units leaderless and wandering in the wilderness. Nor do we know what the US war plans are. We do know that the tonnage dropped in the conventional bombings during the 1991 Gulf War was equal to seven-and-a-half Hiroshimas; in the impending invasion, bombings are likely to far exceed that tonnage, and whereas only 10 per cent of the weapons during the Gulf War were precision-guided, 80 per cent will now be precision-guided. A report on the American CBS network in late January began: 'if the Pentagon sticks to its current war plan, one day in March the Air Force and Navy will launch 300 to 400 cruise missiles at targets in Iraq'. They may then launch the same number the next day; 6,000 of these missiles are now stockpiled around Iraq.

This is part of a strategic plan known as 'Shock and Awe' which Pentagon officials spelled out for CBS, with the exultant claim: 'The sheer size of this has never been seen before, never been contemplated before'. The architect of this scheme, Harlan Ullman, was reported as saying: 'you have this simultaneous effect – rather like the nuclear weapons at Hiroshima – not taking days or weeks but minutes'. And, even though it can achieve the same effect through conventional weapons, the US is now talking of perhaps using nuclear weapons for deep-penetration bombings, on the pretext that that's the way to get to the bunker where Saddam Hussein shall be hiding and at the factories for producing weapons of mass destruction – which, for some odd reason, the UN inspectors simply cannot find, despite having complete access to anything in Iraq they wish to inspect and having at their disposal all the latest technology and equipment for the most thorough search.

Other reported plans suggest that saturation bombings shall be conducted in Baghdad itself and the area from Baghdad to Tikrit (Saddam's ancestral home), while the rest of the territory shall be quickly taken over by ground forces; British troops, in particular, are tipped for taking over the oil fields, where risk of death shall be the highest. Extensive reports in the US media, including such mass media as *Time* magazine, suggest that US special forces as well as CIA's secret armies have been operating already throughout northern Iraq as well as some central zones, to facilitate precisely such an occupation.

In earlier versions, Iraq was expected to be divided into three entities: a Kurdish one in the north, Shia in the east, and the Sunni one in the remaining area. The oil fields are conveniently located in the northern and eastern zones. It then transpired that Turkey would not tolerate a sovereign or even semi-sovereign Kurdish entity on its borders, and that a Shia entity on the Irani border was much too risky. In recent versions, the US seems to be guaranteeing the territorial unity of Iraq as it presently is, infuriating the Kurds who were supposed to do much of the fighting in the offensive from the north, in lieu of (semi)independence and a share of the spoils by way of some role in managing the Kirkuk oilfields. In these new plans, the US seems to have agreed to have the Turkish army operating in the Kurdish zones; how it will treat the Kurds, and when it will leave, remains unclear; its history of genocidal cruelties against Kurds living inside Turkey do not promise a safe future for Iraqi Kurds. And, then, there are the oil fields located in Iraqi Kurdistan, which Turkey regards as an Ottoman province and therefore its own long-lost territory.

The fate of Iraqi oil is likewise unclear. That the US will control it, and that it is building a 'coalition of the willing' by promising a share of the spoils to Russia, Italy etc, is clear enough. However, earlier reports used to suggest that a consortium of US oil corporations would 'hold it in trust for the Iraqi people', would restore and expand production and perhaps help the Iraqis pay for the costs of the war against them – anywhere between $ 2 billion and $ 2 trillion – before restoring the remaining resources to their own government assembled by the United States. New reports suggests that Iraqi oil shall be privatized fully, on the model of the privatization of public sector assets in Russia after the collapse of the Soviet Union. On this issue, however, Iraqi clients of the US are themselves beginning to rebel, with the lofty rhetoric that privatization is good but the privilege of ownership should be allotted to Iraqi nationals only, not to foreigners; they have suddenly become patriots, like any national bourgeoisie.

So, we don't really know what the war is going to be like and what comes after it – if there actually is an 'after'. Perhaps the Americans themselves have been postponing the full-scale invasion because they are unable to predict the future. But four things we do know, as we keep inching toward the holocaust. One, the Security Council is too slippery an entity to bank upon. Second, the savagery shall be strictly unimaginable for those who are not its victims. Third, the Americans shall undoubtedly know how to get in but they may not know how to get out. Fourth, ground shall have been prepared for the whole region to explode. The empire might be overreaching far beyond what it can manage.

28 MARCH 2003
War, Oil and the Dollar

The war on Iraq and its occupation by the Anglo-American axis is now as likely as ever, just more imminent. Here, we shall first detail the further deepening of the anti-war upsurge, which now runs all the way from the Pope to the UN weapons inspectors in Iraq, and from the largest labour confederations in Europe and the US to the governments of France, Germany, China and Russia. We shall then comment briefly on the remarkable unity of the US ruling class behind the far-right cabal of the Bush administration. This unity itself can be explained by the fact that the coming war is not only a far-right offensive within the power structure of the United States but indeed vital for continued economic dominance of the United States over the rest of the world, not only by controlling the strategic oil and gas resources around the world but also, equally importantly, by re-furbishing the dollar-sterling currency complex against the challenge mounted by the Euro, the new currency of the European Union which has risen to challenge the hegemony of the dollar, for the first time since the Second World War.

The anti-war upsurge we reported in the previous piece continues, in the wake of the 15 February demonstrations which had brought out 15 million people, in 2,000 cities of the world, to demonstrations and marches against the war. The Pope has written a personal letter to Bush the born-again Christian President of the United States who never tires of invoking God on his side, pleading with him not to make war, and he has asked one billion Catholics of the world to join him on Ash Wednesday in a prayer for peace. In an extraordinary move which the Turkish press called 'an earthquake', the Turkish parliament rejected their government's bill that sought to allow the US to station 62,000 troops on Turkish soil. The parliament thus acted in defiance of their Prime Minister as well as the overseeing military leaders alike, but in solidarity with the 94 per cent of the Turkish people opposed to the war and with the 100,000 who were demonstrating at that very time just a mile away from the parliament building.

In Britain, 120 Labour MPs rose in revolt against their own Prime Minister, Tony Blair. In the United States itself, AFL-CIA, the largest labour federation which had staunchly supported the US war in Vietnam, passed an anti-war resolution, saying that Bush had failed to make the case for war and that the issue of Iraq's purported Weapons of Mass Destruction (WMD) was a calculated diversion from the dire economic situation that the working people of the US were facing. Three of the four major newspapers in the United States – *Los Angeles Times* and *Boston Globe* more explicitly, the *New York Times* somewhat grudgingly – have been opposing the war and systematically publishing leaks from inside the Bush administration which undermine the positions of the administration. It was indeed the *New York Times* which said editorially after the 15 February demonstrations that the world now had two superpowers, with the United States on one side, and world public opinion on the other. Even the American Chief of Staff has testified in Congressional hearings that an occupation of Iraq might require as much as 400,000 troops for 10 years, thus implying that the war was unwinnable. His testimony incensed the Pentagon hawks so much that Deputy Secretary of Defence, Paul Wolfowitz, who has dodged military service all his life, went out of his way to say that a military general had no right to present estimates contrary to those put forward by the general's bosses at the Pentagon.

Recent polls show that anti-war sentiment has deepened across Europe, and leading newspapers are predicting that the outbreak of war will bring about an onrush of public protest which will be incomparably bigger than even the 15 February demonstrations and will include mass civil disobedience, work stoppages of all kinds, strikes and so on, which are being prepared already by the network of organizers who had coordinated the global protests of 15 February.[1] The ETUC Executive Committee (EC) met in Athens the 6th and 7th of March and confirmed the opposition of the trade unions to the war and to appeal for work stoppages everywhere in Europe on 14 March at midday. A foretaste of what is to come if war were to actually break out can be had in the movement in Italy which is currently busy stopping trains which are carrying war materials from American bases on Italian soil to the ports where American ships are docked. Such actions are likely to become far more numerous, much more widespread, and, in some cases, inevitably, violent as well.

---

[1] That, alas, was not to be. Once the invasion began, the size of demonstrations shrunk everywhere and then petered out, with few exceptions in countries like Greece. London witnessed one quite large demonstration after the war but majority of the population switched to loyalty to their soldiers in foreign lands. This dramatic decline demonstrated the limits and unpredictability of spontaneous mass actions in the absence of revolutionary politics. During the Vietnam years, there was a revolutionary wave throughout the Third World which had given rise to sustained and militant left movements, especially among the students, in the core imperialist countries as well. Now, the moral outrage against US savagery could not attach itself to affirmation of revolutionary resolution, and the despondent mentality of 'there really is no alternative' set in fairly quickly. Only the emergence of an Iraqi resistance and the post-occupation failures of the US on the ground were to give rise to any semblance of practical opposition, some months later, as we explain in a later piece in this book ('Resistance in Iraq, Disarray in the US').

Meanwhile, a special session of countries of the Non-Aligned Movement (NAM), the summit of the Arab League, and the Organization of Islamic Conference (OIC) passed unanimous resolutions rejecting the option of war, while the Secretariat of the Organization of Petroleum-Producing Countries (OPEC) has been predicting utter chaos in the oil markets in the event of war. The Canadian Prime Minister, a close and loyal ally of the United States, has said that Resolution 1441 of the Security Council speaks only of inspections and disarmament of Iraq, but neither of war nor of 'regime change'. He said that the idea of 'regime change' through war on another sovereign member of the United Nations is 'a dangerous idea', bound to lead to instability across the world. Three of the five permanent members of the Security Council – France explicitly, Russia and China implicitly – have threatened to use their veto powers against any resolution either condoning war or even including a deadline for Iraq to abide by. They, along with Germany which sits on the Security Council but without a veto, argue forcefully that Iraq has shown sufficient degree of cooperation, and that inspections necessarily require many months of work, so that any such resolution would be unwarranted; France's threat of using its veto of course represents a joint Franco-German position.[2] Indeed, many countries, led by France in this argument, have suggested that once the Security Council has come to be involved so extensively in the matter of inspections and disarmament, any unilateral action by the United States (or the Anglo-American axis) will fatally undermine the United Nations, leaving the world with no institution through which international law could be upheld collectively.

[2] This position too plummeted toward the end. Just before the war began, France proposed that the inspectors be given just another thirty days after which it would agree to a resolution favouring war. Bush, however, cold-shouldered this change of position pointedly, preferring to act unilaterally and keeping all the power in the hands of the US.

In the midst of all this have come the most recent reports of the chief United Nations inspectors in Iraq, to a Ministerial Session of the Security Council on 7 March, which made mince meat of the arguments the US has been peddling. Even before appearing at the Security Council and directly in response to Bush who had said on the eve of the meeting that the US shall be pushing for a resolution authorizing war, Hans Blix, the chief UN weapons inspector and head of UNSCOM in Iraq said that the co-operation on the part of Iraq was 'active, even pro-active' and inspections should be given more time. Within the Security Council, he took up directly the US position that a resolution for war was needed because Iraq had not complied with Resolution 1441 demanding 'immediate, unconditional and active co-operation'. Blix conceded that Iraq's co-operation was not 'immediate' but then went on to say that so far as 'unconditional' was concerned, Iraq had sought to initially put conditions but then had accepted every condition that the inspectors had put forward. As for 'active co-operation', he repeated his words of a few days ago: Iraq's co-operation had been 'active, even pro-active'.

Hans Blix even spoke of 'Iraq initiatives' in making possible 'professional, no-notice inspections all over Iraq' and 'substantial measure of disarmament'. Despite this 'proactive co-operation' on Iraq's part and 'inspections all over Iraq', and even with the use of most advanced radar technology, no underground facilities of chemical and biological weapons had been found- thus directly rebutting a claim the US has made repeatedly. In other words, there was no evidence that Iraq was in 'material breach' of Resolution 1441, as Bush and Blair have been claiming. Two of his concluding remarks were even more significant. In implicitly challenging the United States which has been claiming that it *knows* that such facilities exist, Blix said that countries which have the means to assemble such information should present that evidence to the inspectors. And, responding to the Anglo-American proposal that a notice of just a few days be given to Iraq and then, if it does not fully comply, the attack could begin, Blix said 'Disarmament, and at any rate verification, cannot be instant. It will not take years, nor weeks, but months'. In short, he upheld the Franco-German-Russian-Chinese position: inspections were working but should be given considerably more time, because the scope and technical nature of the work was such that it could not be done in days or even weeks.

Mr El Baradei, Director-General of the International Atomic Energy Agency and the chief UN inspector in Iraq on the nuclear issue, followed Blix and flatly declared that there was no evidence that Iraq has revived its nuclear weapons programme. He said that the documents, on which the US had based its claim that Iraq had been secretly purchasing uranium from Niger, presumably for producing nuclear weapons, had been examined by international experts and were found to be fraudulent. He then proceeded to refute each of the allegations the US has put forward, without naming the US of course. Unlike Blix, El Baradei did not concede a single claim of the US.

Seeing that the whole case that the Anglo-American axis had put forward was unravelling under the weight of the inspectors' reports, Colin Powell made a petulant speech, upbraiding the inspectors, but left the substantive matter of the proposed ultimatum to the histrionics of the British Foreign Secretary, Jack Straw, a former Trotskyist who has turned into an abject servant of the empire. He is the man who said in a press conference last week that Europe must co-operate with the US because the US would otherwise wreck the international institutions such as the United Nations and the International Monetary Fund. If Europe does not co-operate, he said, it 'will reap the whirlwind'. He was in fact quite right, in a paradoxical sort of way, on two counts.

First, as France has argued most notably, we can salvage the fundamental architecture of the UN and the international law associated with it if only the much lesser powers occasionally ignore its resolutions but the UN will have been shown to be utterly ineffective if the United States, the supreme global power, ignores its will *even while the mechanism for peace put in place by the Security Council with full knowledge and initial cooperation of the US are indeed working.* Second, more crucially, the coming war is not only against Iraq but also the first war that the US is fighting for its own interests which are partially in conflict with the interests of the European Union (EU), as we shall argue below. The British view is that Europe should surrender and accept US supremacy for the foreseeable future; the Franco-German position is that this may well be the time to challenge the more extreme forces of unilateralism inherent in that supremacy and to demonstrate that the US does eventually need the co-operation of its NATO allies beyond Britain, and even the formal co-operation of the Security Council itself. Franco-German calculation seems to be that (a) if the Americans win this war easily the Euro shall remain a second-rate currency for the foreseeable future, and (b) chances are that the US shall not score a quick victory but will enter a quagmire, which will give the EU the prospect of future gains not just in relations with Iraq but with OPEC as a whole. In one of its many aspects this is also a mini-war between the Euro, the currency of the European Union, and the dollar-sterling nexus, the currencies of the two great empires of the past and present, i.e. the Anglo-American axis. Global capital, especially global finance, is now too deeply integrated for there to emerge the kind of inter-imperialist rivalries that used to exist before the Second World War, when capital tended to be essentially national in character and the national bourgeoisie of the core capitalist countries would get locked into opposing – at times, warring –

camps. However, with the Soviet bloc eliminated and EU emerging as a distinct entity within the global system, some degree of sustained competition between the US and the more powerful countries of EU is now likely.

To that we shall return in a moment, and then we shall discuss the economic imperative which is the main force driving this coming war. Let us first comment on the power structure within the United States which is in fact highly favourable to the warmongers. We have written at great length in earlier articles on the nature of the far-right, quasi-fascist group that wields power in Washington these days, in the White House as well as the Pentagon. Second, there is the lamentable role of the Democratic Party, the supposedly liberal opposition party, which has utterly failed to organize any sort of opposition to – indeed even any debate on – the impending war, on false pretences of patriotism, which requires that all parties fall behind the government in matters of war. This is the mirror-image of what happens in India where the Congress as well as all the other opposition parties simply fall behind the BJP as soon as national security, terrorism, etc. are invoked.

Then, there is the US Congress, which is controlled by the Zionist lobby, the Christian fundamentalists, the petrodollar and weapon-dollar industries, and corporate corruption; Enron, for example, was the largest contributor to Bush's electoral campaign and there is not a single Congressional district (electoral constituency for the Lok Sabha, in Indian terms) which does not have a factory tied up with defence procurement. What General Eisenhower, the right wing US President of the 1950s, said in his farewell speech is true today a thousand times over; there is no industrial complex in the US which is not also a military-industrial complex. In overt and covert ways, the US spends roughly half its budget on the military, an amount greater than what the next twenty-five countries spend on their combined military budgets. This is certainly connected with the mania for world conquest but it also means that there is nothing as lucrative in the US as the business of war and that the dominant sections of the US bourgeoisie tend to be directly connected with war materials procurements.[3] The internal dynamic of US capitalism drives the US toward war as much as does the imperialist drive for global domination.

This war economy, in its internal as well as external aspects, intersects then with the petrodollar economy. *Frontline* has time and again emphasized the direct involvement of Bush himself as well as key members of his administration in the oil corporations (See, for example, V. Sridhar's 'Bush & Co. Private Limited', in *Frontline*, 14 March 2003). Every member of this administration would gain substantially, individual by individual, from any expansion of US control over the world's oil resources. Beyond that, there is the actual character of the oil economy as a whole, which has essentially three aspects: (a) actual resources and their possession, control and their actual utilization; (b) control over volumes of supply and directions of trade, i.e. where the pipelines go and where the oil then ends up; and (c) the currency in which oil trade, by far the biggest trade in the world, is carried out, and in which, therefore, the accumulation of wealth generated by this trade takes place. Each of these aspects is worthy of some explanation.

First, the volume of resources and consumption patterns. The largest chunk of the world's known oil resources is in the

[3] Dick Cheney, Defence Secretary under Bush Sr. and Vice President under Bush Jr., is the former CEO of Haliburton, the largest firm among defence contractors. The main business the Carlyle Group, whose Board of Directors includes Bush Sr. as well as his Secretary of State James Baker, commands an immense weapons procurement business around the world. Such examples can be multiplied *ad infinitum*.

Middle East. However, the Caspian Sea Basin is becoming increasingly attractive, with estimates of oil resources there fluctuating widely, between 35 billion and 300 billion barrels; the upper end of this estimate would mean that the region has more reserves than Saudi Arabia and half as much as the entire Middle East. By contrast, the US itself accounts for just two to three per cent of the resources but, with only 5 per cent of the world's population, it also accounts for a quarter of the world's oil consumption, half of which is imported. Caspian oil has a special place in these calculations because whereas oil is state property in the Middle East where US oil corporations have been hired essentially as contractors, oil resources in the Caspian region are still private property and can be owned directly by US corporations. However, it also has two major drawbacks. First, the resources are very undeveloped, even largely uncharted, and the oil is hard to extract; estimates for developing the requisite infrastructure and extraction facilities go up to $ 60 billion, a sum that even the richest corporations find forbidding. Second, and even more significantly, it is yet to be legally determined as to what share of this oil belongs to which of the new statelets bordering the sea. This situation is further complicated by the fact that Iran can refer to treaties with the Soviet Union which specified the Caspian Sea as a 'joint lake' between the two countries; it can thus lay claim to a substantial portion of this oil, and the successor regimes in the region must negotiate with Iran in accordance with international law.

Iraq occupies a special place in this calculus of resources. Its *known* reserves account for some 16 per cent of the world's total, second only to Saudi Arabia and vastly greater than the *currently known* reserves of the Caspian region. Second, decay of the oil industry in Iraq over the past two decades is such that it is currently producing roughly two million barrels a day as compared to eight million in Saudi Arabia, which means, that its reserves have been preserved much better even as its capacity to produce oil has declined (Iraqi oil industry has not had new computers installed since 1979, for example). Third, US oil corporations have been barred from this resource-rich country for well over a decade and shall not be allowed in unless there is a 'regime change'. Fourth, there are strong rumours that after the occupation of Iraq is completed the US will seek to privatize Iraqi oil, either under its own military administration or through the puppet regime it will then install; the willingness of particular clients to do this job may determine as to which ones get elevated to run the changed regime.

Then, there is the question of pipelines, which substantially determine which way the oil flows and who immediately benefits from it. For example, the Caspian Basin during the Soviet period had pipelines going only toward Russia and part of the US design there is to change the direction of this flow. The US would like to build pipelines through Afghanistan toward the Arabian Sea, keeping Russia as well as Europe out of these supply routes, but the problem is that Afghanistan is landlocked and the pipelines in this direction must then pass through Iran (the shortest route) or Pakistan, neither of which the US currently finds reliable. Hence the possibility of intensification of the so-called 'war on terrorism' in Pakistan and the mad plans for 'regime change' in Iran. In the interim, the US prefers the building of a system of oil-and-gas lines starting through Kazakhstan and Turkemanistan, then running under the Caspian Sea to Baku, then through Georgia and Turkey to the Mediterranean. This would keep Russia out but would facilitate supplies to Europe. The main point in any case is that the direction of pipelines is of great geo-political importance. For example, under a different dispensation of global power, pipelines could conceivably be constructed from the Caspian Basin to the Chinese province of Xinjiang, which China would like to develop 'industrially'. Those same pipelines could conceivably be extended across China to take oil and gas to its coastal regions and then, beyond that, to Japan. The construction of such pipelines would be very expensive but, as a result, China and Japan could be substantially free of US domination over their supplies. The US would never allow that because such possibilities feed into one of its two worst nightmares, namely that Chinese and Japanese interests would one day converge and, together, they would lead a vast zone of industrialized countries of East and Southeast Asia in a bloc that could outdo the US itself within a foreseeable future.

The other, and most immediate, nightmare for the US is that the EU shall fast emerge as a rival bloc. That, however, can only happen if Europe itself can emerge from under the dominance of the dollar which is currently the primary, virtually exclusive, reserve currency for the entire world. That, in turn, cannot happen unless the Euro becomes the primary currency for the world's largest trade, namely oil trade. A lot of dollars which are not petrodollars nevertheless gain their value and centrality in the world from petrodollars. The cardinal sin of Saddam Hussein is neither production of weapons of mass destruction nor promotion of terrorism but that, exasperated by ten years of American-imposed UN sanctions and Anglo-American bombings of large parts of his country, he made Iraq, on 6 November 2000, *the first oil-producing country to shift from the dollar to the Euro as the currency for trade in oil and hence the primary currency for its foreign trade in general,* showing to the other OPEC countries that they could break the dollar dominance by shifting to Euro or at least diversifying their reserve currencies. At the time Iraq made the shift, the Euro was worth 82 cents to a US dollar; today it stands at $ 1.5 – gaining by 17 per cent. Iraq's decision was a key element in making the

Euro a competitive currency for the first time. If the other oil producing countries were to shift accordingly; the US economy would face the prospect of immense shrinkage, even collapse.

This is how it works: since the dollar is the world's reserve currency, every country is forced to import dollars, which means that it must sell its goods and services to the United States, which can just go on printing more and more dollars, thus getting its imports at little cost. That's how the US can go on running its economy on huge deficits without any adverse effect of the deficits on its own economy. Oil being the largest single import for most countries, they need increasing amounts of dollars for their purchases. In turn, the oil producing countries accumulate immense amounts of dollars which then go back to – mostly US-based – banks and become what we call petrodollars. If oil trade were to shift to the Euro, there would be a glut of dollars in the world, which will have to be exchanged for the Euro, at declining prices for the dollar. These value-depleted dollars would then have to be honoured by the US Federal Reserve. The more dollars are thus cashed, the lower their value shall be. The US would no longer be able to run its economy on deficits as it has been doing for decades. Indeed, as the world's biggest debtor nation and one whose own currency was now in much less demand, the US would have to start paying some of its debts, without any capacity to just go on printing more dollars. Meanwhile, America's productive capacity and urban infrastructures are in advanced stage of decay, and its states and cities are as much in debt as is the federal government itself, not to speak of the citizenry at large, which is wedded now to a credit card economy. The US may well face a crash. It must therefore make sure that the oil-producing countries do not shift to the Euro, even if that requires occupying some of them and continually threatening the rest. What happens, for example, if Chavez of Venezuela makes the same decision as Saddam Hussein and shifts to the Euro, considering that Venezuela is a major supplier of oil to the US itself?

This currency war is as much an element in the contemplated war against Iraq and the 'regime change' there as is the question of capturing its oil resources. What we are witnessing, in fact, is a possible crack in the whole system of dollar dominance that had been put together by the advanced capitalist countries some fifty years ago, under US guidance. When France warns that the unilateral will of the US to go into this war will ruin the United Nations, we are reminded of how the Nazi excesses had spelled the doom for the League of Nations. The heightened tension between the US and core EU economies, indicated by this currency war, illustrates how the disappearance of the Soviet Union has served not to bring greater stability to imperialism but to accentuate the inner conflicts of the system; retrospectively, in fact, one can see all the more clearly that it was only the existence of communist states that had brought the advanced capitalist countries into a stable alliance and that stability itself may become brittle after the disappearance of the communist rival. Meanwhile, as the US conquers Afghanistan and then discards it to a rubbish heap, as it now prepares to make war on Iraq's people and their resources, and as it issues warnings of making war against another half a dozen countries to bring about 'regime change' in all of them, the US itself begins to look like – more than anything else – a Fourth Reich.

This analysis of the economic imperative underlying the coming war also helps explain two other factors. We can now see, first, why the US is so determined to make war even in opposition to a global coalition of anti-war forces so huge as to have no precedent in past history. At the same time, it also helps explain the otherwise seemingly senseless and knavish behaviour of Blair & Co. One can understand the ideological basis for the Italian and Spanish governments supporting Bush; like the US, Italy and Spain are also ruled by the far right. But why a Labour Prime Minister in Britain? It is the structural intimacy between the dollar and the sterling, which explains the personal intimacy between Blair and Bush, as well as the tension between the Anglo-American and the Franco-German blocs. It's all about money.

11 APRIL 2003
War of Occupation Begins

The expected, the dreaded, the unspeakable has begun. The Anglo-American axis has waged a wanton war of destruction and starvation against Iraq and its people for well over a decade now. What has begun now is the new and climactic phase which turns it into a war of full-scale occupation. Already, as I write this on the fourth day of the war, Baghdad has suffered the worst bombings in human history: 1,000 cruise missiles dropped on a city in one night. When the authors of the so-called 'Shock-and-Awe' strategy proposed that Baghdad be hit by 800 cruise missiles on the first two days, they said that this intensity of bombing will have the same effect as that of the atom bomb at Hiroshima. In that one night alone, 'Hiroshima effect' was exceeded by 200 additional cruise missiles. A night of relatively – only relatively – lighter bombing followed. Together, on the two nights, Us aircraft flew one thousand bombing sorties, in addition to remote-controlled missile attacks from land- and sea-based launchers. More cruise hurricanes are in the offing.

The bizarre fact is that the targets themselves – the presidential palace, headquarters of the defence ministry and the intelligence services, the houses of Saddam's family, and so on – make no military sense. They must have been evacuated long ago. The intent is simply to terrorize the population, to demonstrate that if the most majestic buildings in the city can go up in balls of fire and sky-high splinters of debris, then everyone of the inhabitants of the city can also meet the same fate unless they flee or surrender immediately. What the Americans want is that by the time their Marines walk into it, this city of five to six million people – until recently one of the proudest and most prosperous cities of the Arab world – become a city of corpses and ghosts. American lives are too precious for the more familiar kinds of urban warfare.

So transparent is this intent to terrorize that even the phalanxes of so-called experts and strategists who have been lining up in the studios of TV channels have taken to calling it 'psychological warfare' as if thousands of cruise missiles raining down on a city had the same effect as the dropping of leaflets. One has been quite used to this kind of gibberish on the CNN which has long served as an echo chamber of the Pentagon but BBC too seems to have gone through an overnight transformation and has now taken up a position somewhat to the right of the CNN. A poor man's CNN as it were! Most of the real news about the war now comes from the alternative media assembled by anti-war groupings on the Net, through their websites and server lists. It is only there, for example, that one learns that the three helicopters which have come down, accounting for about 40 deaths among the US and British military personnel, were indeed shot down and not lost in accidents, as the invading axis has claimed. Only from this other media, does one learn that people have defied their tyrannical governments throughout the Arab world and directly clashed with the police all the way from Yemen and Bahrain to Cairo and Amman; that three people were shot and killed in the Yemen during these demonstrations; or that militant sermons are being delivered not just by jihadi elements in the Muslim world but also throughout the world of the traditionally and historically pacificist Islam, all the way from Al-Azhar, the most prestigious and sedate seminary of Sunni Islam, to the mosques of Mecca and Medina in Saudi Arabia, otherwise so savagely controlled by the monarchical clients of the US. The dominant electronic media, on the other hand, has shied away from telling us any of that, or that Ayatollah Khamenai, the current head of the Irani state has used the word 'satanic' for the US designs, having abandoned such language after Khomeini's death; or that it is not only China but also President Megawati Sukarnoputri of Indonesia as well Malaysia's Acting Prime Minister Abdullah Ahmad Badawi who have said that, in Megawati's words, 'the use of military action against Iraq is an act of aggression which is against international law'.

It is not from the big-business media that we can learn that every city in Greece has been rocked with demonstrations or that 200,000 marched in Athens in the largest rally in a generation; or that over 100,000 marched in Paris or close to a hundred thousand in Berlin while every city of any consequence in Germany had rallies; or that a notable feature of these rallies is the participation of tens of thousands of schoolchildren with placards saying 'Not in Our Name'. Only from the website of *CounterPunch* magazine did I learn that the number of arrested in San Francisco exceeded 1400 and that helicopters whirred over the city while police beat up demonstrations across the town throughout the day. The staid print media has become so disoriented that this morning's electronic edition of the *Guardian* says in its headlines that 200,000 marched in London and New York but in the detailed story the number rapidly dwindles to 100,000 in London and 20,000 in New York. That same feat of taking off a zero to reduce the actual size of the rally to one-tenth of it was achieved by the police in Milan where a march of some 150,000 was declared to have drawn only 15,000. It took the CNN well over twenty-four hours to even start coming clean and devote a couple of minutes to the actual magnitude of the London demonstration (half a million according to the organizers, 200,000 conceded by police) or the demonstration in New York (estimated at 200,000). All this on the fourth day of the Baghdad bombings, in hurriedly organized events.

From a media that either simply ignores the protests or relies mainly on police estimates, we shall never know of the size of the turnouts from Turin to Melbourne and from Sydney to Karachi, nor of the persistence of this turbulence, the ebb and flow of it, day after day as the war grinds on. As Stan Goff put it: 'This hasn't been an easy time for Bush and his killer clowns. It hasn't been an easy time for a lot of so-called liberals either. An anti-war movement came onto the scene, and not just any anti-war movement. It is now the fastest and broadest international movement of its type in history. It involves anarcho-kids, olde tyme lefties, and pacifists to be sure, but it also involves soccer moms, Black preachers, Italian dock workers, women who write books, nerds, doctors, Indian garment workers, Nigerian intellectuals, Brazilian coffee pickers, Japanese students, Haitian peasants, Filipino street cleaners . . . every damn body!'[1]

As the BBC itself becomes to the CNN what Blair has become to Bush, the crisis of the Anglo-American liberals, and their dominant media in particular, becomes increasingly more palpable. While the London march was in full swing, all one got on the BBC was an aerial shot lasting about five seconds, before it resumed its cheerleading of the invaders. One can hardly expect from such a media the information that numerous officials of the

---

[1] I owe a public apology to Mr Stan Goff for having used harsh and unwarranted language about him in the original piece as it was published in *Frontline* which I have now deleted. Watching the American scene from the distance of New Delhi, I was aware of his extensive background in the US Armed Forces but did not know of his subsequent work in the anti-war movement generally and among the veterans more particularly. He is currently doing magnificent work in organizing the families of the US militarymen currently on war duty in Iraq, to help build a movement to end the occupation and bring back the US troops.

US intelligence and military services, past and present, stand outside the charmed circle of Bush's happy genocidists and believe, rather, that the project of planetary conquest these genocidists are pursuing is unsustainable, contrary to America's own national security interests, and contrary perhaps even to the larger interests of the Republican party itself which might lose its luster if the war doesn't go the way it is envisioned. This domesticated and paid-for dominant media does its utmost to suppress the fact that America's chief terrorism expert, assistant to Condoleeza Rice, resigned in disgust from his post at the National Security Council as the first bombs fell on Baghdad. And it has simply not told us that three US diplomats have resigned already, or that army chaplains are reporting large-scale disaffection with the war aims among the soldiery itself. It will not tell us that Hans Blix, the UN's former chief weapons inspector, who rendered such sterling service to the United States by destroying what little remained of Iraq's defensive capabilities – notably the Al-Samoud missiles and the attendant delivery systems – now says that the US was always 'impatient to go to war', had no interest in peaceful disarmament from the outset, and provided to the inspectors information that was sloppy or false. Blix's colleague, Joern Siljeholm, who lives in the United States but cannot get a hearing from the US media, said to the Norwegian newspaper, *Dagbladet* about Colin Powell's claims at the Security Council that 'It did not match up at all with our information. The whole speech was misleading. . . Much of what has been claimed about WMDs [weapons of mass destruction] has proven to be sheer nonsense'. One will never hear this on BBC or CNN which are as much part of the 'psychological warfare' as is the raining down of the cruise missiles on Baghdad and Mosul.

Today, fourth day of the war, even these cheerleaders on BBC and CNN have come under three pressures. First, the sheer size of the opposition is so great and so very, very widespread across the globe that the media would lose all credibility if it were to ignore this continuing anti-war upsurge. Far from subsiding after the great global uprising of 15 February which had brought perhaps as many as 15 million marchers to the streets of the world, the anti-war movement is picking up again, growing more militant, recruiting new marchers, especially among the young and the very young. Street fighting between protesters and the police are being reported from across the world, from New York to Brussels, and from Bahrain to Mexico City. This resurgence can no longer be ignored.[2]

Secondly, many of the myths the American disinformation agencies had cooked up are getting exposed. A thousand cruise missiles, thousands of bombings sorties, to 'Shock and Awe', and yet there has been no exodus of the people out of Baghdad. Four days of armour-and-infantry race into the Shia zones of eastern Iraq, which was said to have been just waiting for the Anglo-American liberators, and no one has come forward to greet them and not even the smallest town has yet fully fallen to this greatest power in human history: instead, we see a battered and starving people just holding out as long as they can. The small town of An-Nasiriyah, which the invaders claimed to have captured two days ago is still fighting on as I write these words.

And, third, while every claim made by the Iraqis has either proven to be correct or judged credible, stories put out by the Anglo-American axis are proving to be wrong. They claimed that the 51st Division had surrendered, then said it was a battalion, then the commander of the brigade, then again the full brigade – but failed to produce material evidence; it was obviously a lie, or in a more polite language 'disinformation'. They claimed that certain

---

[2] As we have noted elsewhere, this re-energizing of the anti-war upsurge was not to last beyond the fall of Baghdad, which stunned most people into confusion or despondency or just silence.

towns had fallen, which have not. A grenade attack on an infantry encampment could not be denied; they have put out the story that a temporarily deranged American soldier had himself done it. When the first helicopter was shot down, they said it was an accident. When two of UK's finest, newest helicopters were shot down, they said the helicopters had collided by mistake. When the Royal Air Force (RAF) lost a plane, they first remained silent for some hours, then said that a US missile had shot it down by mistake. They announced that the little border town of Umm Qasr had been captured and Basra, the second largest city in Iraq, was about to fall. Twenty-four hours later, Umm Qasr was still holding out and Basra, which sustained such heavy bombings in the city centre that 77 civilians were killed and 366 injured in one night, was so far from falling that another story was put out saying that the city had just been surrounded and bypassed. Meanwhile, again, there has not been so far any exodus of the population out of Basra despite all the aerial bombings and the ground attack, and despite the fact that its predominantly Shia population was supposed to be just waiting to rise to greet the Anglo-American 'liberators'.

    Faced with these pressures of a resurgent mass anti-war movement, as well as the myths and lies of the invading forces, even the dominant media has begun now to take some distance from its assigned role as mere an echo chamber of the warmongering officialdom. BBC has now inducted at least one commentator who keeps the skepticism alive.

So, why has the war come, and what are the likely consequences? About the larger US objectives we have written in previous articles. We shall return to these objectives and will amplify our argument further. It needs to be stated at the very outset, however, that the Security Council, the United Nations Secretary-General, and the so-called 'international community', including France and Germany who are now waxing eloquent, have been fully complicit as three successive US administrations – Bush Sr., Clinton and now Bush Jr. – have supervised US policy in Iraq. It was by resolution of the Security Council that sanctions were imposed and maintained, which have cost Iraq deaths of one and a half a million of its citizens, have ruined the health and life chances of its citizenry, withheld from them essential commodities such as medicine, led to the decay of its oil industry as well as every other branch of its industry, and to the collapse of its infrastructure. During these same years, this same Anglo-American axis imposed so-called 'no-fly zones' in large parts of Northern and Eastern Iraq, whereby Iraq could not fly its own aircraft over its territory but the Anglo-American axis could and did at will, in utter violation of international law governing the sovereignty of nations. The Security Council did nothing and implicitly condoned this decade-long violation of the UN Charter. Hardly a week has passed during this decade when this axis has not bombed something or the other in Iraq, without the Security Council ever holding a single meeting to condemn, or even consider, this weekly lawlessness.

The US demanded, the Security Council resolved, and every country in the world, without exception, parroted the nauseating demand that Iraq be 'disarmed'. Iraq has not occupied any foreign territory since the Gulf War; Israel has occupied (even 'annexed' by its own national law) Syrian territory for close to forty years, but Israel is not to be disarmed. Britain and the US have bombed Iraq, supplied military materials and advisors to separatists and US-nurtured 'opposition' in Northern Iraq, and even the *Time* magazine has reported several weeks ago that secret US armies, including its Special Forces, have been operating in various parts of Iraq for many, many months. But neither Britain nor the US were to be 'disarmed', nor even condemned, no matter how much they flouted the sovereignty of Iraq or inflicted bombs and death on its citizens.

Not only that. The US has been shouting from rooftops for well over a year, as loudly and frequently as possible, that it will invade Iraq at a time of its own choosing, with the sole objective of 'regime change' (i.e., overthrow of a lawfully constituted government of another sovereign country through a unilateral act of war), regardless of what the inspectors did or did not find. Yet, knowing all this perfectly well, this same Security Council sent in the inspectors and authorized them to destroy what little defensive capability Iraq still had, so as to make the war of conquest so much easier for the Anglo-American axis. When the US decided to begin the invasion it sent its orders directly to those inspectors to get out of Iraq; Kofi Annan, entirely on his own and without permission of the Security Council which had sent them in, 'advised' them to abide by the US orders. Just before the Americans withdrew the draft of their resolution from the Security Council in mid-March, Jacques Chirac, the wily and unreliable French President, offered a compromise solution whereby Iraq would be fully disarmed within thirty days or face a war authorized by the UN. Americans were the ones who didn't care for this surrender by the Franco-German bloc because their calendar for war was set neither by issues of disarmament nor by considerations of an already supine Security Council but by weather conditions most suitable for invasion. By mid-April, the big sand storms would have begun and war would have become a bit more difficult.

This outrage continues. We feel pleased that China has issued a strongly worded statement specifically saying that the war on Iraq is a violation of the UN Charter, that Putin has used the words 'aggression' and 'condemn', that Germany and France are repeating their 'warnings' and advising 'caution' so that 'casualties' be minimized, and so on and so forth. None of these permanent members of the Security Council, nor Kofi Annan who is supposed to be the current custodian of the UN Charter, has so far suggested that a unilateral act of war against a sovereign country, the bombing of its cities, the occupation of its territories, the killing of its civilians in city centres are all war crimes for which the leaders of the US and Britain must be tried in the International Court of Justice which has been constituted for precisely this purpose.

Rather, Kofi Annan is known to have quietly appointed a committee some three months ago for planning the delivery of so-called 'humanitarian' aid after the US occupation, and, the day after the bombings began, the same Germany and France began negotiating as to how many of the contracts will they get for 'post-war reconstruction' in Iraq. The day the Americans announced their resolve to invade, Annan put an end to the oil-for-food programme that was being administered by the UN, thus putting an end to the crucial supplies upon which the sanctions-bound Iraq relies for meeting the daily needs of its population; it's Iraqi money, earned through sales of Iraqi oil, but Iraq cannot use it to buy food for its citizens because a UN bureaucrat, upon directions of the US, says so. He also ordered the relief agencies to leave Iraq, leaving the population without that resource. This prospect of starvation was expected to encourage the population to start leaving the country, generating millions of 'refugees' who would be designated as Saddam's victims and to whom then the benevolent UN and the even more benevolent western countries would bring 'humanitarian aid'. Now, ever the loyal servant of the US, Annan is busy drafting a resolution for the Security Council whereby the US shall be allowed to complete the act of conquest but the ugly task of occupation shall be performed in the name of the UN so that the prolonged guerrilla warfare which the Iraqis are most likely to mount after the occupation may be faced not by the US troops but by soldiers of other countries flying the UN flag but doing the US bidding. A plausible legal case can be made against Annan for dereliction of duty as defender of the UN Charter, and for aiding and abetting war criminals of the Bush and Blair administrations.

The only act of substantive dissidence has come so far from Russia. President Putin and his foreign minister, Igor Ivanov, have both been quoted by the Al Jazeera TV network on 22 March as saying that Russia, 'along with other countries', shall approach the legal departments of the United Nations to determine whether or not the Anglo-American invasion of Iraq is in violation of international law, and as to what appropriate actions can be undertaken in this regard. We still do not know how serious the intent is behind such statements. For, this too may turn out to be merely a bargaining point between the US and the opposing members of the Security Council. This is, however, precisely what needs to be done. The four permanent members of the Security Council as well as numerous other countries around the world have said that the Anglo-American aggression against Iraq violates the UN Charter and other founding protocols of international law. These words need to be made credible through deeds.

As for weapons of mass destruction, rule of the thumb is quite simple: if Iraq had them, Americans would not have gone in and taken the risk. They would have left the matter to the inspectors for as long as was necessary. They knew that Iraq did not have any, not at any rate enough to pose a significant problem. Then, week after week, the inspectors further confirmed what the US already knew. They gave the inspectors false and misleading information because they actually had no concrete information pointing to anything real; they just had some suspicions and wanted them removed. Blix obliged.

Conversely, of course, the US will not invade North Korea because the latter actually has developed nuclear weapons as well as delivery systems that can carry the weapons at least as far as Japan. That's what Iraq was trying to develop: a small number of such weapons that could go as far as Israel, as a minimum counterweight against at least 200 nuclear warheads that Israel, the great menace to the Arab world, is *known* to have. The principle was the same: you threaten a key US ally – Japan in the case of North Korea, Israel in case of Iraq – and the US shall not dare invade you. North Korean gamble worked, Iraq's did not – and in this, as in much else, the Security Council, the 'international community' etc, have been solidly on the side of the US and against Iraq.

What, then, are the strategic objectives and the prospects of their realization?

We need to first dispose of the question of the *immediate* prospects in Iraq, here and now. The first thing to be understood here is that Iraq is battered, exhausted, pauperized, with its defensive capabilities already destroyed, enjoying no practical assistance from outside. Two-thirds of its population relied on the direct distribution of essential commodities, such as food and medicine, by the state. The invasion has put an end to that. It is very unlikely that its armed forces can put up for long any kind of conventional defence against the super-high-tech invaders. Iraq's only strength, which is yet to be tested, is the fighting spirit of its people. Will they stand and fight? The Iraqi authorities say that they have armed seven million people, a third of Iraq's total population. Is that true? Will this fuel a popular, long-drawn war of anti-imperialist resistance? Will it lead, in stead, to armed inter-ethnic conflicts? Between members of the Ba'ath party and their opponents? Generalized anarchy as the population, bereft of even food and other essential goods, scrounges around, fighting for mere day to day survival, each against all? It's too soon to tell.

Conversely, all that the US had expected to happen immediately has not happened. There have been no anti-Saddam uprisings, no Shia welcome for the invaders, no Shia-Sunni tussles, no exodus of people out of the cities. People have seen thousands of bombs and missiles, equal to hundreds of thousands of tons of TNT, fall on their city, and they have not moved. Indeed, there are reports of Iraqi embassies in Lebanon and Jordan getting flooded with applicants who want to go and fight in Iraq, against the US. Even CNN has shown pictures of Iraqis in Amman packing their cars to drive to Baghdad and be in their city as the bombs fall. Americans had predicted splits in the army, splits in the ruling party, splits in the regime itself. They are still claiming to be in negotiation with senior military and party leaders who wish to come over to their side. They have been saying for months that they will absorb the whole of the Ba'ath party into their own apparatus if Saddam is ditched. None of it has happened yet. Maybe it will happen, maybe not.[3]

---

[3] The sudden surrender of Baghdad without a fight did suggest – and now we know it to be a fact – that part of the military and political establishments did in fact make a deal with the Americans while the remaining part of the regime quickly retreated into hiding. Saddam Hussein's daughters were eventually given asylum in Jordan and said in interviews that their father was betrayed by the generals he trusted the most. The nature of the resistance that emerged so very quickly on the one hand, and, on the other, the appearance of quite large numbers of security personnel who are willing to work with the Americans, again shows similar splits in the lower ranks, although it is far from clear that all this personnel shall indeed be – and will remain – loyal to the Americans.

Meanwhile, even as their monstrous military convoys rumble toward Baghdad and the aerial bombardment of the city continues, the nightmare for the Americans is that they will have to fight in direct combat, street to street, house to house, with US and British casualties mounting. They know that public opinion in UK is already overwhelmingly against the war, with the ruling party itself deeply divided on the issue. A prolonged war with significant American casualties shall erode the pro-war sentiment in the US too, quite fast; in the case of Vietnam that erosion took years, in the present case it may take mere months. However, unwillingness to take significant casualties puts the Anglo-US bloc in a dilemma. Conventional armies surrender, but what does the invader do with armies which simply melt into the populace and fight without fixed positions? Well, if conventional combat on the ground is deemed politically too costly on the home front, the only other choice is a war of extermination: kill the whole lot, from up high. The invaders certainly have the military means to accomplish that. But the political consequences of that are even more unthinkable. One night of terroristic bombings of carefully selected uninhabited buildings have brought out perhaps as many as three million people on to the streets across the globe, with street fights breaking out in a couple of dozen cities. Entire populations being incinerated, and on television at that, will rip apart certainly the Middle Eastern and European cities, possibly some American ones as well, and an unstoppable movement will be born to try Bush and Blair as war criminals.[4]

So, the Americans are still hoping that something will

---

[4] The quick surrender of Baghdad ended the possibility of that kind of urban warfare as well as the need, on part of the US-UK alliance, to undertake that kind of war of extermination. It may also be the case that the kind of technology the US now commands no longer allows the more traditional kind of house-to-house urban warfare. That technology is far less effective against hit-and-run guerrilla attacks, however, which is what we have witnessed since the occupation.

work for them: the populations will flee, politicians and officers will shift loyalties, somebody will produce Saddam's dead body, or some such thing. The US-UK alliance says that its forces will reach the parameters of Baghdad on 27 March. Some of the answers shall then start coming in.

What has this alliance achieved so far? Well, their forces are moving along through the desert, but they have achieved little else in the war at this time of writing, on fourth day of the assault. Elsewhere, three of their gains have been substantial. First, they have secured the home front, substantially. In the US, where the population was split before the war, patriotic fervor has helped Bush in winning three-fourths majority to his side, and when the Democratic Senator Byrd, who has served in the US Congress for close to fifty years, longer than anyone else, rose to deliver his solemn denunciation of this war – 'Today I weep for my country' – the Senate Chamber was virtually empty and many of his own party colleagues did not bother to hear him. In UK, the much-longed for rebellion in the Labour Party did not materialize; 139 members of parliament voted against him but Blair won by a comfortable majority in his own party and overwhelming majority in the House, with solid Tory support.

Secondly, the United States has managed to split the EU, a major political aim at the moment, with UK, Spain, Italy, Portugal and a number of the smaller countries supporting them against the Franco-German position. In addition, half a dozen Arab countries have provided them basing facilities (including Jordan which has done it very quietly) while others have given them tacit support, with the exception of Syria. This is really the core of what they call a 'coalition of the willing' and for which they claim a membership of 45 countries; most of those 45 are insignificant little dependencies such as Eritrea, El Salvador and Estonia. If in consequence of this war, the US can also stabilize the dollar as the exclusive currency of the oil trade, against the challenge from the Euro, this split in EU can have long-term consequences.

Thirdly, they have rendered the United Nations irrelevant or worse, not by getting authorization from the Security Council but in bypassing it, and doing their dirty work at the UN through Kofi Annan and his bureaucracy. The other members of the Security Council now have the choice of gulping it and merely asking for a share in the future dispensation, or concretely challenging the very legality of the US-UK aggression and forcing them to be answerable to international law, on terms chosen not by themselves but by courts that have international jurisdiction. The United Nations thus can become 'relevant' again in one of two ways. It can become relevant the way it has usually been relevant, as a tool of the Americans, with 'allies' following suit. Or, it can indeed refuse to play that role and bring the US to book. All that will depend on two factors. First, we have to see if the Franco-German alliance is committed deeply enough to defending the Euro against the dollar, in a do-or-die political battle at this time. Secondly, we have to see whether the Franco-German-Sino-Russian coalition which emerged fleetingly during the recent Security Council proceedings really has any long-term significance as an enduring bloc against unilateral US domination over the globe. Neither of these developments is likely. The fact that the US-UK alliance has pointedly defied and bypassed the Security Council and no other permanent member has even asked for a session to be held to discuss this grave matter would seem to indicate that the will to take on the United States at this point is lacking. This too is a matter which will have to be watched carefully. In the unlikely event that Russia does make good on its threat to have the international agencies determine the issue of the legality of the current aggression against Iraq, then we shall have entered a new phase of the struggle over the global balance of power.

As for the long-term strategic aims of the US we have written previously about the larger geo-political design driving this politics and about the politics of oil and the associated war of currencies, the dollar versus the Euro. We have repeatedly emphasized that the US foreign policy under Bush is being formulated primarily not at the State Department or even the CIA but at a cluster of think-tanks of the far right among whom the Project for New American Century, the home base of the current top officials of the Pentagon, is pivotal but which also include such other think-tanks as the Heritage Foundation and the American Enterprise Institute. In considering what comes after the conquest of Iraq, we might as well conclude with a quotation from a piece that Michael Ledeen, who holds the Freedom Chair at the American Enterprise Institute, contributed to the *New York Sun* of 19 March, just as the invasion began. The article is entitled 'After Baghdad: Tehran, Damascus, Riyadh' and says in part 'Once upon a time, it might have been possible to deal with Iraq alone, without facing the murderous forces of the other terror masters in Teheran, Damascus and Riyadh, but that time has passed . . . their doom is sealed. It would then be only a matter of time before their people would demand the same liberation we brought Afghanistan and Iraq. . . . Iraq is a battle, not a war'.

So, we know where the cruise missiles shall be raining down next.

25 APRIL 2003
Barbarians at the Gate
THE BATTLE FOR BAGHDAD BEGINS

The sacking of Baghdad by the Mongols is vivid in Arab memory as the moment when the decline of their splendid medieval civilization began, paving the way for eventual domination and colonization by Western powers after the Ottoman interlude. That is the memory, combined with the more recent memory of the occupation of Iraq by the British in the first half of the 20th century, which is now being re-lived across the Arab world. For, the Arabs are passing through a remarkable moment in their modern history. For the first time since the creation of Israel more than half a century ago, an Arab country, with that same Baghdad as its capital, faces the threat of actual occupation and, in effect, colonization by a non-Arab power. Those who watched with horror the televised destruction of Beirut by the Israelis in 1982 have now had to watch the much more spectacular and savage bombings of Baghdad since the very first night of this ongoing war of occupation. Faced with the prospect of a prolonged siege of the city by the invading forces and the impending defence of their city by the battered and poorly armed population, under a regime of indifferent merit, some have already taken to referring to Baghdad as a likely 'Stalingrad of the desert'. That is implausible. In the end, Baghdad may well come to resemble not so much Beirut or Stalingrad but Algiers during the war of liberation against

French colonial occupation: an occupied city slowly organizing itself for resistance.

Intoxicated by myths of their own making, the Anglo-American axis had undertaken this war of occupation with a variety of delusions. They had made themselves believe, for example, that the Shia majority would rise up to greet them as liberators from Sunni autocracy. Instead, Ayatollah al-Husainy al-Sistani, the most revered among the Shia clergy in Iraq, has declared from his seat at the holy city of Najaf that resistance against this foreign invasion is a 'religious duty' for all the Shias of the world. He was then quickly followed by the religious scholars and ayatollahs of Qom, the main seat of Shia Islam in Iran, who issued a joint proclamation to the same effect. The invading axis certainly has its Iraqi clients, ranging from Ahmed Chalabi, the convicted criminal who is their favourite for succeeding Saddam, to such comprador intellectuals as Kenan Mekiya of Harvard University, who has declared that the sounds of the bombs falling on Baghdad are, in his words, 'music to my ears'. But they had also deluded themselves that their invasion would provoke a series of uprisings, in town after town, against Ba'athist rule. In reality, no Arab group has come forward to be 'liberated' into colonization and none is fighting on their side, while thousands are said to have streamed into Iraq – from Jordan, Syria and Iran – to join in the defence of Baghdad. Far from invoking any rebellion in the predominantly Shia'ite southern Iraq, the US-UK alliance has so far failed to capture any town of any significant size in the whole region.

Similarly, the invasion has served to bring together the two factions of the Ba'ath party which have been bitter rivals for some forty years as they have ruled Iraq and Syria respectively. The US Defence Secretary has accused Syria of supplying military equipment to Iraq, including night-vision goggles of Japanese and US make, and Ariel Sharon, the criminal Prime Minister of

Israel, has threatened an invasion of Syria. Indeed, as long ago as December 2002, as the US perfected its invasion plans, Sharon took to charging that Iraq had transferred its so-called 'weapons of mass destruction' to Syrian territory – a charge that the US-UK alliance may yet utilize in order to justify an invasion of Syria in the foreseeable future. Those charges are as fictitious as the charges that Iraq still had such weapons in the first place. What we do know is that Syria has allowed an indeterminate number of Arab fighters to cross into Iraq from its own territories, risking US and Israeli retaliation.

More significantly, reports are now emerging of new levels of cooperation among Syria, Iran and Turkey on the question of northern Iraq and the American designs to reward their Kurdish clients there with an autonomous, perhaps even semi-sovereign region/statelet of their own. This is significant, considering that Turkey and Syria were on the verge of fighting a military duel in that region in 1998, thanks to policy differences on the Kurdish question, and that Turkey and Iran have had very tense relations since the Islamic revolution in the latter country a quarter century ago. There is now mounting evidence of increased policy coordination and sharing of intelligence reports among these hitherto mutually hostile countries, albeit on the Kurdish question alone, while hostilities of other kinds remain. Iran is of course being accused by the US-UK invaders of introducing into northern Iraq elements of Iraqi nationality who are loyal to the Irani regime but wish now to fight against the Kurdish clients of the invaders on the side of the Iraqi army. Meanwhile, Turkey, a member of NATO and heretofore a reliable US ally in the region, has allowed to the US the use of its territories to supply its troops in northern Iraq while also preparing to defend the Turkish (the so-called Turkoman) population of northern Iraq against likely violence by the Kurdish separatists.

From the battlefront itself, real information is virtually impossible to obtain. Americans never tire of preaching freedom of the press but they have not allowed any independent journalists to cover their actions or verify their claims. Instead, as the virtually sexual phrase they have coined, journalists are 'embedded' inside their own units, having signed the contracts to say nothing without the prior approval of the axis commanders. So, we have the remarkable display of round-the-clock coverage on television, led by CNN and BBC, which is comprised of either the lies of these 'embedded' journalists or commentaries by the not-so-embedded journalists far from the actual fighting, so that the viewer is reduced to culling little pieces of information from the press conferences held by Iraqi officials, intelligence reports emanating from Russia, or bits of news filtering through the Arab channels, notably Al-Jazeera. Faced with vast discrepancies between their claims and what seems to be happening on the ground, American officials have said publicly that 'disinformation' is a legitimate weapon of war, very much in line with precepts first laid out by Hitlerian propaganda, and they have gone so far as to hack and bloc the website of Al-Jazeera, the independent news channel which is watched by 45 million in the Arab world and which has gained four million new subscribers in Europe since the beginning of this war of occupation.

For all this fierce control of the news, the axis powers are facing a yawning credibility gap. Ken Adelman, the US arms control director under Reagan, wrote in the *Washington Post* in February 2001 that 'regime change' in Iraq 'would be a cake walk'. Senior members of the Bush administration, Vice President Dick Cheney and Defence Secretary Donald Rumsfeld in particular, have been promising a short campaign of two to three weeks. Gen. Tommy Franks, the man leading the current military assault on Iraq, has said time and again that the war has been proceeding according to plan and on schedule. Tony Blair has said so in parliament. The evidence they are presenting as these lines are being written on 18th day of the assault, is that the axis forces have moved rapidly through southern Iraq and the US troops have indeed arrived on the parameters of Iraq. They claim that the Saddam International airport has been captured, the city encircled, elite squadrons of the US forces operating in the centre of Baghdad.

Facts would appear to be otherwise. The fall of Umm Qasr, a small port town near the Kuwait border, was announced on the second day of the assault; the fall of An-Nasiriyah, a somewhat larger town of 500,000 also close to the Kuwait border, was announced two days later. Both are still holding out, fierce battles being reported especially from the latter while the British hold over Umm Qasr is constantly undermined by periodic explosions and frequent sniper fire. Indeed, even as the US troops have raced through huge stretches of the desert to reach the outskirts of Baghdad, no town of any significance has fallen to them and Iraqi resistance is operating in all of them as well as along the whole length of the 450-kilometre Iraqi-Kuwaiti border. The holy cities of Najaf and Karbala, which the Americans regard as vital for defence of their thinly scattered supply lines across the desert, have reported hand-to-hand street fighting.

The US claims that the six divisions of the Republican Guards, the core of the Iraqi defence forces have been decimated or otherwise rendered inoperational and upward of 9,000 Iraqis have so far surrendered. However, even those western journalists who don't have to have their stories approved by the Anglo-US authorities have testified that there seem to have been no significant battles involving those Republican Guards. Nor is it clear how many of the 9,000 POWs are civilians. What is significant, however, is that even the US command claims to have captured only one General and that on the very day that the US announced that 2,500 Iraqi troops had surrendered, the authoritative intelligence bulletin issued by the Russians said that the total number of surrenderies in the whole week had not exceeded 1,000. Similarly, when the US announced that it had captured Baghdad's international airport Iraqi authorities took a busload of journalists to within 150 metres of the airport to show that there were no US troops there, and when the US announced that its forces were operating in central Baghdad – 'to stay there', they said – one of BBC's two main correspondents in the city reported that he had driven around the whole city, without any obstruction from the authorities, and saw no Americans anywhere in a city that continued to function normally despite the unspeakably savage levels of virtually round-the-clock high-altitude bombings by the US-UK axis.

The US had predicted, and seems to have based its own planning on the assumption, that its policy of so-called 'Shock-and-Awe' – i.e., historically unprecedented intensity of bombings of the capital city as well as Basra – would break the morale of the civilian population and would provoke rapid disintegration of the regime, leading to mass defections. In reality, there have been remarkably few refugees leaving the cities so far, despite the mounting rate of casualties especially in Basra and the rest of the smaller cities of southern Iraq, and the regime has held together, with ministers and high officials appearing regularly on Iraqi television which has shown even Saddam Hussein moving about among civilian residents in the affected areas of Baghdad. Instead, there are extensive reports of confusion, disarray and bickering among the highest officials of the US, with disagreements between some of the senior-most generals and the civilian heads of the Pentagon reaching such intensity that a group of Republican members of the US Congress are reported to have met President Bush to urge him to not rely so much on Rumsfeld and Wolfowitz, the Secretary and Undersecretary of Defence at the Pentagon, and to give serious hearing to the professionals of the armed forces and the intelligence agencies who are deeply skeptical of those ideologues.

We now know that the Rumsfeld-Wolfowitz plans, which are now being executed in Iraq, did not have the support of many of the highest military and intelligence officials and that Rumsfeld had systematically moved many of those officials out of key posts, replacing them with more pliant officials who accepted his plans. Frustration among those dissenting officials was indicated by the fact that during the months leading up to the more recent invasions we witnessed a remarkable pattern of leaks to the press of top secret documents which had advised against plans based on the assumption that towns in southern Iraq shall submit easily, welcoming the American 'liberators', so that they would be able to leave loyal local administrations in the captured towns as they moved toward Baghdad with secured rear and safe supply lines. Those plans had similarly assumed that they shall be able to amass a huge army of their own in northern Iraq through a Turkish corridor. The first shock in fact came when the Turkish parliament refused to allow the projected force of 62,000 US troops to pass through its territory and in effect use Turkey to gain strategic depth. We now have reliable reports that even Tommy Franks, the general commanding the Southern Command and directing the invasion of Iraq, who had been one of the few top generals on Rumsfeld's side of the argument, had come to recommend after the Turkish vote that the planned invasion be postponed until after a much larger force had been assembled in Kuwait. The dissenters had of course argued that military planning based on dubious political expectations of the masses of Iraqis welcoming an Anglo-American invading force and quick disintegration of the Iraqi regime were unrealistic, that the size of the force assembled in Kuwait was insufficient for the occupation of Iraq, and that plans to actually occupy a city the size of Baghdad were probably militarily unrealizable.

That skepticism in fact has a history of its own. Back in 1996, five years after the first Gulf War, President Bush Sr., the father of the current President, had said in an interview on BBC that 'To occupy Iraq would instantly shatter our coalition, turning the whole Arab world against us, and make a broken tyrant into a latter-day Arab hero'. Dick Cheney, the current Vice President and a leading figure in the right-wing, Zionist cabal which is masterminding this war, had been a Defence Secretary in Bush Sr.'s administration and had said in 1997 that if the US were to engage in another Gulf War to remove Saddam Hussein the international coalition 'would come apart', indicating that major European powers shall oppose such a move, as Germany, France and Russia indeed did more recently. Cheney had also said at that time: 'To have brought the war into the populous Iraqi capital of Baghdad where Hussein is based would have involved a different type of military operation than in the desert, and would have put large numbers of Iraqi civilians and hundreds of thousands of our troops at risk of being killed'. On the key question of ousting Saddam, Cheney had at that time said, 'The only way to make certain you could get him was to occupy all of Iraq and start sorting through Iraqis until you find Saddam Hussein'.

That the same Dick Cheney would now be spearheading precisely that kind of war plan, against the advice of some of the seniormost US generals, indicates how much deeper the hold of the far right now is in Washington (at the Pentagon in particular) and how much the current policy is being shaped by a group working as much for the Israeli interests as it pursues its own fantasies of world conquest, in which the occupation of Iraq is conceived of as merely a first step. This war plan was at any rate comprised of two key components. The political component presumed that Iraqis would rise up in rebellion, the Iraqi army and regime shall disintegrate, the loyalist sections of the population shall flee under the shock and awe induced by the bombings, Saddam shall be quickly isolated, and US troops shall walk into Baghdad to cheering crowds, pretty much as the Allied Forces had entered Paris after Liberation from Nazi occupation. The military component, based on this calculation, was that massive bombings, high-tech fire power on the ground, and a relatively small land army sweeping through the country would be sufficient to bring about a quick victory.

Facts seems to have taken a different shape, however. Basra was supposed to fall with no effort – indeed, the city was supposed to welcome the 'liberators' – which has simply not happened. That not even the smallest towns have surrendered means that the forces which were supposed to conquer Baghdad in a lightening attack have had to surround the towns on the way, leaving behind contingents at each town so as to secure the rear, while the supply lines have stretched over hostile territories and a relatively smaller number of troops are now available for the battle of Baghdad. A combination of a sand storm and persistent Iraqi resistance has meant daily casualties and the disabling of large amounts of the equipment available to the invading army. They have had to stop for re-supply and repairs. Now, having reached the parameters of Baghdad, and as we write these lines on the morning of 7 April, these forces are faced with a quandary. They are exhausted from constant movement and persistent skirmishes, and in need of rest, repairs, resupply and reinforcement. Few residents of Baghdad have fled from the city, bulk of the Iraqi fighting forces have been withdrawn into the city ostensibly for prolonged, street-to-street defence, and indeterminate number of new fighters are said to have come in from elsewhere. There have been skirmishes, and even modest battles. The war is now about to begin.

There is likely to be a lull of a few days in which the Americans secure their positions, rest their troops, repair their equipment, get more supplies from Kuwait – and wait for reinforcements, which cannot arrive in appreciable numbers for many days to come. The invaders certainly have the firepower to enter the city, terrorize the population, park their tanks at street corners; they do not have the numbers to occupy the city in any meaningful sense. Rules of the thumb for any guerrilla warfare are two in number: there must be at least six combat troops for each guerrilla, and the occupying force must be ready for fairly large number of casualties, one by one, in attrition, over a period of weeks and months, perhaps years. We still have no measure of the fighting capacities of the Iraqi forces, regular and irregular. They may yet collapse and the American dream of a 'cakewalk' may yet come true. However, the fact that the Anglo-American forces have been unable to securely occupy even small towns would indicate that pacification of Baghdad is unlikely in the coming days. And then there is the weather. If the Iraqis can hold out for another month or so, temperatures will rise to as much as 60C and the swirling sandstorms shall minimize the effectiveness of air power, the mainstay of Anglo-American assault plans. More of theirs may die of heat than in combat, and reduction in air cover shall expose their over-stretched lines to guerrilla actions even in the desert and on parameters of scores of towns. This is not how it was supposed to be, but that's how it is.

More broadly, the Americans have three problems. One is simply of greed. Their eyes are set so much on the immense profits that are expected to accrue after the successful conclusion of this war of occupation that they do not wish to share the spoils with anyone. The US Congress has just passed a bill which explicitly forbids post-war contracts in Iraq being granted to companies owned or even operating from France, Germany, Russia and Syria (though not China). The rest of Europe is not debarred but unhappiness with their European allies in countries like Italy is increasing, owing to their reluctance to share in the costs of war, and the inclination in Washington and London is to go it alone as a purely Anglo-Saxon phalanx, so much so that even as Kofi Annan wants so much to step forward and provide to the US some fig leaf of a UN authority, it is the US itself that is not keen on a UN role beyond what is euphemistically called 'humanitarian aid'.

Secondly, the US has been quite unable to put together anything resembling a credible opposition that can succeed Saddam Hussein. There are of course their clients scattered in the US, London, Kuwait, Doha, what have you, but the expectation that this group of discreditable clients shall be supplemented with new clients recruited from among the welcoming elites in southern Iraq and the deserting officials of the army and the Ba'ath party has thus far proved to be unrealizable. This combination – the greedy push to corner all the profits, the political failure to obtain a broad enough group of clients – is impelling the United States to hold fast to its original plan to oust the Saddam government and establish an Anglo-American, in effect American, administration in postwar Iraq. We have been treated to various versions of this plan over the past year or so. Gen. Tommy Franks, at the helm of Southern Command and chief commander in this war, said many months ago that postwar Iraq shall not only need a direct US military administration but also the stationing of substantial number of US troops on Iraqi soil 'on the model of South Korea', i.e., for decades to come.

Third, the Americans are also burdened with their self-image of having come as benefactors and 'liberators', and cannot quite fathom the inscrutable oriental's wish not to be occupied, colonized and ruled by others. Towns and cities have proved to be ungrateful, unwilling to be either bribed or bombed into submission. Basra was supposed to rise up in rebellion against Saddam and in jubilation at the arrival of the British troops. In reality, the whole military might of Blair's neo-imperialist Britain has been unable to secure even a significant foothold in the city despite unspeakable savagery of its bombings, armored assaults and artillery barrages. The horrendous scale of civilian casualties there shall only be known after the fighting is over; in An-Nasiriyah, a town one tenth the size of Basra but equally unwilling to be occupied, the dead and the injured are already estimated in the thousands.

Then, there's Baghdad. Iraqis have always said that they will concede the desert and fight the invaders in the capital itself. As we have pointed out before, this presents the mighty Americans with an impossible choice. They have to either engage in prolonged urban warfare with its predictably high levels of casualties for themselves, which will erode the domestic American support for this war and the many other wars that the Bush administration is planning. Or, they can bomb the city from above, killing the whole lot – a genocide from the skies, as it were – which will lead to mass-scale revulsion not just in sections of the US population but all over the world, including Europe. Among other things, that might lead to the downfall of Blair and his New Labour – along with its Tory allies – in Britain and the strengthening of the Communist-Socialist-Green alliance in the European parliament. Neither of these options seem particularly favourable to the US. So, they have come up with an ingenious new plan in which, according to the *Washington Post*, a 'victory' shall be declared even when there's no victory.

This 'victory' shall have three components. First, it is surely the case that much of northern Iraq is already effectively under control of the US Special forces and its Kurdish clients, and that much of the desert and the countryside in southern Iraq has also been abandoned to the devastatingly superior American fire power. Measured in sheer kilometers, it can certainly be said that the Anglo-American forces and their Kurdish clients have occupied the bulk of Iraqi territory outside the fertile Tigris-Euphrates heartlands; oil resources conveniently lie in the occupied territories. Secondly, towns and cities are indeed encircled and under constant attack. With further reinforcements and fresh supplies, this encirclement can be sustained in the foreseeable future and the besieged towns – deprived of food, water, electricity and health services – are likely to succumb sooner rather than later. Thirdly, as for Baghdad, the US may simply prolong its encirclement and siege, with periodic incursions and withdrawals, with the hope of exhausting and starving the population, accelerating the decay of its infrastructure, and inflicting enough casualties with sufficient regularity to generate more and more refugees, with the hope of the city eventually surrendering at a future date.

With these three elements in place, the US may simply declare 'victory', represent the war of position around the cities as a 'mopping-up operation' in a war that will be said to have ended already, and establish a US military administration not in Baghdad but outside it, perhaps on its outskirts, or even in some places like Basra if and when that falls. In the media, then, the attention shall be shifted away from the daily, relatively low-intensity warfare around the cities and in the countryside, and focused instead on the doings of the US military administration, its so-called 'reconstruction' activities, the occupation and revival of the oilfields by the US corporations and their local clients, and so on. War shall thus be institutionalized and even naturalized, as something ordinary and largely invisible, as war on Iraq, especially on its northern zones, for the past decade or more had been made invisible. The so-called 'international community' – Kofi Annan, the Security Council, the CNN-BBC disinformation regime, etc. – shall be expected to accept that coming war of the next decade as they had willingly, even enthusiastically embraced the sanctions and the war of the past decade. The sanctions, fully supported by every single member of this so-called 'international community' killed a million and half Iraqis and exposed another about a third of the population to malnutrition, epidemics, miscarried pregnancies, declining life expectancies, disappearing drinkable water, disabled schools and hospitals. These atrocities may be multiplied in the coming years of what shall soon be billed as 'postwar reconstruction' in which even the Schröders and the Chiracs shall participate gladly.

That at least is what the Americans seem to be planning for now. Gen. Richard B. Meyers, chairman of the Joint Chiefs of Staff has said that once Baghdad is isolated from the rest of the country it will be 'almost irrelevant' and that 'whatever remnants are left would not be in charge of anything except their own defence and it would be fairly small compared to the rest of the country and what's happening'. Many of the top officials of the US administration are already citing the example of Hamid Karzai whose government has been accepted by governments of the world although that government controls only a small part of the territory of Afghanistan, and even though even the personal security of Karzai himself is in the hands not of Afghans but a unit of the US Special Forces. In this scenario, then, Iraq shall not be formally partitioned but there shall be, in effect, dual authority, that of the current Iraqi government among forces and sections of the populations in the towns and cities under siege, and that of the American military administration in the areas under their control, notably the oil-producing regions. It is also likely that the US-controlled area shall gradually become a mosaic of local fiefdoms, autonomous zones and shifting loyalties, very much on the pattern of present-day Afghanistan, while the Americans are free to do with the oil as they wish.

This is the revised war scenario that is leading to an otherwise absurd situation that despite the inability to take even a single significant town, let alone the big cities, the US is already announcing the skeletal structure of this military administration, euphemistically named as 'the Office of Reconstruction and Humanitarian Assistance', which is headed by Jay Garner, a retired General, currently making his money in arms trade, and whose core officials have been named already. In one variant of the plan we hear that perhaps as many as 23 'ministries' shall be established, each headed by an American official. We are back to the heyday of colonial conquests, crown colonies, Mandates sanctioned by the League of Nations, imperial administrations resting on local chiefs, and the rest. Not the least of the ironies in the situation is that if the first Gulf War was fought in the name of 'liberating' Kuwait from the Iraqis, so as to restore princelings to their shiekhdom, now it is from Kuwait itself that Iraq itself is being 'liberated' from itself and into full-scale foreign rule, with Blair imagining himself as the rightful proconsul of Iraq, in the good old British colonial tradition, but in the service of the new colonial masters in Washington.

This at least is the current American dream. We are yet to see if and how and when the Iraqis will puncture it. For, we may be witnessing not the making of a new colony but simply another Palestine. Imperial dreams do have a way of becoming nightmares.

9 MAY 2003
Wars Yet to Come

Umm Qasr is a small town of a couple of thousand inhabitants, close to the Kuwaiti border and barely a few miles from the point from where the mighty Anglo-American forces entered Iraq. It was the first town that those forces tried to take, but the town held out in a fierce battle that raged for two weeks. During those same weeks, the Iraqi forces held out throughout the Fao peninsula against massive armour and ferocious air attacks, with no air cover for themselves. Battles raged during those two weeks around An Nassiriyah, Basra, Kerbala, An Najaf and scores of other towns and cities, large and small, and none fell. That same story was being repeated in the North which had been largely under Kurdish control, thanks to ten years of Anglo-American bombings which had favoured their Kurdish clients against Iraqi state administration and armed forces. Neither Kirkuk nor Mosul fell during those weeks of resistance.

Encircling of the southern towns and cities had required deployment of large contingents of troops and weaponry, so that the Anglo-American forces which raced through the desert toward Baghdad kept getting depleted and came to have intolerably long and exposed supply lines behind them. Most military observers believed that two weeks of fighting and traversing hundreds of kilometres had probably tired out the remaining forces, that the invaders would probably need fresh supplies and another at least one hundred thousand troops before mounting an assault on Baghdad, that there would be a lull of perhaps three weeks in preparation for an assault on a city of perhaps six million people which was also the citadel of a government that had yet not used its air force, most of its armour and artillery, most of its famed and feared Republican Guards, the Fedayeen-e-Saddam, the Ba'athist irregulars who were said to be fully armed for urban warfare. Short of a Dresden-style firebombing of the city on even a much larger scale, Baghdad was expected to be a fortress-city that would have to be won in a prolonged battle with a much bigger army than the Anglo-American alliance had when they reached the suburbs.

But there was neither a lull before the assault, nor even an assault of any great scale, nor any fighting even on the scale of the small towns from the invaders had been held at bay. The Americans just kept driving, some of their tanks wandered into various parts of the city, then more came, occupied one part, then another, and then another. Baghdad did not fight back. The invaders celebrated their victory in this non-war by allowing and inciting a sacking of the city quite the equal of – in some respects worse than – the sacking of Baghdad by the Mongols in the 13th century. The regime simply disappeared. The accumulated treasures of a civilization were looted, and libraries burnt, on a scale that even the marauding Mongols had not dared – not just in Baghdad but in town after town, which now fell, after the Surrender of Baghdad.

This is worth repeating. Umm Qasr, a dusty border town of no military significance, fought back for two weeks. Kerbala and An Najaf, sleepy towns of shrines and seminaries and holy men, fought back for two weeks. So did scores of others. None fell. Baghdad fell, the whole of it, in three days, without a fight. A myth is now being made in front of our eyes, lapped up by the more gullible even within the anti-war movement, that Baghdad collapsed in the face of superior weaponry, greater firepower, the historically unprecedented ferocity of the bombings which began on the first night. The fact of the matter, however, is that Baghdad fell not to that weaponry but thanks to a deal that the Ba'athist regime made with the Americans where they renounced the defence of the city in exchange for a whole variety of favours – to the Ba'athist leaders and ministers, the military commanders including the commanders of the elite Republican Guards, to possibly Saddam himself and his family – the details of which are yet unknown but which can be easily surmised: secret transportation to safe havens, treasury chests and payoffs, and, for many, lucrative posts in the new post-Saddam regime that the US is now putting together.[1] The Americans have said all along that they shall absorb much of the Ba'athis party and bureaucracy in the new regime – and so it shall be.[2]

Saddam Hussain had begun his savage, ignominious career in treason, as a 22-year old paid agent of the CIA who had been hired in 1959 to assassinate Abdel Karim Kassem, the man who had led the anti-monarchical revolution the previous year. Once the Ba'athists firmed up their grip on power in 1968 and Saddam

---

[1] In retrospect, this has turned out to be somewhat too sweeping. That many of the top generals and the core of the Ba'athist regime made a deal is clear enough. However, it is equally clear that enough remained loyal to Saddam Hussein personally and committed to the defence of Iraq more generally for there to be an orderly retreat and the gradual unfolding of precisely the kind of resistance we had predicted in this piece, written immediately after the occupation of Baghdad.

[2] By September 2003, the US had not only re-employed the higher officials but also large number of the police and security personnel, as well as – more notoriously – personnel of the *mukhabbarat*, the much feared and hated secret service of the Saddam regime which is known to have run a hideous regime of terror and torture for decades. By November, Rumsfeld was claiming that 100,000 Iraqi security personnel were now under training by the US. This policy of 'Iraqization' is likely to be even less successful than that of 'Vietnamization' under Richard Nixon, and is likely to start unravelling quite soon. The Ba'ath party will probably infiltrate these outfits quite effectively, and the rest would be mercenaries hardly interested in dying for the Americans.

seized positions as Vice President and deputy head of the Revolutionary Command Council, he used lists provided by the Western intelligence agencies to execute communists. It is widely believed that the US assisted him in his seizure of power in 1979 in a palace coup against President al-Bakr because the US had wanted to build him up against the new Irani regime after the Islamic Revolution, and he indeed invaded Iran the next year, in close collusion with the United States which supported him in a variety of ways, including supply of technology for production of chemical and biological weapons, in its own bid to get Iran weakened and have both Iraq and Iran, major oil producing countries opposed to Israel, weaken each other. He fell afoul of the Americans only when he invaded Kuwait, a close US ally, in an attempt to capture Kuwait's vast oil resources and thus emerge as the strongman of the Middle East. In this respect, the recent US determination to oust him resembles earlier cases of Diem in Vietnam, Marcos in the Philippines, or Noriega in Panama, who were all agents and allies but became liabilities later on. In the perspective of this past history, it is only fitting that Saddam's regime collapsed thanks to a deal made with the United States. Whether the deal was made by him to save his own skin, or by his subordinates who acted against him, is unclear. It is also unclear as to who brokered the deal. Probably Putin's men did it, just as Yeltsin's men had eventually persuaded Milesovic to give up. It is often the case that traitors are eventually betrayed by their own friends.[3]

[3] 'Traitors are betrayed by their own friends'. When I wrote these words I did not know how true they were. A month later, the daughters of Saddam Hussein (the 'traitor' in question here) were to give interviews from their newly found safe haven in Amman saying that their father had been betrayed by his most trusted generals. We might add that King Abdullah, whom the Americans groomed before putting him on the Jordanian throne, would not have provided safe haven to those daughters without prior American approval. It might take as much as a generation to uncover even the bare contours of the elaborate and many-faceted intrigue involved in the Surrender of Baghdad, before and after.

Some of the details of that deal are now beginning to emerge, though all the relevant facts are still shrouded in mystery. The circumstantial evidence pointing to a deal is overwhelming nevertheless. The entire political and military high command have disappeared without a trace. Indeed, most of that high command disappeared from sight immediately after the war began. Key leaders like Saddam's two notorious sons, Vice President Taha Yassin Ramadan, the Deputy Prime Minsister Tariq Aziz, and ministers of defence, health, etc. have all become invisible. The US Defence Secretary Rumsfeld kept repeating in his statements over the past several weeks that the US was in 'negotiation' with senior leaders of the party and senior military commanders, offering safe passage to all, jobs to others in the post-war dispensation. Is that why we don't see those eminences of yesteryears? No one knows what happened to the Republican guards; they just melted away, and even the 'embedded' reporters and photographers have reported no big battles or scenes of military carnage – as we had seen on television when the retreated Iraqi army was decimated by US bombings during the Gulf War of 1991, with US bulldozers pushing thousands of the dead into mass graves. Saddam Hussein had made a spectacular bonfire of oil wells during that earlier war; this time they were wired (just in case the deal didn't go through) but never put to flame (because the US did come through with the deal).[4]

Iraq was said to have some 500 military aircraft and, as

[4] Retrospectively, one might speculate that once the defence of Baghdad became unfeasible (thanks to the betrayal) and Saddam, together with the loyal elements within his inner circle, decided on an orderly retreat and guerrilla warfare, they were also shrewd enough to realize that a spectacular bonfire of the oil wells would give them far less political mileage than persistent sabotage of production facilities and pipelines so long as the US occupation and rule of their proxies continues. No documentary evidence has yet surfaced to clarify the process whereby the decision was made not to set afire the bridges and pipelines that had been wired.

the destruction of the World Trade Centre demonstrated, airplanes can be used as missiles that crash into targets, even if they cannot take on the superior US-UK air forces. None was used. US tanks drove on highways which were never mined, not even in the vicinity of Baghdad; they crossed into the city over bridges which were wired for destruction but never detonated. They came on to the boulevards, and encountered the most sporadic of small arms fire. They parked their tanks in squares, and nothing happened. They just sat on the tops of their tanks, watching the burnings, the lootings. From the first day to the last, independent journalists who were working in Baghdad on their own, were mystified why they never could see any preparation for the defence of the city even as Mohammed Saeed al-Sahaf, the unspeakably brutish Information Minister, kept making all kinds of claims about battles impending in the city – until he too disappeared, slipping into an obscurity which might have been prepared for him in advance.

Understanding that Baghdad failed to fight back not because of the overwhelming military superiority of the US but because at least key elements in the regime cut a deal even before a battle for Baghdad could begin is a matter of great political importance. This fact tells us at least three things. First, the Saddam regime was so barbarically repressive, so unwilling to tolerate any force independent of it, that the regime alone – and no one else – controlled all the resources and therefore had the wherewithal to wage a battle for the defence of Baghdad; once the regime disintegrated and/or disintegrated thanks to that deal, there was no alternative force to organize a defence of that magnitude. Second, and most crucially, it means that the *removal of that regime* – i.e., the sifting off of those of its top political leaders and military commanders who were colluding with the US – is in fact the *precondition* for the emergence of a popular struggle. Third, and by the same token, the quick surrender tells us nothing about the will of the Iraqi people to fight for their freedom or even the preparedness of the lower levels of the armed forces or of the ordinary cadres of the Ba'ath party itself. They are probably relieved by the demise of the regime even as they are revolted by the re-colonization of their country. Their resistance has been deferred, and their war is yet to come. And the leadership for that shall emerge over the next few months. The US is planning to formally announce a victory in a few days. That's too soon. The war isn't over; it hasn't even begun.

In a sense, though, this new war has actually begun – in the shape of an extraordinary expression of mass resentment against the US presence as such. The tone was set already on April 15, just as the occupation and sacking of Baghdad was fully under way and the US tried to hold a meeting of some of its top clients in An Nassiriyah, the first since the beginning of the invasion and certainly the first on Iraqi soil. Jay Garner, the retired General and currently an arms dealer who has been appointed to lead the US administration in Iraq, opened the conference, held near the city of Ur, the biblical birthplace of prophet Abraham, with the grand statement: 'What better place than the birthplace of civilization could you have for the beginning of a freer Iraq?' Well, much to his dismay, his little meeting was greeted by 20,000 protesters in that small town, chanting 'No to America, No to Saddam'.

When the Ba'athists came to power (briefly in 1963, more lastingly through a coup in 1968), Iraq had a huge Communist Party, the largest in the Arab world, which then faced mass arrests, torture, execution, exile and general decimation. Other modern political forces met the same fate as Saddam perfected his brutal monopoly over power and politics in civil society, but he failed to entirely suppress the religious opposition which took refuge in its mosques and seminaries, its informal civil networks, its monopoly of shrines and pilgrimages. Now, with the demise of the Saddam regime, there is no secular force organized enough to fill the vacuum and, for the first time in modern Iraqi history, the mosque is emerging as the site of opposition, the focus for anti-colonial organization, and as contender for construction of a parallel system of governance rooted in civil society, in opposition to the colonial administration and a subordinate network of clients that the US is putting together. Less than two weeks into the colonial occupation, Friday prayers have become the occasion for mobilizing a mass insurgency.

On Friday, April 18, Sunnis and Shias offered prayers together in the Abu Haneefa Al Nu'man mosque in Baghdad (a veritable Sunni mosque, and one whose dome was smashed by American bombing), listened to anti-American sermons and erupted into the streets, marching peacefully and calling for a united struggle of Shias, Sunnis and Kurds against foreign occupation, some of them chanting 'No Bush – No Saddam; Yes to Islam', and other carrying banners in English and Arabic saying 'Leave our country. We want peace' and 'We reject American hegemony'. The mostly Sunni organizers are calling themselves 'the Iraqi National Movement'.

Meanwhile, in the poorer part of Baghdad where the Shia predominate, local militias hostile to the occupation forces are reported to have sprouted everywhere, taking control of the streets at night and organizing welfare activities – food supplies, medical aid, funeral arrangements – by the day. In faraway An Najaf, the city where Khomeini spent some 15 years in exile and from where he plotted his revolution for Iran, the venerated clergy has come together as a decision-making body, organized a nation-wide system of communications for instructions imparted through messengers, and have initiated the formation of defence committees in neighbourhoods throughout Iraq, ostensibly for restoration of normalcy and provision of aid for the suffering population but obviously in a move to create a parallel, grassroots administration which is designed to function as a parallel state and a network of local organizations for popular armed struggle as the US creates its own administration at the top and pretends to put in place a supposedly 'democratic' government comprised of its clients. In some towns, such as Kut, some more enterprising clergymen have simply walked into mayorial offices to take over local administrations, with remarkable degree of popular acceptance. Checkpoints are coming up inside cities and on roads linking various cities in southern Iraq which are manned by these new groupings, and there are already reports of confrontations with Americans who are simply unprepared for this kind of challenge on the ground. Militants from a variety of Islamicist groupings are in evidence, and some are reported as saying that in case the Americans oppose them on the ground they are willing to use themselves as suicide bombers. Most of the groupings that have emerged are Shia, but more Sunni groups are likely to emerge as well. Reports also suggest that entirely secular armed groups are also emerging in particular neighbourhoods. All these shall be the militias of tomorrow.[5]

We said in our previous essay in these pages ('Barbarians at the Gate', *Frontline*, April 12-25, 2003), that far from acting like a 'Stalingrad in the desert' as some people fancifully expected

---

[5] Soon after this article was written, evidence began mounting that Iran was pressing those prestigious sections of the senior Shia clergy who were aligned with it to distance themselves from the more radical forms of protest and to offer at least minimal cooperation to the Americans and their proxies, to influence the outcomes as insiders of the evolving order rather than as uncompromising belligerents. This role of Iran in moderating the resistance of very substantial sections of the Iraqi Shia can be understood in terms of its own immense anxieties as the neoconservative cabal in the Pentagon, as well as the Sharon regime from Israel, started pressing Bush Jr. for diplomatic isolation and military action against Syria and Iran as well.

Baghdad to become, it was more likely to resemble Algiers under French occupation, Palestine under Zionist occupation, Beirut in the time of Israeli occupation and the prolonged civil war. Not a city defending itself against siege by a foreign army which is then repulsed after some weeks or months, but a city actually under full occupation where costs of occupation become unbearable only over a period of time and which engages in a type of warfare against which the most modern weaponry is largely useless. And a city, moreover, which is surrounded by a rebellious hinterland of other cities, towns, villages. But then, also, like Beirut, a city riven by its own communal divides, its warring militias fighting for turf, arms merchants flourishing by feeding the multiplicity of militias – the more warring factions there are, the more splendid the arms bazaar becomes. Not the sheer brute power of American weaponry but the internal communal divides shall be the largest challenge to anti-colonial unity in Iraq during this new phase. For, just as the establishment of a colonial administration shall serve to bring together the various opposing groups, the sudden collapse of the central authority and the lack of a successor central organizing force shall serve to accentuate the communal divides and mutual competitions over scarce resources.

For, what the Americans have brought with them is not only the gift of colonization but all the paraphernalia of communalization and factionalization of Iraqi society: dividing the Turkoman against the Kurd, the Kurd against the Arab, the Sunni against the Shia, and indeed one Shia faction against the other, not to speak of the Ba'athist against the non-Ba'athist, the torturers of yesterday against a battered people, the clients against the patriots. The one positive aspect of Saddam's authoritarian rule was its militant commitment to secularism against religious strife, not to speak of a state-centred nationalism against divisive localisms. With that nationalist cement gone, collapse into fiefdoms of local power in the name of primordial loyalties is very probable, and the colonial power is likely to do all it can to accentuate these conflicts since these conflicts are the surest means through which anti-colonial forces can be disorganized and the presence of colonial authority, as keepers of the peace among communities, can be justified. Far from being an unintended consequence of colonization, this emerging communalization of Iraqi society is something the US has foreseen and wanted to achieve. A foretaste of the bloody nature of this communalization has can be had in the ethnic cleansing of Arabs that is already under way in northern Iraq, at the hands of Kurdish zealots.

Intoxicated by the scale and ease of victory, the US had already begun to make ominous statements against Syria. Within one week, Bush, Powell and Rumsfeld accused Syria of harboring fugitives from the Iraqi regime, manufacturing chemical and biological weapons, and providing bases and training facilities to a variety of 'terrorist' organizations such as the Hizbollah. Each of them warned of reprisals and Rumsfeld ordered the Pentagon to make contingency plans for invasions of Syria. That planning shall indeed continue and Syria certainly faces the threat of invasion, especially now that it has refused to submit to the charade of inspections which paved the way for the invasion of Iraq. It also seems probable, however, that with the emergence of widespread religio-political opposition in Iraq, and with the religious establishment already launched on creating structures of dual authority even before the US has put together its own administration, the Americans have come to understanding that the pacification of Iraq shall be infinitely harder than the military conquest. The neoconservative cabal at the Pentagon and the think-tanks may well be restrained in their designs for swift conquest of other countries in the region (Syria, Iran, even perhaps Saudi Arabia), and an invasion of Syria may well be postponed until after the US Presidential elections of November 2004. The fate of Syria shall be in any case decided in Iraq. If the resistance is slow in emerging and if the US feels confident of containing it, the invasion shall come sooner rather than later.

Meanwhile, the structure of a unilateral colonial occupation and administration is being put in place with great alacrity, with Iraqi clients assigned a much more subordinate role, the United Nations being kept out of any significant decision-making process, and even Britain being given only a marginal role. Jay Garner, who is to head the colonial authority, has been flown in already and sections of the US media have appropriately taken to referring to him as 'viceroy'. He is a retired general and an arms contractor specializing in missiles, closely aligned with Israel and known to get non-competitive contracts from the Pentagon. This year alone, he obtained a defence contract worth $ 1.5 billion, as well as a contract for building Patriot missile systems in Israel.

Garner shall supervise a total of 23 ministries, all headed by US top brass and each of the heads of ministries assisted by three assistants and eight advisors – all Americans. The 'reconstruction' of Iraq, currently expected to generate $ 100 billion worth of contracts, is being monopolized by the US Agency for International Development which is distributing these contracts among US transnationals. A whole range of these corporations, from the little ones like Stevedoring Services of America to giants such as Bechtel and Haliburton – all closely aligned with highest officials in the Bush administration – are already grabbing these contracts. In the process, everything that has been in the state sector in Iraq – ports, waterworks and power grids, building of roads and bridges, trains and telecommunications, pharmaceuticals and medical facilities, and so on – are to be privatized and opened to foreign, principally American investment and ownership. The

Iraqi dinar is being provisionally discarded as an unreliable and worthless currency and dollars are being spread as part of the so-called 'humanitarian aid' packages and remunerations of various types. The dollar is already a parallel legal tender in Lebanon; the US would like it to be so in the much larger, oil-based and lucrative economy of Iraq. If Saddam had the temerity to adopt the Euro as the currency for its foreign trade and foreign currency reserves, the US is retaliating by making the dollar even a *domestic* currency for Iraq.

Deputy Defence Secretary Paul Wolfowitz, the supreme commander of the neoconservatives and the real godfather of this war, declared in early April that direct US rule shall last at least six months and 'probably . . . longer than that'. Ahmed Chalabi, a crony of Wolfowitz and head of the US-sponsored Iraqi National Congress, has been flown into Iraq along with a number of other Iraqi clients from London, New York and elsewhere. Echoing his Washington bosses, Chalabi has said that there can be no role for the UN in Iraq and that direct US rule may be required for as much as two years. All the basic economic decisions shall have of course been made during these two years, putting in place an entirely new, privatized, neo-liberal economic structure dominated by US transnationals. Plans for privatization of Iraqi oil are also afoot. A lesser member of the Chalabi clan, Fadhli Chalabi, a former Iraq petroleum ministry official, has said: 'we need a huge amount of money coming into the country. The only way is to partially privatize the industry'.

This privatization of Iraqi oil assets and their sale to transnationals has been a major objective driving this war, as a first step in the campaign – backed by military campaign, if necessary – to privatize oil in Iran, Saudi Arabia, Kuwait and elsewhere, including of course the Caspian Sea Basin. Not the least aspect of this restructuring of the Iraqi oil industry is that a pipeline is sought to be built quickly to supply Iraqi oil to Israel, which is currently boycotted by Arab states and purchases most of its oil from distant Russia. A direct pipeline from Iraq is expected to cut down the Israeli oil bill by about a third, while more gains are expected from the plummeting of oil prices once the Iraqi production has been fully restored. A veritable tripartite Iraq-Jordan-Israel axis is envisaged in this regard, with Iraqi oil being delivered at the Jordanian port of Aqaba, across from the Israeli port of Eilat.

In the face of these grand designs, it is turning out to be virtually indecent to ask just what happened to all the rationales that were trotted out to justify the invasion. Saddam Hussein was supposed to be sponsoring 'international terrorism'; the only 'terrorist' the Americans have captured so far is an ageing Palestinian whose last action dates back to 1984. Predictably, the so-called weapons of mass destruction have not been found and the US seems neither in a hurry to look for them nor embarrassed by their non-existence. Saddam Hussein's 'tyranny' was the other plank. Instead of toppling a regime the US made a deal with its commanders, promising to integrate most of that regime in its own administration. The US was said to bring in 'democracy'. Instead, what we have is a veritable colonial administration which is already being projected for two years. General Tommy Franks, who led the invasion, has said that US troops shall be stationed on Iraqi soil for many, many more years, 'on the model of Korea'. Meanwhile, the Americans don't really like the democracy they are beginning to encounter on the streets of Iraqi cities, in the form of popular protests and emergence of grass-roots administration opposed to the US design.

We have deliberately not tried to outline the scale of atrocities and suffering that this invasion has inflicted upon the Iraqi people and the criminal silence of the so-called international media in which these atrocities have been shrouded. For the first time in the history of modern warfare, journalists from the entire spectrum of these international media, from CNN to *Le Monde*, agreed to become subordinates of the military command structure, voluntarily giving up their right to report what they saw. This internationalized vow of silence has had a mafia-like quality to it, and only from the margins did a few brave ones tell the story of at least some of the gruesome details of mass civilian killings, organized looting of the national heritage and its treasures, the bonfire of books and rare manuscripts that would have impressed even the Nazis. Every single article of the Geneva Convention and the UN Charter was violated, and a whole range of war crimes committed, with impunity. Yet, not a single member of the so-called 'international community' has come forward to say so: not Kofi Annan and his bureaucrats at the UN, not the leaders of the Franco-German alliance or any other member of the Security Council, not the head of any Arab state. The moral bankruptcy of the whole state system of the world is there for all to see. This global complicity is what made the invasion possible in the first place.

And yet, in the distant and dingy alleyways of that battered and occupied country, a resistance is in the making. It will take some months to take organizational form, more months to make a transition to credible forms of armed resistance. In the long run, though, the US may have made for itself not just a client state whose assets can be bought up for a song, but a veritable Palestine writ large. As the whole history of anti-colonial movements has shown, history does not end with conquest. A different history then begins.

15 AUGUST 2003
Resistance in Iraq, Disarray in the US

In an article I published in *Frontline* immediately after the US occupation of Baghdad ('Wars Yet to Come', 9 May 2003), I wrote that 'the quick surrender tells us nothing about the will of the Iraqi people to fight for their freedom or even the preparedness of the lower levels of the armed forces or of the ordinary cadres of the Ba'ath party itself. They are probably relieved by the demise of the regime even as they are revolted by the re-colonization of their country. Their resistance has been deferred, and their war is yet to come. Leadership for that shall emerge over the next few months. The US is planning to formally announce a victory in a few days. That's too soon. The war isn't over; it hasn't even begun'.

President George W. Bush duly announced 'victory' on May 1st even as the new war – the war of resistance – was just beginning. As I now draft the present report some three months later, on 28 July, some of the officially acknowledged statistics on American casualties in Iraq are worth re-iterating.

Fourteen US soldiers have been killed in Iraq over the past eight days, at an average of close to two per day. A month ago, the average was one every two days. By now, more US soldiers have died since that announcement of 'victory' than had died in the course of the technologically spectacular Anglo-American war of occupation during the three weeks of March and April. Almost as many have been killed since this 'victory' as the total number of US soldiers who died during the first Gulf War. The number of the seriously wounded since the occupation of Baghdad on 9 April exceeds the total number of the dead during the three weeks of the invasion prior to that. This much is officially acknowledged. Not every attack by the forces of resistance gets acknowledged, however, for the simple reason that not every Iraqi attack leads to the killing or wounding of an American soldier. Numerous reports suggest, furthermore, that casualties are already so high that the US is systematically under-reporting the wounded.[1] According to one count, the Americans are facing an average of 13 attacks per day. Most of the attacks are mounted in central Iraq. Families living in Mosul and Basra, in northern and eastern parts of Iraq respectively, told this writer earlier this month that they heard repeated, often persistent, gunfire every night.

US officials no longer know how to represent these attacks. Before the invasion, they had been predicting a US direct occupation lasting 30 to 60 days and installation of an Iraqi government of their choice thereafter, with no more than perhaps 30,000 troops remaining after that, for a few months. Now, more than a hundred days later, half of the US global combat strength is still bogged down there, backed by 17,000 'allied' troops and with another 30,000 on the way. Meanwhile, the US is pressing a variety of countries around the globe, including India, Pakistan and Bangladesh, to provide another 30,000 troops. Under Secretary

---

[1] A month after this piece was drafted, the *Observer* published a well-researched report that a total of approximately 6,000 US soldiers had been evacuated from Iraq to various hospitals in the region. That gives us a rate of over a thousand wounded or otherwise disabled for each month since 'victory' was announced. The number of attacks per day have now risen to thirty-five, and have recently included the downing of US helicopters and a blistering attack on the US occupation forces' headquarters in Baghdad in which Assistant Secretary of Defence Wolfowitz barely escaped. When Bush visited Iraq for a photo with the serving GIS, as a public relations exercise, he was whisked in and out under maximum security and without prior announcement, for fear of getting killed.

of Defence and dean of the neoconservative cabal at the Pentagon, Wolfowitz, says that things are going better in Iraq than he had expected and Saddam Hussein is hiring people from his hideout to kill American soldiers; he refers to them as 'contract killings' which shall soon cease, as soon as Saddam is killed or apprehended. By contrast, the newly appointed US military commander in Iraq, Gen. John Abizaid, describes the war of resistance as a 'classic guerrilla-type campaign'. Defence Secretary Rumsfeld, boss to both Wolfowitz and Abizaid, typically speaks from both sides of his mouth, describing it as the 'last gasp' of 'Baathist remnants' but also as 'guerrilla action'; he also blames this 'disorder' on thousands of criminals who fled Iraqi prisons after the US occupation.

Professional militarymen are, as usual, more realistic than the civilian ideologues of the far right who supervise them. Weeks before the war, the outgoing Army Chief of Staff, Gen. Shinseki, had told a panel of the US Congress that 'several hundred thousand' troops would be required to occupy Iraq for an indefinite period following the invasion, and Gen. Tommy Franks, the head of the Central Command who led the invasion of Iraq, had similarly predicted that US troops would have to stay for years and perhaps even decades, on the model of Korea. Some seven weeks after the 'victory', Retired Air Force Col. Richard Aitchison told the *Washington Post* on 27th June: 'I thought we were holding our own until this week, and now I'm not sure' just as Retd. Marine General Carlton Fulford predicts 'a long, tough haul in Iraq. The longer this goes on, the more violent these events will become'. Retired General William Nash, former commander of US forces in Bosnia and now a senior fellow with the Council of Foreign Relations, told *The Observer* on 22 June that the occupation of Iraq 'is an endeavour which was not understood by the administration to begin with. [W]e are now seeing the re-emergence of a reasonably organized military opposition – small scale, but it could escalate'. He says that opposition is not confined to Saddam supporters: 'What we are facing today is a confluence of various forces which channel the disgruntlement of the people'.

Undeterred by the advice of professionals, the neoconservative cabal moves on. Paul Bremer, the civilian American proconsul in Iraq, himself a veteran of The Heritage Foundation, the conservative think tank, and a former member of Kissinger Associates, exults: 'We are going to fight them and impose our will on them and we will capture or . . . kill them until we have imposed law and order on this country. We dominate the scene and we will continue to impose our will on this country'. To this end, he has appointed a 'governing council' of 25-30 Iraqis of his choice. Elections or even broadly consultative procedures may further de-stabilize the country, he says, and he has issued a proclamation outlawing any 'gatherings, pronouncements, or publications' that call for either the return of the Ba'ath party or for opposition to the US occupation. So much for 'bringing democracy' to Iraq!

Signs of stress and disarray are emerging in a thousand ways, however. Numerous serving soldiers have given interviews to journalists and written letters to their senators demanding that they be brought back to the United States, on the plea that they were trained for combat in war, not to serve as occupation army against a hostile population. One of them said on TV that if he ever met Rumsfeld he would ask for the Secretary's resignation. An infantryman by the name of O'Dell told the *New York Times*, 'You call Donald Rumsfeld and tell him our sorry asses are ready to go home'. Quite a few women serving in the US army in Iraq are coming home on the plea of unforeseen pregnancy. Families of serving soldiers are known to have become so violent at a military base in Georgia that the officers who were addressing them had to be taken away by a military escort. Some British troops have said that they are reluctant to go on serving in Iraq for fear that they may later be hauled in front of the International Court on charges of war crimes.

Meanwhile, the actual evidence of war crimes is mounting. A single report in *Rolling Stones*, a US publication, documents the cases of several US soldiers who have directly confessed to killing civilians out of fear and even killing the wounded in their custody. Psychiatrists and chaplains attached to the US forces are reporting widespread cases of emotional breakdown and unwarranted killings. One chaplain, disgusted by the willingness of US soldiers to go on killing sprees, remarked that 'Christ is a doormat' for these soldiers. None of it is 'winning the hearts and minds of the people', as the phrase in US propaganda machinery has it.

All this is further complicated by the fact that the US has a voluntary army and half of its 1.3 billion strength is comprised of reservists. Mounting casualties, increasing perception that the occupation is illegal, and persistent report of widespread physical and psychological stress among serving troops may break the morale so badly that, as many US military experts now fear, the military may face mass resignations and a wholesale exodus. This morale is already under stress thanks to the well-known fact of tens of thousands of veterans from the Vietnam War still suffering from psychological trauma while numerous veterans from the first Gulf War of 1991 are reporting a wide variety of disorders caused by their exposure to various chemical substances in the US weaponry itself.

That is at the base of the armed forces. At the top, Thomas White, a retired general who was serving as the army secretary, was sacked in May for siding with the Army Chief of Staff, Gen. Shinseki, on the estimate that 'several hundred thousand troops' would be required to occupy Iraq. White now charges that the Administration is 'unwilling to come to grips' with the facts.

Shinseki himself was allowed to retire in private bitterness and semi-public disgrace. Gen. Tommy Franks, the 'conqueror of Iraq' and widely tipped to be the next Army Chief of Staff, suddenly resigned at the height of his glory. Shinseki's vice chief, General John Keane, is widely reported to have turned down the offer of being promoted to the position of the chief. This too is happening in the midst of much bickering over fundamental issues of strategy. Rumsfeld and his crew had taken over with the plans to vastly extend the US military presence across the globe while *simultaneously* cutting down the size of the army and making it better equipped technologically with all the weaponry of the automated battlefield, Star Wars, etc. The occupation of Iraq and the growing resistance there has eroded that planning.

Half of the US combat strength is already bogged down there, another one-third is spread thin across the globe, and no one knows how many more troops shall be required in Iraq itself in the near future. The Pentagon is already speaking of the possible need for a considerable *expansion* of the armed forces, and experts are wondering if the kind of expansion that is required for the stated objective of fighting several theatre wars simultaneously can be achieved without re-instating compulsory military service. The present US army is overwhelmingly the army of the poor and the racial minorities, who seek military jobs out of financial need and with fantasies of power that compensate for the real misery of their lives. Disenchantment is likely to set in very quickly among many of them as the misery of the war itself mounts, and it is not at all clear that, with mounting casualties in a war with dubious and illegal foundations, the white, college-educated, middle class youth would be willing to accept involuntary and compulsory military service.

The civilian front for the Bush-Blair duo is not in appreciably better shape. Unwilling any more to defend lies on a daily basis, press secretaries for both of them, Ari Fleischer and Godric Smith respectively, resigned on the same day in mid-June. A single article that I came across at that time lists several other Bush administration's political and career officials who have quit: Richard Haass, who as the director for policy planning, was number three at the State Department; Christine Todd Whitman, Environmental Protection Agency administrator; Rand Beers, the senior National Security Council director for counter-terrorism; Charlotte Beers, the State Department chief for International Public Diplomacy , and State Department career Foreign Service officers John H. Brown, John Brady Kiesling, and Mary A. Wright. On the other side of the Atlantic, Blair lost his Foreign Secretary and former leader of the Commons, Robin Cook, even before the invasion began and then his Development Secretary, Clare Short, soon after the invasion as the scale of the deception became unbearable even for her. This is significant because both these luminaries had remained loyal servers of Blair's regime of untruth during the war over Kosovo which had been waged with no less squalid level of deception. Their shrewd and cynical calculation was that no one was much interested in uncovering the lies that they and their boss told about Kosovo but that Iraq was going to blow up in their faces.

The revolt, or at least dismay, of a section of the professionals in the military and diplomatic services of the Anglo-American bloc has been, if anything, exceeded by the persistent dismay of the professionals in the intelligence services. It was, after all, the information *they* had provided which has been twisted and even falsified by the Bush-Blair combine and *their* careers and reputations are the ones that would be at stake in the inquiries that are now being instituted – gradually, grudgingly, belatedly – by the US Congress and the British Parliament. As preparations for invasion were being mounted on the basis of false claims, both sides of the Atlantic began witnessing an extraordinary set of leaks of secret and even top-secret documents from a variety of intelligence services, ranging from the CIA and the Defence Intelligence Agency (DIA) in the US to the MI-6 and MI-5 in Britain. The list of leaked documents that systematically refuted several of the key claims of the US and UK governments is long indeed, and it is widely rumoured that Sir Richard Dearlove and Eliza Menningham-Buller, heads of MI-6 and MI-5 respectively, threatened to resign over Blair's claim that Iraq had the capacity to launch a chemical/biological attack on Britain within 45 minutes – the statement that has now come to haunt the liar that runs the British government these days. These leaked documents also show that the CIA had consistently argued that there was no credible link between Saddam Hussein and either Al-Qaida or the attack on the World Trade Centre; that claims regarding Iraq's chemical and biological weapons were unverifiable and exaggerated; and that Chalabi, the principal source for the false information and Rumsfeld's favourite for succeeding Saddam, was not only a convicted criminal but also a political fraud. It is also well known by now that reports coming from CIA and DIA were so contrary to what Rumsfeld wanted to hear and/or have manufactured as justification for the invasion that he created a special agency inside the Pentagon, the Office of Special Plans (OSP), specifically to re-mould the available information in accordance with what he and his neoconservative colleagues desired. So bitter is the animosity between CIA professionals and the OSP ideologues that Larry Johnson, a former CIA officer, described OSP, US Defence Secretary's favourite outfit, as 'dangerous for US national interests and a threat to world peace'.

With these rudimentary facts in hand, let me draw closer to the argument of the present essay. The singular achievement of the Iraqi resistance is not that it has killed and wounded so many of the occupying troops, even though its other achievements would not have been possible without this ability to confront the enemy militarily and inflict daily casualties. Domestically, the chief achievement is that it has surfaced even more rapidly than we had anticipated, is more widespread than was believed possible in so short a time, seems to include very diverse elements of Iraqi society instead of cultivating a sectarian or specifically religious base, and is fast moving from sporadic hit-and-run episodes to a concerted strategy of daily attacks across quite large areas of the country. It has ruined the US plans to install a client regime before mass anger explodes, to restore oil production and begin the corporate exploitation of Iraqi resources, and to widen global coalition behind itself. This resistance has provoked the Anglo-American troops into the kind of widespread search-and-seize missions, arbitrary killings, generalized hostility toward the civilian population and the morale-breaking round-the-clock vigilance typical of occupation armies and counter-insurgency operations. It has pinned down a force of over one hundred and fifty thousand personnel, forcing them to extend missions of duty for the deployed personnel and to need reinforcements and raise the prospect of engaging a much wider part of the US forces in Iraq on rotation basis.

Externally, this resistance has immediately relieved the pressure on Syria and Iran. Rumsfeld and co. had envisioned a quick pacification of Iraq as a prelude to invasion and occupation of those two countries, or, at the very least, an occupation of Syria and unbearable pressure on Iran. They had also imagined that as Iraq becomes their main military base in the region, they would withdraw most of their troops from Saudi Arabia before popular Saudi revulsion against those troops explodes into a revolutionary situation. Instead, Saudi Arabia, Qatar and Kuwait have remained the bases for the aggression against and occupation of a major Arab country which is now itself fighting a war of liberation against the US, with incalculable political fallout in the neighbouring countries.

Further afield, this resistance is provoking a full-scale institutional crisis in the US and UK states as they are presently constituted. In Britain, Blair had faced mass opposition in the broad public and a sizeable dissent within his own Labour party before the invasion; once the invasion began, British society closed ranks behind the leader, mass opposition collapsed, and popularity ratings for the war shot up to above 80 per cent. It is the Iraqi resistance after the fall of Saddam, rising casualty rates as months go by, and the prospect of continued deployment there that has brought about a full-blown crisis in which everyone of Blair's words, past and present, is being scrutinized and a third of the British population now says that they will not trust anything he says or does. His lies were always known to be lies. It was common knowledge well before the invasion that the dossier on the Saddam regime which he had presented to parliament as justification for invasion was so fraudulent that it combined big swath of worthless information drawn from a ten-year old Ph.D dissertation with other bits circulating on the internet and manufactured claims that were discredited by his own intelligence services. None of it mattered then. Had there not been armed resistance of any consequence in Iraq, he would have shrugged off the matter of the so-called weapons of mass destruction and got the British to swell with pride over bringing the gift of 'democracy' to the grateful Iraqi barbarians. British troops dying after the 'victory' is what brought back the pressure on him, and he again stands exposed as a liar.

The institutional crisis that is developing in the US may become worse, and may complicate matters not only for Bush but also for Blair, and many others as well. Mere three months of occupation, with the casualties mounting by the day, have eroded the morale of the US army, turning some of the troops into pacifists and others into psychotic killers. Strategic planning lies in ruin, generals cannot agree with their civilian superiors, one intelligence agency wants to protect itself from the other, and no one yet knows whom to blame for the debacle and the quagmire which the US has walked into. Again, there's nothing new about the information which is now being used to question the veracity of the President of the United States and his highest officials. The charge that Iraq had bought materials from Niger that could be used for the making of nuclear weapons, which Bush has used time and again and which has now so enraged the mainstream media in the US, was rejected as fraudulent well before the invasion by the UN's chief nuclear inspector on the floor of the Security Council. Even Iraqi defectors had testified years ago that Saddam had destroyed his remaining chemical and biological weapons in 1995. Years of UN inspections thereafter did not produce an ounce of such materials. Yet this same media had accepted all of Bush's claims, because the media, especially the electronics media, were united behind the policy of invasion. It is only now, after the spectacular failure of that policy as it is brought home to the US in the shape of daily corpses, that the unity of imperial purpose has been blown apart, so that even John Dean, the legal counsel to Richard Nixon who blew the whistle on Watergate, now says that Watergate 'may pale by comparison' with the lies Bush has been telling and that the case for impeachment in this instance may turn out to be stronger than the case which led to Nixon's resignation.

Facts were well known, for four reasons. First, some courageous investigative reporters for established newspapers such as the *Guardian* and the *Independent* in Britian – and, less frequently, such as *Los Angeles Times* in the US – had kept on uncovering them and publishing them; electronic media were much more subservient globally but the Qatar-based Al-Jazeera TV station mounted a valiant and effective challenge to such disinformation machineries as Fox News, CNN and BBC. Second, the Internet served as an irrepressible alternate media, and what got to millions upon millions through these channels of democratic dissent across the globe could not be made to just disappear. Third, the UN inspectors, no matter how taciturn or circumspect, did not corroborate the Anglo-American claims and occasionally contradicted them. Fourth, some professionals serving within machineries of state in the US and UK saw that their bosses were overreaching on the basis of falsified reports and sought to warn the public through leaks. This last fact lies at the heart of the death of Dr. David Kelly, the British microbiologist who had worked with UN inspectors. He knew that the claims put forth by his Prime Minister were false and agreed to meet with investigative journalists without the express permission of his superiors so as to reveal at least some of the truth as he knew it. He was found dead on a rainy afternoon. Whether he slit his own wrists or someone else did it to him is, for present purposes, irrelevant; he died under the weight of the lies he knew to be lies told by his government – just another victim of New Labour and its insufferable Prime Minister. The relevant fact, for our purposes, is that there are numerous such people, on both sides of the Atlantic who have done the same thing and may come forward with more facts if serious inquiries were instituted in Washington and London. The further relevant fact is that such knowledge of the invasion of Iraq being based on a heap of lies would have faded away from memory if the Anglo-American design had been successful. It is the Iraqi resistance, and the crisis it has precipitated, which has given to this knowledge a new lease on life. The very people who had lapped up the lies, in the mainstream media and the political establishments of the two countries, wish now to scrutinize them because the lies have led to what is clearly becoming a quagmire of historic proportions.

As it becomes clearer for publics across the globe that the case for invasion was based on falsehoods, that Iraq possessed no weapons of mass destruction and posed no threat to American or European countries, that the Anglo-American armies are seen there not as welcome liberators but as hated occupiers, and that Iraqis are now engaged in a war of national resistance and liberation, other governments shall also be in trouble, from Australia and Denmark who contributed troops to the army of occupation, to Spain and Italy who did not contribute troops but became cheerleaders of the occupation.[2] The US had hoped that it would do the conquering and would then assemble a global imperial army, on the model of the British army of the colonial days – with soldiers coming mainly from Asian and African dependencies – to enforce its will in Iraq. As casualties mount for the present army of occupation and the will of the Iraqi people hardens, numerous other countries shall have to re-consider the wisdom in sending their men to die for the US imperium in another Third World country, whether or not the UN lends its flag for legitimizing Anglo-US occupation, as it is about to do.

The resistance in Iraq seems to be sinking its roots into the soil and it has already precipitated what appears to be a global crisis of belief in legitimacy of Anglo-American actions, at the highest levels. The road ahead, however, is going to be even more difficult. Iraq is a society battered by an Anglo-American assault that has been unremitting since 1991, under Tories as well as Labour in Britain, Democrats and Republicans alike in the US. Whether or not such a wounded society can mount a sustained

---

[2] In an extraordinary move, the Australian Senate has more recently censured its own Prime Minister for taking Australia into the invasion of Iraq on the side of the US on false grounds.

war of liberation over months and years to come cannot be predicted, one way or another. On the other hand, the ruling class consensus in the US and Britain seems intact. Even as the mainstream media now sizzles with doubts and queries, only the former president Jimmy Carter and a couple of high officials in his Administration have squarely denounced Bush Jr.'s policy while the rest of the Democratic Party establishment, including notably all its potential Presidential candidates, have either remained non-committal or actively supported him on the matter of Iraq; none ever questioned the lies Bush was telling.[3] It is indicative of this bi-partisan unity on the question of Iraq that Clinton has yet again supported Bush even as the latter faces a storm of criticism from elsewhere. On the other side of the Atlantic, the Tories, Blair's official opposition, are even more committed to him than half of his own party.[4] Within the Arab world, every country is dominated by illegitimate minority regimes which would rather see Iraq sink into the sea than help a national liberation movement grow in their midst; even Syria is known to have expelled Iraqi dissidents so as to please the United States and save the existing domestic power structure headed by President Bashara Asad, a man committed to anti-imperialist struggles even less than his late father. A variety of countries, from Germany and Japan to India

---

[3] Among the Presidential hopefuls in the Democratic Party of the US, Governor Dean of Vermont is trying the hardest to ride to power on the wave of disaffection against the war which is now rising in the US. It is indicative, however, that even he has said that now that the US is already in Iraq any 'precipitate withdrawal' before 'normalization' can only do harm.

[4] Blair's troubles in his own Labour Party have failed to bring forth an antiwar candidate and have served only to strengthen the competitive position of his Chancellor of Exchequer, Gordon Brown, whose own positions are hardly distinguishable from those of Blair. Robin Cook, Blair's former Foreign Secretary and leader of the House at that time, had resigned in the hope of leading the anti-Blair campaign inside the Labour Party after the dimensions of the fiasco became clearer. Even that has not transpired.

and Pakistan, seem to be just waiting for the UN to fully identify itself with the task of occupation before they send in their own troops. We may yet live to see Indian and Pakistani soldiers fight side by side, as comrades-in-arm, in the service of Pax Americana and to quell the Iraqi resistance.[5]

I wrote in my previous article immediately after the US soldiers entered Baghdad that it is not Baghdad that will come to resemble Stalingrad, a city under prolonged siege, but Iraq as a whole that may come to resemble Algeria under French occupation, or Palestine under Zionist occupation. In Iraq today, there's no peacekeeping, only war; and when India decides on the question of sending our soldiers to Iraq, we should first decide whether the Indian soldier shall fight on the side of the colonizer or the colonized. Indian soldiers went to Iraq about a century ago in the service of the British. Shall our soldiers go again, to serve the same masters of yesteryears, and now their transatlantic cousins as well? Do we have no shame, as a nation, even to be discussing such a possibility?

---

[5] Turkish parliament recently passed a resolution allowing for Turkish troops to be sent to Iraq on the side of the US with or without UN authorization, in the teeth of a population among whom opposition to the war is running at 90 per cent, according to public opinion polls. Even so, Turkish troops could not be despatched owing to opposition from the US-appointed Iraqi Governing Council itself. In Japan, debate over despatch of troops to serve the Americans released such passions in Parliament that the Prime Minister barely escaped from getting thrashed on the floor. Governments of Pakistan and Bangladesh would love to send troops but are afraid of their own populations. In India, the military itself seems to be perturbed by the thought of committing troops in a country where Americans themselves are taking so many casualties. Meanwhile, spectacular attacks on UN offices and personnel inside Iraq has led to the withdrawal of the UN personnel from Iraq and taken the will out of even Kofi Annan to give the Americans what they want out of the Security Council.

26 SEPTEMBER 2003
Afghanistan: The Forgotten War

The scale of the horror and atrocities visited upon Iraq – and now the scale of the emerging Iraqi resistance – are such that all our attention tends to be currently focussed on that tragic country and we tend now to forget the ongoing war – and resistance – in Afghanistan where America's infamous 'war on terrorism' first began. In his fateful speech of 20 September 2001 Bush referred to this 'war' as 'a task that never ends', and one that might be fought in as many as 50 or 60 countries. Some two years later, the reality is that the forces of the US-led coalition are bogged down in unending conflicts in both countries – Afghanistan and Iraq – which first came into the eye of this storm, so that other countries – notably Syria and Iran – which had been slated for immediate invasion and 'regime change' have been spared for the time being, thanks to this deepening quagmire.

    The fate of these two countries has been intertwined from the very onset of this war. On the morning after the 11 September attack on the World Trade Centre, the US Secretary of Defence Donald Rumsfeld advocated an immediate focus on war upon Iraq whereas the Secretary of State Colin Powell persuasively argued that Afghanistan was a softer target and easier to immediately identify with Osama bin Laden, Al Qaida, and so forth. Attack on Iraq could wait. A campaign to associate *both* countries with a global network, centred on Al Qaida, was launched immediately and intelligence agencies of the US and Britain were instructed to provide the proof. Indeed, Niaz Naik, the former Foreign Secretary of Pakistan, was to claim on BBC a bit later that American diplomats had told him in July that military action against Afghanistan was being prepared for 'some time in October'. Powell was thus simply arguing that there be no change in plans: Afghanistan first, Iraq next.

Once the decision to invade Afghanistan had been thus made, nothing could make the US deviate from its path. As late as 23 September, barely two weeks before the invasion began, *The Observer* was reporting, 'The thousands of intelligence, security and police officers investigating the attacks on America on both sides of the Atlantic are racing against an unknown deadline: they have to produce enough evidence of Osama bin Laden's involvement to convince world opinion before Western military action begins. . . . Sources in all the principal agencies – the American FBI and CIA, and Britain's MI6 and MI5 – insist that, at present, there is nothing approaching the standard of proof that would be required to persuade a jury in a criminal court of law'. It was in fact even more difficult to link the Taliban themselves with the events of 11 September; they denounced the attack immediately and promised in no uncertain terms to help find the culprits. Lack of evidence at that time did not matter any more than it was to matter later, regarding Iraq's purported 'weapons of mass destruction'.

The US demanded that Osama be turned over to them. The Taliban first asked for some evidence, on the ground that without evidence of criminal activity no principle of extradition applies. When the US refused, they dropped even that demand and offered to hand over Osama to the Pakistani authorities and under the collective jurisdiction of the Organization of Islamic Conference (OIC, involving 52 countries) to stand trial 'in accordance with Islamic laws of evidence'. The agreement had been negotiated between heads of two Pakistani religious parties and Mulla Omar, the Taliban head of state, and was explicitly approved by Osama himself. General Musharraf, the Pakistani head of state, turned down the arrangement, under pressure from the US which was interested not in catching Osama but in occupying Afghanistan. Significantly, the Taliban had made a similar offer much earlier, in February 2001, well before the World Trade Centre bombings, in which they were willing to surrender Osama in exchange for official recognition of their government by the US and some economic aid. The US had turned down the offer at that time as well. This again is not altogether different from the US insistence on inspections in Iraq and then going on to invade Iraq even after the Iraqi authorities had given the inspectors unrestricted access to any site they wished to inspect and to destroy whatever they thought was in violation of the UN sanctions.

In other words, both wars were eminently avoidable. Indeed, had the United States accepted the earlier offer of the Taliban to extradite Osama in exchange for official US recognition of them as the government of Afghanistan, the tragedy of 11 September itself may not have happened – presuming that Al Qaida was indeed behind that attack. What was at stake for the US, however, was not the avoidance of war or misery for war's victims – it had indeed been making different kinds of war against those two countries for many years previously – but a very elaborate imperial design. I have written extensively about this imperial design in several articles pertaining to Iraq and, indeed, the two articles I published immediately after the September 11 events ('Responding with Terror', *Frontline*, September 29, 2001, and 'Re-mapping the Globe', *Frontline*, October 27, 2001). This design is itself evolving rapidly and new elements of it come into view from time to time. A key element that is becoming increasingly apparent is the gradual formation of a historically new kind of imperial army that shall be led by the United States but shall be comprised of soldiery drawn from diverse countries, to enforce the will of global capitalist imperialism as a whole. This too has become clearer in Afghanistan already but is designed to take on massive proportions in Iraq in the foreseeable future.

As the US made up its mind to invade Afghanistan, it deliberately ignored the Security Council as well as its NATO allies with the exception of the Anglo-Saxon cousins in UK. Once the Anglo-US occupation of Afghanistan was achieved in October 2001 it assembled its Afghan clients in Bonn, under the benign eyes of the German Chancellor Schröder, got the clients to elect Hamid Karzai as the head of an 'Interim Authority' and then got this 'Authority' to 'request the United Nations Security Council to consider authorizing the early deployment to Afghanistan of a United Nations mandated force'. The 'Bonn Accord' further specified that 'This force will assist in the maintenance of security for Kabul and its surrounding areas. Such a force could, as appropriate, be progressively expanded to other urban centres and other areas'. The Security Council of course complied, thus bestowing legitimacy on the Anglo-American conquest and its creature, the 'Interim Authority'. Troops for this International Security Assistance Force (ISAF) were then provided by a bunch of NATO countries, notably Germany which took up much of the policing functions so that the American troops would be free to consolidate their conquest. This is the first time that German troops have been deployed in a war zone since the Second World War.

That was extraordinary enough. In an even more extraordinary move, NATO itself has now taken over, as of 11 August this year, command of the ISAF in first such deployment outside Europe in its 54-year old existence. The name itself – North Atlantic Treaty Organization – has always signified that North America and Western Europe were the regions of its operation. Then, after the collapse of communism in southeastern Europe, NATO has been broadened to include a number of countries from that region as well and countries as far-flung as Uzbekistan have now applied for membership in what NATO calls its 'Partnership for Peace'. Meanwhile, NATO was of course the chief military instrument in the final destruction of Yugoslavia. As the invasion of Afghanistan was being prepared, reports began to circulate of Tajik and Uzbek troops being trained at US bases in Alaska and Montana while US Rangers began training troops in Kyrgystan and perhaps Tajikistan as well (*Guardian*, September 26, 2001). In other words, these statelets were not only providing bases but also preparing their troops for participation in the wars of the core imperial army itself. This has now become altogether clear in Iraq where Polish and Ukrainian troops have come in without any discussion of Security Council approval and, significantly, NATO has provided guidance to the Polish-led division even though it has yet not assumed any direct role there.

Several aspects of this direct NATO takeover of the ISAF in Afghanistan are notable. First, as NATO's deputy secretary general, Alessandro Minuto Rizzo, noted in Kabul: 'This new mission is a reflection of NATO's ongoing transformation, and resolve, to meet the security challenges of the 20th century'. Key words here are 'transformation' and 'security challenges'. What is being announced here is that NATO is being 'transformed' for a global role far beyond the region for which it was originally designed, while 'security challenges of the 21st century' is short-hand for what Bush calls 'terrorism with a global reach'. This puts in perspective the true grievance of the Franco-German alliance as it fleetingly opposed the unilateral US decision to invade Iraq at the time and in the manner of its own choosing. These countries had been party to the destruction of Iraq over more than a decade through US-mandated sanctions under the UN aegis and the illegal US-UK bombings of Iraq all those years. Nor did they disagree with the idea of US invasion of Iraq; Germany had indeed offered its air space in the eventuality of such an invasion some five months before it happened. Their grievance was that the US did not sufficiently recognize that even though it was the hegemonic imperial power on a global scale, the fact was that, in the present phase of global capitalism, the US bourgeoisie was itself part of a fully integrated trans-Atlantic ruling class along with the European bourgeoisies and that Europe should therefore be given an appropriate role in the management of empire.

The second aspect of NATO's takeover of the ISAF command is that it has deliberately been announced as 'indefinite'. They are there to stay until the realm has been fully secured. Thirdly, Germany was the country most insistent that NATO take over the command directly and the first commander under the new dispensation is indeed a German general. Finally, their jurisdiction shall be confined initially to Kabul and its environs, the Security Council mandate specified for the ISAF, but this jurisdiction is expected to get extended to other parts of Afghanistan over time. Afghanistan is supposed to have general elections in June next year, and it is likely that the government which then emerges will be as much a client as the present one and will then formally request NATO for an expanded role, bypassing the inconvenience of seeking a new Security Council resolution, even though the UN special envoy in Afghanistan, Lakhdar Brahimi, has himself been asking for an expanded role for this security force.

Why this shift at this time? The obvious reason is that the resistance against US occupation has gained enormous momentum over the past year or so. Taliban really had no understanding of the kind of firepower the US could bring to bear upon them and seem to have thought, until the invasion really began, that they would withstand the US attack just as the so-called mujahideen had been able to withstand the Soviet firepower, forgetting that it was the US weaponry which had made the war against the Soviets possible in the first place and they had no such weaponry against the US. But they seem to have learned fast. After a couple of set-piece battles in which many of them got slaughtered, the regime and its main forces did manage to withdraw and melt away, into the mountains of Afghanistan and northern Pakistan. When the Americans began their saturation bombings of the mountain strongholds they again did not initially know how to hide or fight back and suffered uncountable casualties. Over the next few months, though, they and their allies – some old allies and some new ones – managed to re-group and start fighting a very different kind of guerrilla war.

The occupation of Afghanistan had been swiftly accomplished in October/November of 2001. Less than a year later, international media was again rife with news of resistance across a wide swath of the national territory. By then, Hekmetyar, the former Afghan premier whom the CIA and the Pakistani ISI had used as their main conduit for arms and men against the Soviet troops, had re-emerged from his Irani exile and joined up with the Taliban, now de-emphasizing the Islamic character of the resistance and focusing on the issue of national resistance to foreign occupation and a rightful place for the Pashtuns who comprise roughly 40 per cent of the Afghan population. Security situation under US occupation and the client regime that was dominated by the gang of thugs and rapists of the Northern Alliance had deteriorated so sharply that large part of the populace, opposed to foreign occupation any way, began to recall wistfully the rule of the Taliban which had guaranteed more personal security than the Afghans have experienced at any other time since the American jihad against the Soviets began some twenty years ago. Meanwhile,

Taliban-style groups started re-emerging in numerous smaller towns and villages.

By September 2002, Hekmetyar's Hezb-e-Islami-e-Afghanistan (HIA) was getting organized with new command structures on both sides of the Pakistan-Afghanistan border, with substantial support in the provinces of Kandhar, Ghazni, Kunar and Logar, while the rule of Karzai's gang is so tenuous in the outlying provinces that local administration has no choice but to cooperate with the resurrected power of this group throughout eastern Afghanistan. There is some reason to believe that Ismail Khan, the Governor of Herat who runs perhaps the most efficient administration in today's Afghanistan and is close to both Russia and Iran, has reached some kind of understanding with HIA. Many reports emanating from Afghanistan also suggest that the institutions of Karzai's own regime are thoroughly infiltrated by the Taliban as well as Hekmetyar's men. For Karzai personally, the situation is so grim that he does not trust Afghan soldiers and is protected by 46 bodyguards drawn from the US Special Forces.

A remarkable story in *Washington Post* of 8 November 2002 began with the words: 'The US military is losing momentum in the war on terrorism in Afghanistan because the remnants of Al Qaida and the Taliban have proven more successful in adapting to US tactics than the US military has to theirs, the chairman of the Joint Chiefs of Staff said this week'. There is of course that wonderful word 'remnants' referring to Taliban here just as all the acts of resistance in Iraq are supposedly carried out by 'remnants' of the Ba'athists. The report in any case quoted the CIA assessment that 'security was most precarious in smaller cities and some rural locations', far from where the ISAF has any jurisdiction. Then, using the all-purpose term 'Al Qaida' for anyone in Afghanistan who dares to resist the US the report then went on to say that 'A detailed analysis just released by the US Army War College reported that Al Qaida fighters have been quick to adapt to the high-tech weaponry the United States used in its attack on the network'. Stephen Biddle, the report's author, has said that already by March last year these forces were successfully using all the classic guerrilla tactics of cover and concealment, camouflage discipline, dispersion, communications security, and so on.

Three days later, on 11 November, a report in *Time* magazine began with the bald statement, 'The US concedes it has lost momentum in Afghanistan, while its enemies grow bolder' and ended with 'Is Afghanistan slipping out of America's control? It's an especially relevant question at a time when Pentagon planners are holding up Afghanistan as a template for possible "regime change" in Iraq'. That was four months before the full-scale US-UK invasion of Iraq got going, and by now of course resistance in Iraq has surfaced even more quickly than in Afghanistan. Such headlines and reports were to become routine over the next several months. By February 2003, a month before the Iraq invasion, Robert Fisk, the splendid and authoritative British reporter, was writing of 'the near-collapse of peace in this savage land and the steady erosion of US forces in Afghanistan – the nightly attacks on American and other international troops, the anarchy in the cities outside Kabul, the warlordism and drug trafficking and steadily increasing toll of murders'. In a more recent column in *New Statesman* (19 June 2003), Fisk was to again report: '"We are in a combat zone the moment we leave this base", an American colonel told me at Bagram airbase, near Kabul. "We are shot at every day, several times a day." When I said that surely he had come to liberate and protect the people, he belly-laughed. American troops are rarely seen in Afghanistan's towns. They escort US officials at high speed in armoured vans with blackened windows and military vehicles, mounted with machine-guns, in front and behind. Even the vast Bagram base was considered too insecure for the Defence Secretary, Donald Rumsfeld, during his recent, fleeting visit.'

A specific aspect of this quandary for the Americans is that three-quarters of the so-called Special Forces personnel in Afghanistan now are actually members of the National Guards and the Reserves, since the bulk of the special forces personnel there has been withdrawn for duty either in Iraq or some other place from where troops have been sent to Iraq. This too is probably very much a part of the situation in which NATO has decided to take command of ISAF directly, preparing no doubt for a much wider combat role for NATO in the near future. What Americans can't do, their European cousins shall. Or so they hope.

It seems most unlikely that they will succeed. Afghans have never taken kindly to foreign forces. Hamid Karzai, the US-appointed head of the provisional government is a non-entity and is widely hated even among the Pashtuns whom he is supposed to represent. He studied in India, then drifted to Peshawar where he once used to own a little restaurant. It's not clear as to when the Americans picked him up but he is known to have been close to the Taliban when the US was patronizing them and broke with them when they clashed with the US. At some point, he moved to the US, helped his brothers and sisters to open several restaurants there, and re-emerged as a consultant with UNOCAL, the US energy corporation during the years when it was trying to negotiate an oil pipeline through Afghanistan with the Taliban government. Zalmay Khalilzad, the special US envoy to Afghanistan who engineered Karzai's ascendancy as head of state, was also a consultant with UNOCAL. The writ of this gang does not run much beyond Kabul, so that the rest of the country is a patchwork of about two dozen regional administrations run by local strongmen commonly referred to in the media as 'warlords'. These are men of shifting loyalties and alliances, and they will work with any power centre, domestic or foreign, which seems to be ascendant in their own region, be it Iran or Pakistan or India, Taliban or Hekmatyar or the Kabul gang.

The only lucrative business in Afghanistan today, other than gun-running, is the opium/heroin trade. Taliban had banned poppy production which is now flourishing again under US occupation and with full participation of its clients in the Northern Alliance. United Nations statistics suggest that Afghanistan is again the world's leading exporter of heroin, supplying to Central Asia, Europe, and the US. Billions of contraband dollars are involved, and every warlord has stakes in it, above all the ones most closely allied with the Karzai dispensation. Underneath all this wealth and corruption and warlordism is the real country which was poor and underdeveloped enough even previously but has been ruined more and more since the Americans started assembling their jihadi force in 1980. Roads and bridges, schools and hospitals, homes and farmlands are all ruined. Six to seven million Afghans, roughly a third of the population, were at the point of starvation when the US invasion began, and the invasion created more refugees. Since then, the prospect of immediate starvation has receded but two million refugees have returned to a country that is largely a huge mass of rubble and dust; the US bombing of Kandahar was so severe that roughly 80 per cent of the population of the city fled and most buildings simply collapsed. Afghanistan has buried in it more land mines per square mile than any other country in the world; the road from Kabul to Kandahar, the country's major highway, is largely unusable thanks to these mines. Only 5 per cent of the rural population have access to clean water, 17 per cent have access to medical services, 13 per cent have access to education, and 25 per cent of all children die by the age of five. Life expectancy is 43, half of what it is in the NATO countries that have taken over as occupiers.

Talking of elections in a country that does not even have an administration is a cruel joke; if held, they will produce an assembly of anointed notables, allies and enemies of each other simultaneously. Speaking of 'development' is an even more cruel joke. The occupying benefactors can hardly leave their own compounds, imprisoned as they are in their own power bases. The native collaborators they have chosen, largely from the Northern Alliance, are crooks and criminals, more interested in rape and child abuse and heroin sales than 'development'. Then, there are the technocrats, discredited by the company they keep and at odds with fundamentalists within the regime itself; the only woman in the cabinet has had to go and is so afraid for her life that she has to be kept under elaborate guard. Taliban arose and were widely welcomed with relief because of the anarchy and criminality of the very people who have now returned to power; those same Taliban are now becoming national heroes because their demise was brought about by foreign occupiers and their friends. Indeed, the Taliban have become so confident that they are revealing the names of their regional commanders to journalists, and, surprisingly, most of their new commanders of the underground forces are the same who occupied key posts under the Taliban's government. It is astonishing how very many of them have survived the savage US-UK bombardment not only of the cities but even of the mountain fastnesses. And then there is Hekmetyar, potentially far more powerful than Osama bin Laden, since he is a Pashtun leader and a former Prime Minister who has a base within his country of a kind that no foreign 'guest', such as Osama, could ever have. A combination of the Taliban and Hekmatyar's HIA, if it lasts, is likely to be too much for NATO. European populations are unlikely to have a stomach for the kind of war that is now beginning. And Hekmatyar is clever; he is talking now not of jihad but of national liberation.

We shall have no sense of a historical perspective if we do not see the parallels between Afghanistan and Iraq, otherwise countries very different from each other. Both have been devastated by roughly twenty years of American interference. Every brand of fundamentalist in Afghanistan who tasted power in Afghanistan did so thanks only to the US-organized anti-communist jihad, just as the Ba'ath itself rose to power through American sponsorship of it there against the increasing power of the Iraqi Communist Party. Just about the time, around 1980, when the US was organizing its fundamentalists for jihad against the progressive and secular government of the Peoples' Democratic Party of Afghanistan (PDPA), it was instigating Saddam Hussein to invade Iran and, together with the British, supplying him with all kinds of weapons including the technology to manufacture chemical and biological weapons. That war, instigated by the US-UK combine, ruined Iraq during the 1980s, just as the US-instigated jihad of the 1980s ruined Afghanistan. Hekmetyar came to power in Kabul with American backing, as did the Taliban some years later, as did Saddam in Baghdad many years earlier; eventually, they all became enemies, as did Osama, the Saudi millionaire who too was recruited by the CIA. The Northern Alliance, which preceded Taliban and has now returned to power as a dominant faction in the Karzai government, was far more rapacious than Saddam himself, if that's at all possible; Chalabi, Rumsfeld's favourite candidate for rulership of Iraq, is a criminal who has been sentenced on several counts of embezzlement etc. by a Jordanian court.

Both countries suffered from US-dictated, UN-enforced sanctions, Iraq for a longer period and with constant bombings by the US-UK alliance, Afghanistan not for so long. However, society and economy in Afghanistan were much poorer, far more fragile, so that it had been thoroughly devastated already by the war of the 1980s and the subsequent civil wars among factions originally created by the US. So, sanctions against the Taliban only made worse a situation already dire. However, one-third of the population on the verge of starvation there by the time the invasion came compares with the million or so Iraqis who died owing to the sanctions in that long-suffering country.

The decision to invade Afghanistan and Iraq predates the events of 11 September 2001. The neoconservative/Christian fundamentalist/Zionist cabal that came to dominate the US administration under Bush had been urging Clinton to invade Iraq throughout his Presidency and the US Congress passed the Liberation of Iraq Act as far ago as 1998. And we know from unimpeachable sources that the US had been threatening Afghanistan with an invasion throughout 2001, starting in February but especially vociferously during the summer that year, well before the attacks on the World Trade Centre and the Pentagon.

Once the decision was made to carry out the respective invasions, some time in late September 2001, nothing at all could dissuade the governments of the US and UK from doing so. On the very day that Blair was telling Parliament that there was no peaceful way to get Osama, his country's press broke the story of Taliban's repeated offers to extradict Osama. As the two governments made their case for invasion on the basis that the Taliban were responsible for 11 September, their own intelligence agencies were saying that there was no credible evidence, just as intelligence agencies warned their respective governments that there was no credible evidence that Saddam had weapons of mass destruction that could endanger the UK or the US. Bush and Blair issued dossiers of what they called 'evidence' before the invasion of Afghanistan as well as Iraq. In both cases, scholars dismissed the dossiers with contempt and intelligence services were embarressed. In both cases, the basic strategy was the same: massive aerial bombings, attempts to play ethnic groups against each other, clients flown in from the US (Karzai, Chalabi), 'Interim Authority' in Afghanistan, a hand-picked Governing Council in Iraq, and so on. And, the same rhetoric – 'we come not as occupiers but liberators' – which colonizers have used for some two hundred years. And when a national resistance begins to take shape, we constantly hear of 'remnants' – of Taliban, of the Ba'ath – while the 'civilizing mission', the 'white man's burden' continues on its infernal march.

The wonder is that in countries so deeply injured and exhausted, a quagmire for the world-conqueror has opened up so fast. So, a new kind of imperial army is to be assembled. The entrance of NATO into Afghanistan would be laughable if its expected consequences were not so grim. This same cynical drama shall be played out in Iraq on a much larger scale, and the recent bombing of the UN compound in Baghdad, with its casualties that included a very fine international civil servant of Brazilian origin, shall undoubtedly be used now to beef up such an army. Kofi Annan and his ilk are incapable of confessing that the Security Council is hated in Iraq because it was the sanctions mandated by the Council which killed half a million Iraqi children. In stead, the word will now go that we need an international armed force but not under UN aegis because the UN blue flag no longer guarantees safety for those who carry it. Similarly, the more recent assassination of Ayatollah Mohammad Baqir al-Hakim, the senior Shia cleric in Iraq who had come to represent the tacit US-Iran understanding in Iraq, shall be used to argue even more vociferously in favour of the internationalization of the security forces in Iraq against the 'remnants' of the Saddam regime, without any recognition that the Ayatollah's having joined the US-imposed Governing Council might have something to do with his getting targetted – not necessarily by those so-called 'remnants' but by any one of the numerous forces in Iraq today, including powerful

Shia groupings, that are opposed to the collaborators of the US occupation forces. In an atmosphere where any act of war by the national resistance can be portrayed as 'terrorism', we may well have a Security Council resolution authorizing the formation of an international military outfit comprising of soldiers from all corners of the empire, mandated by the UN, led by the US, guided by NATO and so on – a true imperial army representing not this or that imperialist country alone but the combined will of the ruling classes of this world as well, to finish a war that the US started but is incapable of finishing on its own. The 'international community', the 'Free World', is always there to do the bidding of its leader, which is on its own incapable of fighting even a bunch of half-literate mullahs in towns and villages of Afghanistan because, for lack of an alternate leadership, these mullahs have come to embody the national will.

III

The Imperialism of Our Time

> Horkheimer, reacting early against the whole conception of 'totalitarianism', wrote: 'Anyone who does not wish to discuss capitalism should stay silent about fascism.' Strictly speaking, this in incorrect: it is he who does not wish to discuss *imperialism* who should stay silent on the subject of fascism.
>
> Nicos Poulantzas[1]

I begin with the phrase 'the imperialism of our time' as a homage to Michal Kalecki who wrote his seminal essay 'Fascism of Our Time' at the juncture when the American far right had made a serious bid for the Presidency with the emergence of Barry Goldwater as the Republican candidate in the 1964 US election.[2] Kalecki did not refer to Mussolini directly, although he might have, since it was after all Mussolini who first said that fascism is simply that form of rule in which government unites with 'corporations' – a term which for Mussolini meant something not unlike what President Eisenhower meant when warning of the US government's convergence with the 'military-industrial complex'.[3] Kalecki's

---

[1] Nicos Poulantzas, *Fascism and Dictatorship*, London: New Left Books 1974 (tanslation from French of *Fascism et dicature*, Paris: Maspero 1970).
[2] Michal Kalecki, 'The Fascism of Our Time' (1964) in *The Last Phase in the Transformation of Capitalism*, New York: Monthly Review Press 1972.
[3] Mussolini's actual words are: 'Fascism should more properly be called corporatism, since it is the merger of state and corporate power'. It is in light of this particular

analysis did suggest, however, that in its extreme form industrial capitalism does have an inherent fascist tendency in it, and he wondered what fascism would look like if it ever came to the United States in conditions of prosperity and stable electoral democracy. Kalecki's intent was not to suggest that the US was becoming fascist, on the model of Nazi Germany or fascist Italy, nor do I mean to imply that. Nonetheless, one of the salient features of the present conjuncture is that the United States, the leading imperialist country with historically unprecedented global power, is today governed by perhaps the most rightwing government in a century, and that the wars it is currently waging are much more nakedly and immediately in the interest of specific corporations than were the wars of Indochina, for example, where 'containment of communism' was more fundamental than monopoly over strategic resources. In the process, the chickens of the most hysterical forms of authoritarianism that the US has been routinely exporting to large parts of the globe seem to be coming home to roost, with national as well as global consequences, including military consequences.

I also use the simple phrase 'imperialism of our time'

---

understanding that I have argued elsewhere that fascism is (a) an inherent tendency in the whole history of modern imperialism, from the 1880s onwards, and (b) it is a global tendency, in the imperialized countries as much as in the imperialist ones. See my 'Structure and Ideology in Italian Fascism,' in *Lineages of the Present: Political Essays*, New Delhi: Tulika 1996. In a footnote to Section 3 of that essay I have also offered a rough periodization: 'Schematically, we might say that the fascisms of the interwar period corresponded to the crises of accumulation brought about by the maturing of imperialism itself as it made a fuller transition from the competitive to the monopoly structure of capital – an explanation that Baran and Sweezy, among others, and Poulantzas in his own way, have accepted – whereas the *fin-de-siecle* fascisms of today correspond to the Late Imperial period of full globalization of the capitalist mode in which the mode has provisionally triumphed over communist states but faces internal crises of stagnation in the core countries and unmanageable social tensions in the less industrialized countries brought about precisely by that imperialist globalization.'

with the more modest aim of avoiding terms like 'New Imperialism' which have been in vogue at various times, with varying meanings. Imperialism has been with us for a very long time, in great many forms, and constantly re-invents itself, so to speak, as the structure of global capitalism itself changes. What is offered here is a set of provisional notes toward the understanding of a conjuncture, 'our time', which is itself a complex of continuities and discontinuities – and, as is usual with conjunctures, rather novel. I shall first offer a series of proposition and then, in the remaining space for this article, some further elaboration of these points.

I

The fundamental novelty of the imperialism of our time is that it comes after the dissolution of the two great rivalries that had punctuated the global politics of the 20th century, namely what Lenin called 'inter-imperialist rivalry' of the first half of the century as well as what we might, for lack of a better word, call the inter-systemic rivalry between the US and the USSR that lasted for some seventy years. The end of those rivalries concludes the era of politics inaugurated by the First World War and it is only logical that the sole victor, the United States, would set out most aggressively to grab all possible spoils of victory and to undo the gains that the working classes and oppressed nations of the world had been able to achieve during that period.

This new phase of imperialism arises not only after the dissolution of the great colonial empires (British and French, principally) and colonial ambitions of the other, competing capitalist countries (Germany and Japan, mainly) but also the definitive demise of the 'nationalism of the national bourgeoisie' in much of the so-called Third World (anti-colonialism, wars of national liberation, the Bandung project, non-alignment, the protectionist industrializing state) which had itself been sustained considerably by the existence of an alternative pole in the shape of the communist countries.[4] The three objectives for which the US fought a war of position throughout the twentieth century – the containment/disappearance of communist states, its own primacy over the other leading capitalist countries, the defeat of economic nationalism in the Third World – have been largely achieved. Consolidation of its dominance over possible competitors and a permanent disarray of Third World nationalism are the current objectives.

Far from being an imperialism caught in the coil of inter-imperialist rivalries, it is the imperialism of the era in which (a) national capitals have interpenetrated in such a manner that the capital active in any given territorial state is typically comprised, in varying proportions, of national and transnational capital; (b) finance capital is dominant over productive capital to an extent never visualized even in Lenin's 'export of capital' thesis or in Keynes' warnings about the rapaciousness of the rentiers; and (c) everything from commodity markets to movements of finance has been so thoroughly globalized that the rise of a global state, with demonstrably globalized military capability, is an objective requirement of the system itself, quite aside from the national ambitions of the US rulers, so as to impose structures and disciplines over this whole complex with its tremendous potential for fissures and breakdowns.

Empires without colonies have been with us, in one corner of the globe or another, throughout the history of capital,

---

[4] I offer an analytic narrative of the triangular relationship between capitalism, socialism, and nationalism between 1945 and 1990, i.e. from the end of the Second World War up to the dissolution of the Soviet Union, in the opening essay, 'Introduction: Literature among the Signs of Our Time,' in *In Theory: Classes, Nations, Literatures*, London: Verso 1992; New Delhi: Oxford University Press 1994.

sometimes preceding military conquest (commercial empires), at other times coming after decolonization (South America after the dissolution of Spanish and Portuguese rule), and sometimes taking the form for which Lenin invented the term 'semi-colonial' (Egypt, Persia, etc., in his time). However, this is the first fully post-colonial imperialism, not only free of colonial rule but antithetical to it; it is unlikely that the current occupation of Iraq will translate itself into long-term colonial rule, however long the quagmire may last and even if the superhawks of the Pentagon take US armies into Syria, Iran or wherever. It is not a matter of an ideological preference for 'informal' empire over 'formal' empire, so-called. It is a structural imperative of the current composition of global capital itself. The movement of capital and commodities must be as unimpeded as possible but the nation-state form must be maintained throughout the peripheries, not only for historical reasons but also to supplement internationalization of capitalist law with locally erected labour regimes so as to enforce what Stephen Gill calls 'disciplinary neoliberalism' in conditions specific to each territorial unit.

The singular merit of Luxemburg's theory of imperialism was that, much more systematically than Hilferding or Lenin or Bukharin, she sought to ground her theory in the larger theory of the capitalist mode of production itself and therefore focussed on the question of the relationship between industrial and agricultural production which had been a notable feature of the Marxist theory of capitalism as such. One of her key propositions was that colonialism was not a conjunctural but a necessary aspect of the globalization of the law of value because capitalist zones require non-capitalist zones for full realization of surplus value; but she also went on to say that once capitalism has reached the outer reaches of the globe a crisis would necessarily ensue thanks to the increasing disappearance of non-capitalist zones. This latter inference would appear to be unwarranted, historically and even logically. Combined and uneven development does not strictly require that the peripheries remain 'non-capitalist', i.e., outside the global operation of the law of value. In actual history, the era of classical colonialism divided the world between an industrial core and a vast agricultural hinterland. Then, however, the dissolution of the great colonial empires and the postwar restructuring of global capital opened a new era in which the world was increasingly divided between advanced and backward industrial zones, while the formerly colonized countries and continents were themselves divided between islands of advanced forms of finance and industrial production, on the one hand, and forms of agricultural production, on the other, that were governed by the capitalist law of value even in the most backward zones. At the extreme poles within the so-called 'Third World', one witnessed not only the stunning capitalist breakthrough in countries like Taiwan and South Korea but also, in contrast, the regression of parts of sub-Saharan Africa to levels below those obtaining at the time of decolonization. This transcontinental production of extreme inequalities is rife with potential for perennial violence, hence the need for state systems that guarantee extreme forms of extra-economic coercion. Meanwhile, one can witness across large parts of Asia and Africa all the processes of primitive accumulation and forced proletarianization that Marx specified in his famous chapter on the question, with reference mainly to England, and one remembers the central role he assigns to the state in the process, which, in his words, 'begat' the conditions for capitalist production 'hothouse-fashion'. To the extent that relatively similar processes are duplicated in a number of countries under regimes of both nation-state and globalized management (the World Bank, the WTO, etc.), in a system that is itself trans-national, a supervening authority above national and local authorities is again an objective requirement of the system as a whole; hence the tight fit among the multi-lateral institutions, the US state, and the local managers of other states.

At the broadest level of generalization, one could say that it took two world wars to decide whether the US or Germany would inherit the British and French empires and thus transform itself into the leader of the bloc of advanced capitalist countries, and hence the centre of a global empire. It is significant that while the German vision was mired in the primitive notions of a world-wide colonial empire, the US, already under Woodrow Wilson, was championing the dissolution of colonialism and the 'right of nationalities', an ideological precursor for today's imperialism of 'democracy' and 'human rights'. And, it was after the First World War, as the centre of global finance shifted decisively from London to New York and the Bolshevik Revolution arose to challenge global capitalism as a whole, that the US positioned itself as the leader of the 'Free World', as was symbolized by Wilson's dominating presence at Versailles as well as the leading role the US always played in the containment-of-communism crusades, especially after the Second World War.

Precisely at the time when the US has achieved all its long-standing objectives, including the objective of full dominance over its partners in the advanced capitalist world, there has arisen in some circles the expectation of an 'inter-imperialist rivalry' between the US and EU as competing centres of global capitalist production, with reference mainly to the size of the European economy as well as a futuristic projection of an East Asian power, be it Japan or China or a bloc of East Asian states. On the basis of present trends, this seems rather fanciful. The most the Europeans do in the Third World is look for markets and investment opportunities. There is no power projection, for the simple reason that there is no power. Not only is the US military power far greater than that of all of Europe combined, it also has a military presence in over a hundred countries of the world, in sharp contrast to Germany or even France, and NATO goes only where the US tells it to go.[5] This military supremacy over its would-be rivals is supplemented then by the overwhelming power of its currency and finance, its dominance over the global production of techno-scientific as well as social-scientific intelligentsias, as well as its global reach through its dominance over mass entertainment and (dis)information.

The US fought as hard against radical Third World nationalism, as it did against communism during the second half of the century. Having championed decolonization as a precondition for the emergence of a globally integrated empire under its own dominion, it set its face against national liberation movements, whether led by communists (as in Indochina) or by radical nationalists (as in Algeria); against non-alignment (the rhetoric of 'for us or against us' of Bush Jr. today comes straight out of John Foster Dulles' speeches during the 1950s); as well as against particular nationalist regimes, be it Nasser's or Nkrumah's or Sukarno's or even Prince Sihanouk's in Cambodia. Instead, it kept monarchies in power where it could and imposed dictators wherever it needed to. The failure of the national-bourgeois project in the Third World has all kinds of domestic roots but the implacable

---

[5] The EU as a whole spends less than half of what the US spends on the military, and its actual military capability amounts to perhaps not much more than 10 per cent of the US capability because of equipment duplication, incompatibility of weapon systems, over-all much lower technological levels and R&D allocations – not to speak of the fact that Britain, the major European military power alongside France, is and be likely to remain much more integrated into the US military design than the envisioned European one. Meanwhile, the US is ensuring that the ex-Warsaw Pact countries which are joining the EU get integrated much more into NATO, under US umbrella, than into the Franco-German alliance. An independent European military force is envisioned in any case not as alternative to NATO but as autonomous supplement.

undercutting of it by the US was a very large part of it. One now tends to forget that in his postwar vision, Keynes himself had recommended not only state restrictions on rentiers in the advanced capitalist countries, but also regular long-term transfers of capital to the underdeveloped countries to guarantee real growth, hence domestic peace, and hence stability of the global capitalist system as a whole, not to speak of more prosperous markets for the advanced capitalist countries' own commodities. This latter recommendation was rejected out of hand by the US which kept a tight control over the making of the Bretton Woods architecture. This undercutting of the national-bourgeois project – precisely because the project required high levels of protectionism, tariffs, domestic savings and state-led industrialization, with little role for imperialist penetration – certainly made all those states much weaker in relation to foreign domination but they also made those societies much more angry and volatile, eventually even susceptible to all kinds of irrationalism, with little popular legitimacy for the ruling minorities in the majority of Asian and African states. This phenomenon itself has required not only globalized supervision but also an increasingly *interventionist* global state. Little fires have – more and more – to be put out everywhere and now the whole system has to be 're-ordered', as Bush and Blair keep saying. The Cold War was never cold for many outside the NATO and Warsaw Pact zones, and US military interventions in the Third World, direct and indirect, was a routine affair throughout that period. Now, winning the Cold War has opened the way not to world peace but for an ideology of permanent interventionism on part of the United States: 'a task that never ends', as Bush put it some ten days after the 11 September catastrophe.

Defeat of all the forces whom Hobsbawm cumulatively and felicitously calls 'the Enlightenment left' – communism, socialism, national liberation movements, the radical wings of social democracy – has ensued in a full-blown ideological crisis across the globe. Race, religion and ethnicity – re-packaged as just so many 'identities'– are now where class struggles and inter-religious, inter-racial, trans-ethnic solidarities once used to be, and a politics of infinite Difference has arisen on the ruins of the politics of Equality. Postmodernism is rife with thematics taken over from European irrationalism and with nostalgia for the pre-modern. Indeed, this idea of the pre-modern as the postmodern solution for problems of modernity is even more widespread, with far more murderous consequences, in the peripheries of the capitalist system, be it the ideologies of the Hindu far right in India, the sundry fundamentalisms of Islamic mullahs, or the millenarian ideologies of those who brought us 11th September.[6] Terrorism is now where national liberation used to be, and the US today chases these handful of terrorists as assiduously and globally as it used to chase phalanxes of revolutionaries until not long ago. Nor is it a matter any longer of the peripheries. The United States itself is gripped today by a peculiar, cabal-like combination of Christian fundamentalists, Zionists, far right neoconservatives and militarists which provide the ideological bases and policy formulations for the Bush regime.

It is here that the specificity of this regime in the United States lies. We shall return to the fact that the US has fought a war of position not just against communism throughout much of the twentieth century, not only against radical nationalisms in the second half of that century but also, crucially, for its own dominance over its capitalist rivals and in pursuit of a role for itself as the sole architect of the global capitalist system. In that sense, of course, the current administration continues a much

---

[6] See Aziz al-Azmeh's brilliant piece 'Postmodern Obscurantism and "the Muslim Question",' in Panitch and Leys (eds), *Socialist Register 2003*, London: Merlin Press 2002.

older project, and some of the most aggressive of its policies can be traced back to not only Bush Sr. or Ronald Reagan but to Clinton and Carter as well. Yet, there is also an element of fundamental novelty. The first specificity of this regime lies in the fact that, thanks to the dissolution of the Soviet bloc, this is the first time in human history that a single imperial power is so dominant over all its rivals that it really has no rival, near or far, precisely at the time when it has the greatest capacity to dominate the globe. Clinton in this calculus appears as a transitional figure and Bush Jr.'s Presidency, the first US Presidency of the twenty-first century, seems to coincide fully with this moment when history's greatest concentration of force can be exercised without any restraint imposed by a rival centre of power, as the Soviet Union once did, even with its demonstrably inferior military power. That is the objective moment of this Presidency. The second specificity is that never in the post-1914 epoch has so concentrated a force of the far right taken hold of the governing institutions of the US state, a force so overdetermined in their ideology and projects that they recognize no limits to their own venality or criminality or global ambition. It is this ideological blindness which routinely forces them to vastly underestimate the potential of popular resistance from below, as they are already finding out in Iraq where, fragmented as it might be in its inner composition, the resistance has already torpedoed all their plans not only for Iraq but even for the occupation of Syria and Iran which the neoconservative policymakers in the US had been dreaming of. From the rabidly Zionist Vice President Dick Cheney to the National Security Advisor Condoleeza Rice, and from Defence Secretary Rumsfeld to the Evangelical fundamentalist Attorney General Ashcroft – not to speak of their once-alcoholic and now born-again Christian President Bush – all the key members of this regime are in their own way quite as millenarian as the most irrational member of Al Qaida. Unlike Al Qaida, however, they have power – more power than any other regime in history. Thus it is that their actions by and large conform to the logic of capital but also may well exceed that logic. Thus it is that Ken Livingston, the current Mayor of London, may well be right is speculating that George W. Bush is 'the greatest threat to life on this planet that we've most probably ever seen'.

II

To properly understand where imperialism stands today it's necessary to begin by reconsidering Lenin's conception of 'inter-imperialist rivalry'. His thinking on this subject arose in the course of a conjunctural analysis required by an intense debate over whether a world war was imminent or not, the line that European social democracy was to adopt in case war did break out, the question of voting over war credits in the various countries (notably Germany), the question of what revolutionary possibilities might or might not open up in the event of a war and what kind of a power bloc (class alliances) the revolutionary parties were to try to constitute in that event, and where – if anywhere – the likelihood of a revolution would be the greatest. As an analysis as well as a strategic perspective for action in a conjuncture riven by multiple contradictions, his position proved to be unassailable. The First World War, contrary to what Kautsky, the master theoretician of German social democracy, believed, soon led not to the emergence of a 'superimperialism' but to the outbreak of a Second World War, meanwhile creating a situation where the Bolshevik Revolution could be successful. At the end of the war, countries like Germany and Italy did witness a level of revolutionary militancy that was not to be matched again during the inter-war period. And it was in consequence of that war and the Bolshevik

Revolution that anti-colonial mass movements arose in a number of Asian and African countries, with the alliance of the proletariat, the peasantry and left-wing intelligentsia – which Lenin had recommended at the time – becoming a common feature of those movements, whether led by communists or not. Nor is there much doubt that as a latecomer to advanced capitalism without being a 'colony-holding state' (Luxemburg's phrase), Germany was keen on a re-division of the colonial world. Indeed, classical fascism itself triumphed, provisionally, in precisely those three countries – Germany, Italy and Japan – which had come to advanced capitalism rather late and were the most keen to acquire colonies in their competition with the major colony-holding states of France and Germany.

The acuity of Lenin's *conjunctural* analysis, and the recommendations on matters of strategy he drew from it, has little to do with whether or not he was right on other things, like export of capital, etc.; in the more mature period of imperialism (post-1945), the advanced capitalist countries were to invest much more of their surplus capital in each other's economies than in the Third World. The idea of 'inter-imperialist rivalry' was in fact much more closely integrated with the idea of 'the weakest link' (more revolutionary possibility in Russia than in Germany, for example), the political strategy of multi-class alliances based on the strategic alliance of the proletariat and the peasantry (a great innovation in Marxist revolutionary theory for backward countries: Stalin's fatal error in breaking that alliance through policies of 'primitive socialist accumulation'), and the national-colonial question (the possibility of anti-colonial revolutions thanks to the weakening of the colonizing bourgeoisies, the rise of mass anti-colonial movements after the First World War, general decolonization after the second).

The conception of 'inter-imperialist rivalry', however,

presupposed a stage in the global evolution of the capitalist mode of production in which the national capitals of the advanced countries are essentially discrete in nature and with little interpenetration. And, it therefore presupposed a kind of state that represents the national bourgeoisie as such, in competition with other national bourgeiosies and their states. Rooted as the conception was in a debate over the inevitability and imminence of war among these competing and discretely organized states, 'rivalry' itself had a meaning far exceeding mere competition because it excluded the possibility of even any lasting collaborative competition *in those circumstances*. The idea that war was imminent similarly presupposed some equivalence, or at least illusion of equivalence, in levels of military capability, i.e., the rivals had to be seen to be erecting military structures that were capable of fighting each other.

This brief excursus on Lenin serves to make a point: one cannot lift the conception of 'inter-imperialist rivalry' out of a conjunctural analysis of almost a century ago. As one now revisits those texts, one is struck by their belonging to a different epoch, entirely. The specificity of the conjuncture in the imperialism of our time, as different from Lenin's, is that its core – consisting of advanced capitalist countries – is comprised of neither rivals nor equals. The total population and the collective GNP of the EU is certainly equal to that of the United States, marginally greater in fact. That's where the matter ends, however. It has no centralized state structure even remotely comparable to that of the US, no singular language, no standing army or security structure of its own, no foreign policy that is binding on member states, and its laws supercede national laws in only certain circumscribed fields. Its proposed constitution in 2003 is so bound by conditionalities and ifs and buts that it looked more like a statement of principle and vision than a proper constitution. The

Brussels bureaucracy, the new Euro, and a whole host of good intentions seem to be the unifying factors. Inter-penetration of national capitals, especially in finance, means economic interdependence among the key capitalist countries and regions is the key aspect of this 'imperialism of our time'. Competition is inherent in the very nature of the capitalist state system, and we are witnessing this even as the Euro tries to emerge as a viable world currency alongside the dollar, and as the EU competes with the US for markets; this 'competition' must fall well short of 'rivalry', in the Lenininst sense, because neither the mutual inter-penetration of economies nor the vast discrepancy in relative military power makes 'rivalry' a feasible option for the EU.

All this became transparent during the decision-making process over the invasion of Iraq. Britain threw in its lot with the US, with complete disregard of even procedural consideration for the EU but in keeping with the role of loyal subordinate that the US imposed upon it soon after the Second World War, and from which neither Harold Wilson nor Thatcher nor Blair have ever deviated. Then, as France and Germany sought to distinguish themselves from that position and the US Defence Secretary Rumsfeld dismissed them contemptuously as 'old Europe', everyone from Derrida to Habermas marched to television studios to express dismay on Europe's behalf. Eventually, Rumsfeld did line up Britain, Italy, Spain, Portugal and a host of little/new countries of 'Europe' on his side, and it was in the Azores that Bush announced the final decision to ignore the Security Council and proceed with the invasion. Equally significant is the fact that in the last round of negotiations at the Security Council before the invasion began, the Franco-German alliance proposed a 30-day warning to Saddam (and the inspectors) after which they too were willing to condone the invasion. Bush pointedly snubbed them by keeping to the schedule set by the Pentagon and ignoring the Security Council from that point on. The US instructed the UN to withdraw its inspectors forthwith and Kofi Annan, the Secretary-General of the United Nations, did not even bother to call the Security Council in session, even though the inspectors had been sent there not by the US but by a Security Council Resolution; Annan simply instructed the inspectors to comply with US orders. Hans Blix, the chief inspector, was to say later that he had long believed that Iraq had no weapons of mass destruction and the whole thing was a charade anyway. Once the invasion got into full swing, even the Franco-German alliance began to pray publicly for a quick US victory and, only slightly less publicly, began begging for contracts for European firms in the 'reconstruction' of Iraq. When the US decided to establish itself as the occupying force and grant the UN no appreciable role in it, the Franco-German alliance complied. The puppet regime appointed by the US under the name of Iraqi Governing Council was quickly recognized by the Security Council, *in a unanimous vote,* as 'embodying the sovereignty of the Iraqi people' while that same vote awarded Iraq's seat in the UN to Ahmed Chalabi, the head of that Council and a convicted criminal. How a person and a body wholly appointed by the military administration of a foreign power, designated as *Occupying Power* by the Security Council itself, can embody the 'sovereignty' of the occupied country is a question left to anyone's guess. This gross violation of every conception of international law and the UN Charter was accomplished with full collusion of all the would-be rivals of the US: Russia, China, as well as the three leading countries of the EU, namely Germany, France and Britain who sit on the Security Council.

Meanwhile, on the completely different issue of a Belgian law which grants Belgian courts the jurisdiction to try foreign nationals for war crimes, a stern warning from Rumsfeld that he might move the NATO headquarters from Brussels if the laws were not changed brought swift compliance from the Belgian government. So much for the claim by high-minded European intellectuals that respect for universal human rights is an integral aspect of the emerging European identity. Belgium apparently has no right to have laws of its own even on issues such as war crimes, even though these laws have no relevance to global trade, finance or commercial contracts. The doctrine of limited sovereignty that is emerging as a major component in US policy, with its vast implications for the new imperial constitutionalism, is to be applied, apparently, not only to the Third World countries but even, selectively, to Europe's own ability to promulgate laws for itself.

In the theoretical field, developments of this kind concretely bring into question the Negri/Hardt conception of a supra-national 'sovereignty', which, according to them, has been so thoroughly globalized that it is hard to locate it anywhere in particular, just as this 'sovereignty' is to be opposed by a 'multitude' which too is beyond class or any other determinate identity or boundary. In actual reality, it is of course the United States that claims a sovereign right to act in its own interests (which it calls 'defence') while flouting the sovereignty of others, so that the sovereignty of the imperial state seems boundless. Indeed, it was Ms Albright, a former professor at Georgetown University, who became the first high official of US administration, as Clinton's Secretary of State, to expound the notion that 'nationality' as well as 'sovereignty' belong to an outdated repertoire of political theory and need to be abandoned in view of new structures of globalization and imperatives of 'humanitarian intervention'.

The declaration of the Bush administration that it has the sovereign right to make war – what it calls 'pre-emptive war' – against any or all states that it perceives as a threat, while reserving the right to judge what constitutes a threat, is in fact an extension of a doctrine already in place since earlier administrations. What we are witnessing is the making of an imperial sovereignty claimed for itself by a state which is at once the state of a nation as well as a globalized state of contemporary capitalism. The US arrogates to itself a limitless sovereignty which is arbitrary by nature, and can only exist in so far as its might is so superior to that of all others that its action would necessarily go unchallenged by other components of the global state system however resentful they might be otherwise.

While we are still on the question of inter-imperialist rivalry, as contrasted to the global sovereignty of the US imperium, it is worth recalling that there is yet another, even less plausible and more or less futuristic idea which locates this rivalry not in the Atlantic zone but the Pacific zone, so that the rival arises not from Europe but from East Asia. In an earlier version, the rivalry was to come from Japan but the deeply crisis-ridden nature of its current economy, contrasted with the remarkable growth rates sustained by the Chinese economy over the past more than a decade, seems to have shifted the attention to China. This too is implausible, however. Whatever its recent rates of growth, the scale of the Chinese economy is nothing compared with that of the EU, and whatever the immense size of its land army, the high-tech component of its military capability is still far behind even that of Russia. The preponderant role of its military establishment is internal, with respect to management of civil society and dominance over other institutions of state; for the rest, its war-making capabilities are largely defensive in character. Its capitalistic pattern of economic growth over the past quarter century itself has aggravated internal social contradictions, along fault-lines of class and region, and China will be lucky if it can survive, through this extremely difficult and lop-sided growth period, in its present territorial shape, and may face increasing mass unrest along class lines as well. One can be fairly certain that the US will exploit that internal unrest to foster separatist movements, especially in the outlying regions such as Xinjiang, just as it closely watches Tibet as a possible staging area. Meanwhile, the remorseless export orientation of the Chinese economy has served to integrate it deeply into the US consumer market, so that China today is beset by the nightmare that if there is a full-scale American recession Chinese exports will decline dramatically and its economy will consequently grind to a halt. In a parallel development, China has now become the second largest importer of oil, bypassing Japan; and most of the oil it imports comes precisely from the region where the US is busy, with single-minded brutality, to establish its monopoly over all the strategic resources. Integration of China into the US-dominated global system as a way of increasing its dependency is an imperative that Bush Sr. and Clinton well understood. The current administration may pursue a policy (in which India may well play an important role) of forcing upon China stupendous expenditures on building its military defences, taking those resources away from economic growth and thus exacerbating internal conflicts. In any case, China is extremely vulnerable to the United States, militarily and economically, and any idea of it as competitor is fanciful at best.

III

Unlike inter-imperial rivalry, the question of colonialism is – or should be – central to our thinking today. In the history of imperialism, the role of colonialism – generally conceptualized these days in terms of a contrast between 'formal' and 'informal' empires – remains a contentious issue. Four initial observations can be offered without fear of much contradiction, except from devoutly Westocentric circles. First, colonialism was not an incidental, epiphenomenal or episodic feature of the development of capitalism, and the neglect of this fact has marred much Marxist theory of capitalism; colonialism was from the beginning an intrinsic part of the primitive accumulation of capital and former colonies continue to play this role in the primitive accumulation of capital on the global scale in postcolonial imperialism of even today (primitive accumulation being a *constant* feature of capitalism throughout its history, right up to the present juncture). Second, there is a sharp contrast between different kinds of colonialism, as for example between settler colonialism (which succeeded in the Americas and Australia but failed in Africa) and the so-called colonies which were occupied, administered and exploited by bourgeoisies so external to them that they never put their roots down in the conquered lands (the experience of most colonies in Asia and Africa). Some of the white settlements in the temperate zones made a transition to advanced capitalism (notably North America and to an extent Australia-New Zealand) while others did not (South America). None of the occupied-but-unsettled colonies did, not even India which had fairly advanced levels of mercantile capital as well as sophisticated pre-industrial manufactures at the moment of colonization. Much capital and technology was transferred to the settler colonies, very little to the unsettled ones. All this had rather consequential effects on the class structure of the respective sub-systems. The settler-colonies which made the capitalist transition are marked by the dominance of industry over agriculture, and they have a demographic balance in which the employed greatly outnumber the army of the unemployed; in those which did not make that transition, the army of the unemployed and the indifferently employed tend to exceed the employed sections of the working class.

Third, the so-called 'informal' empire (imperialism without colonies) has been a recurring feature from the beginning, and full-scale colonialist conquest often came as an aftermath of other forms of imperialist exploitation. Coastal outposts in western Africa, combined with raids and incursions into the interior, were enough to empty it of much of its population via the slave trade and to disrupt its economic networks; conquest of the interior came much later. Even the beginnings of extensive territorial conquest of India came very much later than the establishment of coastal outposts for purposes of commercial imperialism, and the full territorial conquest – not to speak of the transition from a possession of the East India Company to a crown colony – took a hundred years; by contrast, ninety years were to elapse between full conquest and decolonization.

Fourth, the global history of 'formal' and 'informal' empires – not to speak of colonial conquest and decolonization – is parallel but non-synchronic. Latin America was fully decolonized well before the interiors of Africa and Asia were fully colonized; the history of Anglo-American rivalry over the 'informal' empire in Latin America after decolonization predates the rise of mass anti-colonial movements in Asia and Africa by roughly a century. The fact that Latin American states originated in settler-colonial formations while most states in Asia and Africa did not experience even the attempt to impose that form has had enormously differentiated consequences for the development of languages, cultures, religions, demographic compositions, etc. in the respective continents. And some of the consequences of imperialism were rather similar in 'formal' and 'informal' empires so far as the colonized territories and the 'semi-colonies' (Lenin's term) are concerned. India shifted to the status of a crown colony in the 1830s; Turkey, never colonized, undertook modern bourgeois reforms under the Tanzimat at roughly the same time; by the 1920s both had developed remarkably similar property relations, legal structures, reform movements, etc., not to speak of the modes of dependence on Europe (e.g., debt servitude) with the difference that India had been colonized and Turkey not.

The United States occupies a unique place in this whole history of colonialism. It was the only former colony that turned itself into an empire, but even during the nineteenth century when colonizing was quite the fashion in Europe, the US sought not to colonize Latin America but to dominate it. Born in genocidal annexation of vast territories, its initial Thirteen Colonies made a revolution, turned themselves into a nation, wrote for themselves a constitution which combined stirring rhetoric of what we today call 'human rights' with defence of slavery, so that the settlers could now go on doing what they were doing anyway – race-based slavery for the plantations, profits from the triangular trade, commerce and industry concentrated mostly on the eastern seaboard, petty commodity mode in New England – without having to share profits with the 'mother country'. The expansionist ideology that arose out of it was annexationist rather than colonial in the European sense; what lay beyond the frontier was there to take, and frontiers could be extended through much of the nineteenth century. To the west, only the Pacific proved to be the limit; to the south and north, borders with Mexico and Canada were determined in warfare and annexation of territory, not conquering these neighbours as colonies. Unlike the 'colony-holding' states of Europe it never had the problem of surplus labour; it constantly accumulated for itself a massive surplus of resources. European colony-holders exported their populations to achieve a favourable demographic balance; the US thrived on importing slaves, skilled labourers and vast intellectual resources from other countries. Its first 'informal' empire was in the Americas itself, while the heart of the empire lay in the annexed territories that were constantly converted into more and more national territory; empire and nation were, in that originating moment, one.

IV

The US entered the First World War not for re-division of the colonial world but as arbiter of European disputes, and emerged out of it as the first among equals. With the European slaughter of that war weakening the colony-holding (Britain and France) and colony-desiring states (notably Germany) alike, and with the centre of finance shifting increasingly to New York while its own industrial base profited from the war, leadership of the capitalist world was there for the taking. It already perceived that order and stability in the increasingly complex capitalist world could not be maintained without concentrating the task of leading it in the hands of the most powerful state, nor communism fought back without that unity behind a purposeful leadership, but the British empire was still intact and Britain was not yet ready to concede that leadership so unequivocally. The US at any rate did not yet have the requisite framework of institutions capable of running an imperial state. So, its first foray into world leadership made a considerable mess. The League of Nations was a fiasco. The burden of reparations which it imposed upon the losers fed into the growing resentment, irrationalism and right-wing hysteria in Germany. The Armistice that ensued increasingly became a period of reprieve and preparation for the second round of the killings. The Wilsonian attachment to the 'principle of nationalities' transformed the map of Europe but did little for progress toward decolonization. Containment/rolling back of communism was recognized as a key task but the US could not organize under its own clear leadership the kind of anti-communist crusade it was to organize after the Second World War; it was still living – to put it in today's jargon – in a multi-polar world. It is, however, significant that the Depression which strengthened the Nazis so much gave rise to the New Deal in the US; one of the aspirants for controlling a global empire succumbed to a retrograde resolution of the crisis, the other chose a progressive one. The Nazis initiated the Second World War with the ambition of turning the whole world into a vast and permanent German colony. Once the US entered the Second World War, it explicitly adopted the goal of persuading – or forcing – all the 'colony-holding' states to unburden themselves of the colonies and get on with the business of joining a unified capitalist empire on the global scale.

It was really by the end of the Second World War that the US had acquired sufficient material resources and institutional structures of statecraft at its disposal to actually undertake a task of such magnitude, and only at that point that the gap between itself and its would-be competitors grew so wide that Britain itself could be swiftly turned into a vassal and Germany partitioned, occupied and turned into an object of reconstruction through American largesse. Even France succumbed to the bonanza of the Marshal Plan, and De Gaulle's subsequent pursuit of an independent foreign and defence policies never had the requisite material clout behind it. Outside Europe, the US was to fight and fund many wars, the most lethal and protracted ones in Indochina of course, but never to colonize, only to obtain client regimes and make the world safe for capitalism. This globalized and punctual policy of military interventions has mystified those on the left for whom contemporary capitalism is a system essentially of transactions among the advanced countries and for whom the Third World is largely irrelevant due to the meagreness of its share in world production and trade. However, as even a third-rate general would know, it is on the flanks that the centre is secured; no flanks, no centre. So, the US has always sought to hegemonize the whole of the tri-continental imperial realm in Asia, Africa and Latin America, so as (a) to monopolize its vast strategic resources and thwart its revolutionary potentials, in a permanent counterrevolution, and (b) to consolidate its dominant position within the zone of advanced capitalism itself.

The post-Second World War settlement was based on a combination of a clear-cut US leadership and a complex network of multilateral institutions. The most useful were the institutions – such as the IFIs and NATO – which the US could control more firmly. The UN was always treated as a necessary and useful nuisance because the USSR had veto power in the Security Council and because membership in the General Assembly was so numerous that, in the heyday of communism and Third World nationalism, majorities were not always easy to obtain; there even came a fleeting moment, in the 1970s, when UN itself became a forum for the pursuit of Third World nationalist projects through such subsidiary organizations as the UNCTAD. Now that those adversaries have been vanquished, a paradoxical situation has arisen in which the UN itself has become much more pliant but the US is now so determined to take the management of the capitalist world into its own hands that it is systematically undermining not only the UN but also, on occasion, the IMF and the World Bank which have been among its chief instrumentalities for governance of, especially, the Third World since the imposition of the postwar settlement. With hindsight, one can now see that the great emphasis on multilaterism in the past was itself perhaps a function of the fact that the US faced challenges from communism and Third World nationalism and needed at least an institutional framework in which to buttress the unity and consent of its chief allies behind its own leadership. Now, with those challenges gone, the leadership firmly secured, and a much more belligerent US administration in office, many aspects of this multilateralism are being allowed to lapse. Bush Jr.'s hysterical assertions of US imperial sovereignty stand in sharp contrast to the trilateralism of his father.

The years immediately after the Second World War were crucial. The gap between a vastly invigorated US and the devastated European countries was so huge, and the latter depended on the former so much for their reconstruction and protection against communist threat from within and without, that the period has gone down in literature on the subject as one of 'US hegemony'. That there was such hegemony is beyond doubt; that it then declined sharply or even disappeared during the 1970s is rather doubtful. What is crucial in any case is not only that the US now had the resources or that the gap between it and its capitalist allies was so great but that a quarter century of sustained prosperity and productivity served to transform the very structure of global capitalism in such a way that the *need* for organizing a distinct centre for the extended reproduction of this new structure and the *material means* to erect an imperial state of that type arose simultaneously. The US was always at the heart of NATO, always the guarantor of the supplies of the world's strategic raw materials to its allies, always the military power that intervened to make the world safe from communism, from Vietnam to Chile; its currency was the own right but also the model for reorganization of capitalist firms across the world; and the US was the one with enough resources to invest so much in its armament industry that the USSR bankrupted itself in trying to match it.

Marx once remarked that a ruling class is stable only to the extent that it presses the best minds of the subordinate classes into its service. A very underrated aspect of the global hegemony the US established after the Second World War was the role its knowledge industry came to play in training and nurturing large elements of the ruling strata in the Third World, directly in its own institutions on US soil and indirectly through 'national' institutions located in the Third World itself, through supply of teachers, syllabi, grants, research equipment, libraries, and so forth. As it emerged as clear leader of the capitalist countries after the Second World War, at a moment when European empires were being dissolved in Asia and Africa, the US developed the largest, best funded, richest academic establishment ever known to humankind, and systematically set out to bring key intellectual strata from the newly decolonized countries into its own academic institutions, across the diverse fields of physical and technical sciences, social sciences and the humanities, arts, diplomacy, jurisprudence, and so on. Many stayed on and became part of the intellectual powerhouse of the United States itself; from the 1960s onwards, certainly, the stupendous 'brain drain' from the Third World (principally Asia) gained momentum as, by contrast, fewer European intellectuals were now inclined to migrate out of their increasingly prosperous and politically stable continent. Those who returned became the home country's economists, scientists, diplomats, bureaucrats, professors, politicians, businessmen. By comparison, the role of the European countries in the intellectual formation of the postcolonial Third World intelligentsia declined sharply, and domestic institutions were re-fashioned to correspond as closely as possible to their American counterparts.

The American imperial project was of course greatly aided by the fact that English became during this period something of a world language, thanks to the fact that it was the language of the two predominant imperial powers of the nineteenth and twentieth centuries. The net result was that large parts of the state institutions in Third World dependencies were taken over simply through the intellectual takeover of many of their key personnel. The American worldview became the practical common sense for those personnel. Nor was this a matter of practical affairs alone.

There was an attendant training of sense and sensibility, of literary and artistic taste, of patterns of consumption, the telecasting and absorption of news, the duplication of forms in the entertainment industry. Most European intellectuals are known in much of Africa and Asia today through their American re-packaging. The only Latin American literature that arrives in the bookshops of Delhi is that which has been translated, annotated, commented upon and published in the United States. The only 'universal' musical forms today are the ones that either come from the US or are local duplicates and variants of the American form. Postmodernization of the world is actually Americanization of the world, with considerable degree of local colour and imitative originality no doubt. A good degree of this imitative originality can be seen in Europe too.

V

That, however, is not the only impact modern imperialism has had on the cultural and ideological spheres in the Third World. A general outbreak of irrationalism across large areas of the former colonies and semi-colonies is the other consequence of the defeat of the original anti-colonial project.

National liberation movements against colonialism and imperialism had risen within a determinate field of force. This field was constituted, on the one hand, by the glaring brutality of foreign occupation as well as the anachronistic hierarchies of their own societies many of which the foreign rulers maintained and even strengthened for their own purposes; and, on the other hand, most such movements derived their inspiration from the radical side of Modernity. This radical side included the Enlightenment ideas of secular reason and the right of every social entity to emancipate itself through the exercise of that reason; the practical example of the relatively emancipated social life in industrialized societies; the ideas of the Bolshevik Revolution which had exploded upon the world just as these mass movements were coming into being and which itself inspired new mass movements. As such, they were, generally speaking, secular reform movements – secularization of religion itself was often an objective – as well as anti-colonial movements. As mass movements, their notable achievement was that they brought into the political field collective social actors which had never acted politically in the past. And as national movements for independence and social change, they sought to bring together diverse elements of society which otherwise belonged to different ethnic, religious and linguistic groups.

This was obviously not the only kind of opposition that grew against colonialism. A traditionalizing backlash in defence of the older social hierarchies was common enough, as hostile to secularizing reform movements as to colonialism. However, as one looks at a broad landscape – from North Africa, through West and South Asia up to Indochina – one is struck by how dominant the secularizing and reforming, even revolutionary, tendencies were. This would include Arab nationalism as much as the Indian anti-colonial movement, and the same was of course true of such reformist regimes as that of Ataturk which founded the modern Turkish state. Mass communist parties were a phenomenon not at all restricted to countries such as Vietnam where the communist-led national liberation triumphed, but also in a whole range of countries, from Iraq and Sudan to India, Malaya and Indonesia. Muslim societies seem to have been rather hospitable to communist ideas, while entities like the Egyptian Muslim Brotherhood and the Indian RSS remained marginal until the last quarter of the twentieth century. One might add that political Islam was nurtured in all those societies by the US from the 1950s onward as a bulwark against communism, with eventually disastrous effects in Afghanistan and beyond.

In class terms, meanwhile, such movements usually represented an alliance of the urban middle classes and the peasantry, and were led by the intelligentsia arising out of the former who were themselves aligned with the national-bourgeois project. What, then, happened to this project after independence? That is a complex story, but as a broad generalization, one could begin this story with the key fact that every national bourgeois regime that arose after decolonization in the larger agrarian societies had a stark choice of alignment between imperialism and the peasantry, and in every instance it betrayed the peasantry. This is a theme of great significance. Gramsci argued that the European bourgeoisie that went through the experience of the French Revolution became thoroughly frightened by the prospect of the peasantry carrying its own revolution to its logical end of merging with the proletariat in a revolution against private property as such, so that no bourgeoisie was ever again to play a revolutionary role against the landholding classes. In the agrarian economies of the larger former colonies certainly, agrarian revolution was the only way out of imperialist dependence and lack of that revolution lies at the heart of the defeat of the national bourgeois project and the eventual acceptance of imperialist dictation and the formation of neoliberal regimes by the local bourgeoisies. This internal factor was certainly decisive in India, where the post-colonial state 'begat' quite a powerful industrial/financial bourgeoisie 'hothouse-fashion' and created a widespread class of rich farmers in the countryside – but never emancipated the vast bulk of the poor and landless peasantries, thus greatly circumscribing the emergence of an extensive home market for the products of this bourgeoisie while the bourgeois-landlord alliance made sure that these dominant classes were taxed as little as possible, causing something of a fiscal crisis of the reformist state. That type of state itself began to decay by the mid-70s, and when the appropriate moment arrived the bourgeoisie cut loose from the project of state-led growth strategies and reconciled itself to a greatly subordinated status in the structure of global capitalism. A major external factor contributing to the fate of the national-bourgeois project was the existence of the Soviet bloc which provided key supports for it in terms of technological inputs, finance and markets; the demise of the Soviet bloc also ended what little had remained of that project. Imperialist pressure was in any case the largest element in the demise of that project.

The defeat and/or decline of the democratic, secular, anti-colonial nationalism has given rise, in a host of countries, from India to Egypt to Algeria, to hysterical, irrationalist forms of cultural nationalism and atavistic hysteria. I have been arguing elsewhere in my writings that in the whole history of modern nationalism, from the early years of the nineteenth century onward, there has been a ferocious struggle between the Enlightenment project of equal citizenship and rational self-emancipation on the one hand, and the romanticist, identitarian, racialistic, religiously bigoted nationalisms. What we are seeing today is that the defeat of the Enlightenment project has necessarily led to the rise of savage identities based on race or religion. As Clara Zetkin once put it, fascism is a just reward for the failure to make the revolution.

This brings us to Al Qaida. In the Arab world, where the Zionist state was a chief instrumentality of US imperialism, it was in the crucible of the Six Day War of 1967 – Israel's professedly 'pre-emptive' invasion of Egypt, instant destruction of its Air Force, occupation of the Sinai – that the radical-nationalist project of Nasserism collapsed; the re-stabilization of the monarchies and resurgence of political Islam in the Arab world can be dated back to that catastrophe. Defeat of the left and of the secular-democratic forces of national liberation in Palestine accounts for the latter-day rise of Hamas and the suicide bombers. In Iran, the destruction of the communist movement and forces of secular nationalism by the joint efforts of the CIA and Shah's secret police paved the way for the Islamic regime to fill the vacuum and hijack the anti-monarchical, reformist sentiments of the Irani people. In Afghanistan, the US sponsored an elaborate, ferocious war against the reformist regime brought about by the communist forces, assembled a huge international force of Islamicist extremists to fight against communism and brought to the world stage the so-called 'mujahideen', the Taliban, Osama bin Laden, and the rest. That is the monster of its own making that came to haunt the United States on 11 September 2001.

VI

We may now, finally, return to the question with which we began, namely wherein lies the specificity of Bush Jr.'s regime. It does not lie, in the first instance, in the invasion of either Afghanistan or Iraq. In the case of Afghanistan, the US has only come back to profit from the war it initiated in 1978, under Carter, against the then new and deeply secular regime of the People's Democratic Party of Afghanistan (PDPA), through their Islamicist proxies who called themselves 'mujahideen' ('fighters of the faith'). Brezinski, Carter's National Security Advisor, has written that he sponsored that war with the explicit objective of drawing in the Soviets – and the Soviets obliged by walking into the trap. Taliban (literally, 'students') arose from among the youngsters and children who grew up in the refugee camps, with the smell of gutters in their nostrils and the rage of displacement in their hearts, that the war itself had produced. They were trained in seminaries established with the express purpose of producing more 'fighters of the faith' in American service, and the regime of their Islamicist faction was foisted upon that wretched and bleeding country some years later, by the Pakistani intelligence agencies upon US advice, after the first set of clients, the 'mujahideen', had slaughtered some 50,000 in the capital city of Kabul and generally plunged the country into chaos, warlordism, rape, plunder, and drug trafficking. The so-called 'Arab Afghanis', among whom Osama was a leader, were CIA agents recruited to fight the Soviets. When the Taliban refused to cooperate fully with the US in its designs on Central Asian oil, the US decided to invade. Niaz Naik, the dean of Pakistan's diplomatic corps, said on the BBC that he had been told by the Americans during the summer of 2001 that invasion would begin in October. The events of 11 September came between the making of the design and its execution.

War against Iraq began not in 2003 but in the course of the so-called 'Gulf War', in 1991, which continued through sanctions and no-fly zones, for over a decade – longer than the combined duration of the two World Wars – under three consecutive US Presidents, two Republicans (father and son) and one Democrat (Clinton, the 'New Democrat' who inspired 'New Labour' across the Atlantic). It was during the Clinton Presidency that the US Congress passed the Iraq Liberation Act, in 1998. When the sanctions regime was estimated by some UN agencies to have killed half a million Iraqi children and journalists asked Clinton's Secretary of State Madeleine Albright whether their death was worth the price of upholding the sanctions, she said 'the price was worth it'. The so-called no-fly zones in northern and eastern Iraq were declared by Boutros Boutros-Ghali, the UN Secretary-General, to be illegal, and yet under that scheme the Anglo-American bombardment of

Iraq became the longest aerial campaign since the Second World War; in 1999 alone 1,800 bombs were dropped and 450 targets hit inside Iraq. (The US instantly turned against Ghali, deprived him a second term and got Kofi Annan to replace him.) Cumulatively, over some 12 years, the tonnage dropped on Iraq came to equal seven Hiroshimas.

'Regime change' is a catchy phrase, and the Bush administration has undoubtedly raised it to the status of a legitimate right of imperial sovereignty. However, the US has been doing it for decades. It did so in Iraq itself when the CIA helped overthrow the progressive regime of Abd al-Karim Kassem in 1964 and brought in the Ba'ath party regime ('We came to power on a CIA train', exulted the General-Secretary of Saddam's parent party), paving the way for the eventual personal dictatorship of Saddam Hussein who remained a close US ally throughout the 1980s when he fought a US-assisted war against Iran. 'Regime change' is what the CIA brought to Iran in 1953 and the US military to Grenada and Panama more recently. And the history of the US coming as 'liberators' and staying as occupiers goes back to the Philippines at the end of the nineteenth century.

What is specific to the Bush regime is the combination of an intensification of such long-standing trends as well as a cluster of novelties which, taken together, amount to something of a historic break. Intensification of trends is obvious enough. What are the novelties internal to Bush Jr.'s Presidency? First, the manner of his election: he was elevated to the Presidency by a judicial decision of dubious merit, combined with widely suspected disenfranchisement of a considerable section of the black electorate in the state of Florida which *happened* to be run by his brother, Jeb. Jeb Bush's other major contribution to Bush Jr.'s campaign was that he was the one who assembled that cabal of the neoconservatives, drawn from the think-tanks of the far right and supervised by Dick Cheney, who came to define the domestic as well as foreign policies, the civilian as well as military structures, of the United States after the elections: they captured the Pentagon, hence the US military machine, just as the Bush brothers captured the White House. (Jeb was the one originally slated to be the Presidential candidate; it is unclear why Bush Jr. was chosen to run for the Presidency instead.)

The second novelty of this Presidency, which distinguishes it from the preceding ones, is the will to radically re-make the United States itself as it sets out to re-map the globe. Dick Cheney's bland prediction that the war against terrorism may last for fifty years or more, and General Tommy Frank's prediction even before the invasion of Iraq that US troops may have to be stationed there fairly indefinitely, on the model of Korea, is matched by a politics of permanent hysteria at home, invoking a mixture of extreme insecurity and atavistic patriotism. The general populace is being persuaded to surrender many of its own fundamental rights, and to endorse distinctions between those born on US soil and the naturalized citizens, between immigrants from one part of the world and another, between 'good' and 'bad' members of one faith, Islam – all this buttressed by a historically new and now very extensive alliance between extreme Zionism and Christian fundamentalism. The assault on American liberties is itself being coded as Patriot Act I and II. This tie between hysterical patriotism and a docile populace whose own rights are being abridged is itself something of a quasi-fascist move. Meanwhile, the already existing policies of shifting incomes upward and offering tax bonanzas to corporations and the rich while bankrupting the social state have been accelerated to a degree that a successor government may not even have the resources to save such things as Social Security for the elderly in its present form even if it had the desire to do so.

What is being reversed, thus, is not only the so-called 'Vietnam syndrome' but even aspects of American social life dating back to the New Deal. In 'Re-Building America's Defenses: Strategy, Forces and Resources For a New Century', a report prepared by an impressive cross-section of the neoconservative elite including Paul Wolfowitz, and issued by The Project for a New American Century in September 2000, the authors remarked that the kind of sweeping changes they are proposing may take some time unless some catastrophic and catalyzing event, like a new Pearl Harbor, were to occur. 11 September 2001 was the event they were waiting for. Condoleeza Rice urged her colleagues the next morning that ways be found to 'capitalize on these opportunities', while Donald Rumsfeld urged immediate invasion of Iraq.

How does one comprehend this peculiar mix of continuities and discontinuities as a whole? One way of putting it is that the rightwing backlash which began in the United States in the late 1960s (in response to the military defeats it was facing in Indochina, on the one hand, and, on the other, the immense successes at home of the Anti-Vietnam War movement, the radicalization of Afro-American politics, and the rise of the women's movement) has finally grown and matured to the point where it has actually captured state power. This offensive was prepared over a quarter century or more and Bush Jr.'s Presidency represents something of a historic break in the sense that these trends had remained scattered and subordinated to other exigencies of power, and its representatives, even as they began occupying positions in the Reagan and Bush Sr.'s administrations, were not in charge of all the key institutions of state, as they now are. One notable feature of this counteroffensive has been the role that think-tanks and foundations of the far right have played in funding, training and delivering the requisite personnel transforming the intellectual climate in the US, and now the state apparatus. Another notable feature is the role that the quasi-messianic Evangelical Christianity has played in preparing a popular sensibilities receptive to all these changes.

A group of New York intellectuals had begun arguing as far back as the Nixon Presidency in the late 1960s that the New Left, the anti-war movement, black nationalism, women's liberation movements, et. al, collectively comprised a disruptive but highly vocal minority and the real task was to organize and mobilize the 'Silent Majority' which was opposed to all that. Milton Friedman at Chicago University formulated an assault on the social state and advanced the ideology of the market as the final arbiter of the social good. His colleague Alan Bloom wrote best-selling books on 'the destruction of the American Mind' by the reforms that leftwing/black/feminist pressures had forced upon the educational system, including the formidable elite universities. Bloom's teacher and senior colleague Leo Straus, whose own highly authoritarian theoretical positions and rightwing critique of liberal democracy went back to Nazi thought via Carl Schmidt, himself trained many of those who were to emerge within the last decade as members of the neoconservative intellectual elite.[7] Hundreds of large and small, inter-locking, neoliberal organizations now dotted the American landscape, and a rash of not very widely known rightwing foundations started appearing – the Carthage Foundation, the Henry M. Olin Foundation, the Phillip M. McKenna Foundation, the Henry Salvatori Foundation, etc., etc. – which then helped to

[7] Literature on (and by) the neoconservatives is vast. The influence of Leo Strauss on figures such as Assistant Defence Secretary Wolfowitz, a key architect of the Iraq policy, William Kristol, Chief Editor of the influential *Weekly Standard*, and Gary Schmitt, founder and chairman of the Project for the New American Century (PNAC), is only now becoming a topic of general discussion. To trace the power of this pernicious influence, one could begin with articles by Alain Frachon and Daniel Vernet in *Le Monde* and Seymour Hersh in *The New Yorker*, a more journalistic presentation by William Pfaff in the *International Herald Tribune*, and the website <www.straussian.org>, not to speak of Strauss's own work.

fund the more prestigious and influential ones: the American Enterprise Institute, the Heritage foundation, the Cato Institute, and the elite of all neoconservative think-tanks, The Project for the New American Century, whose founders include the core of the Bush administration: Vice President Dick Cheney, Defence Secretary Donald Rumsfeld, Deputy Defence Secretary Paul Wolfowitz, Cheney's Chief of Staff Lewis I. Libby, Reagan's Education Secretary William Bennet, and Zalmay Khalilzad, Bush's shadowy representative first in Afghanistan and then in Iraq.

In other words, these tendencies have been long in the making and have been gathering momentum and increasing power over some three decades. With the Bush Presidency, they have seized power. They wish to re-make the US, eradicating from its system of governance all those elements which can be traced back to the New Deal of the 1930s, return it to the kind of brutal capitalism that flourished before the Depression, and turn its liberal-democratic order into something of a National Security State. They wish to re-map the globe through a policy of permanent war, brutalize the Third World, monopolize the strategic raw material resources of the world, and impose permanent subordination on all its potential rivals, in the form of an imperial sovereignty that abides by no law external to itself. This raises the question of 'fascism' with which this article began. If we take Mussolini's own definition of fascism as 'corporatism' in which the state merges with the corporations, that moment has already arrived in the United States and is showing its most brutal face in the wars over oil in the Middle East and the Caspian Sea basin, not to speak of corporate globalization and the globalized militarism which is itself driven by the military-industrial complex.

Racism is equally a fundamental structuring component of the dominant ideology in the United States, rooted in three overlapping histories and far exceeding the historical depth of

German anti-Semitism of the Nazi type. Born in a genocidal extermination of the indigenous population, American conscience accommodates itself easily to mass murder of others in pursuit of what it considers its own security and manifest destiny in the world; be it Hiroshima and Nagasaki or the carpet bombings of Vietnam or the death of half a million Iraqi children under its regime of sanctions,[8] it cultivates amnesia about its own historic guilt and moralizes about genocides conducted by others. An equally potent element in the making of this consciousness is the whole history of race-based slavery which has made racist hatred and violence against people of African origin a permanent feature of the dominant culture of white America; it is with the greatest and virtually natural ease that popular American consciousness can shift its racist hatreds from the African-American to the Arab or Muslim, and then back to its historic object. This ugly underside of American culture is then buttressed by the deeply moralizing tendency that goes back to the Puritan forefathers in which collective life becomes the psychodrama of an eternal duel between Good and Evil in which America-the-Good is always exorcising the demons that are out to devour it. Hence the litany of the past two years, from George Bush down to the smallest outlet in the US media: 'Why do they hate us?' and the pat answer, with a characteristic lack of self-examination: 'because we are good, democratic, prosperous – and Christian!' Racism re-invented now as a Clash of Civilizations.

In the midst of all this, and for some thirty years now, the US media and large sections of the elite intellectuals have

---

[8] The figure of half a million Iraqi children killed by the sanctions must be seen in the perspective of the actual size of the Iraqi population of twenty-five million, which means that even if we count only the children and no adult, one out of every fifty Iraqis was killed by these sanctions. If a similar catastrophe were to occur in India with its population of one thousand million, the figure would come to forty million – that is to say, four crore children killed in twelve years!

colluded with the US and Israeli states to give rise to that other kind of anti-Semitism which focuses mass hysteria and the consequent bloodlust not on the Jew but that other Semite, the Arab; these Arabs – Iraqis and Palestinians in particular – can be killed by the million, but they shall always remain the Barbarians who pose a threat to the security of their killers. Elsewhere in this book, we quote Karl and John Mueller writing in *Foreign Affairs*, the American Establishment journal *par excellance*, and saying that the regime of sanctions created by the United Nations and enforced by the US-UK coalition has killed more Iraqis than had been killed by 'all the weapons of mass destruction in history' but it is Saddam Hussein, whose regime tried to protect the Iraqi population against those sanctions, who is demonized as the barbarian whose possession of weapons of mass destruction became the excuse for the invasion; in the event, no weapons of mass destruction were found but the invasion was nevertheless accepted as a 'humanitarian intervention' and an 'export of democracy' that was good in and of itself. This demonization of the Arab, including American citizens of Arab origin, is now not only part of the dominant ideology but even of the new legal structure abridging the rights of such citizens.

Why, then, does the US not have the political and paramilitary state structure historically associated with fascist regimes of the 1930s? The answer is really quite simple: there is no militant labour movement to require such a state, and the US population is largely quiescent; the 'good American' today is where the 'good German' once was. One needs to remember that the Nazi dream of acquiring a global empire has indeed been realized – but by the United States of America. The imperialism of our time shall not replicate the entirety of the fascistic forms of the first half of the past century, but there is also a fundamental continuity between these two historical moments. The brave individuals and groups in the US who work so hard to build an anti-racist, anti-war, anti-imperialist movement are faced with the whole weight of this history, past and present.

Even so, both the US and UK states are busy erecting regimes of universal surveillance and political control which would abolish the conception of civil liberties that have existed in those countries for a century or more, and even the thought of a military government is being introduced into the popular discourse so that such a thought becomes thinkable. I could illustrate this point with two pieces of news that came my way in late November 2003. The first is the text of an interview with Gen. Tommy Franks, who led the recent US assault on Iraq, in the forthcoming issue of the magazine *Cigar Aficionado*, in which he says that in case of another event such that of 11 September 2001 Americans would be provoked to 'question our own Constitution and to begin to militarize our country'. These are grave and terrifying words from one who is himself a military hero in his country. What does 'militarize' mean in this context? A military takeover, a *coup d'etat* with or without the cooperation of the Bush gang? The second piece of news is that the Blair government in the UK is about a promulgate sweeping legislation, provisionally called the Civil Contingencies Bill, which is closely modelled upon the Patriot Act already in place in the US and other such laws currently envisaged in the US. This new Bill gives the government sweeping powers to define an 'emergency'; the power to suspend the Bill of Rights without a vote in Parliament; to 'prohibit assemblies of specified kinds' and 'other specified activities'; to order destruction of certain properties, and so on. In sum, the Blair government intends to undo the structure of civil liberties under which Britain has been ruled for roughly a century. Developments of this kind speak for themselves and need no further comment.

A word about Evangelical Christianity. When Reagan was

re-elected with the largest electoral sweep in history, losing only one state, it was revealed that only 27 per cent of the potential voters had actually voted in his favour; the majority had stayed home. At the same time, a Gallup poll showed that 27 per cent of Americans subscribed to some variety of Evangelical Christianity, and commentators noted that if all of them were to be mobilized as a voting bloc the US could have a permanent government of the far right. Not *all* of them have been mobilized yet – but that kind of government has now arrived. While Reagan gifted us supply-side economics and Star Wars, and the left thought that he was as bad it could get, the right-wing of the Republican Party thought of him as a Roosevelt democrat. That right wing is now in power.

VII

We may be witnessing an imperial overreach. Overdetermined by their own ideological delusions, Bush's neocons may be pursuing policies that far exceed the logic of global capitalism or the requirements of the imperial US state; even George Soros, the US billionaire of Hungarian origin, whose network of institutions has just managed to stage something of a bloodless pro-American *coup* in Georgia, seems to think so. Two former Presidents, including the current President's father, opposed the invasion of Iraq before it happened. Ever the mildly Presbyterian Trilaterist, Bush Sr. emphasized that the US needed alliance with Europe and the war on Iraq would undermine it. As we have seen, the Franco-German alliance has accepted the consequences, however resentfully. But Iraqi resistance is already sending enough coffins of the US military personnel as well as thousands of injured and disabled GIs, which may yet prove to be a quagmire that cures the US populace of any appetite for the real wars that are fought on the other side of their TV screens; more Americans have died in Iraq in four months than in the first three years of Vietnam, and more have died in November 2003, as I write these words, than in any month since the invasion began in March. They may yet come to comprehend what a menace this administration is for their own security. At the same time, the global revolt against imperial America that we witnessed on the eve of the Iraq invasion may regain momentum; those who have died in the service of the US imperium in Iraq include not only Americans and the British but also Poles, Spaniards, Italians, Koreans and the Japanese. This moment of neoconservative extremity may yet pass as one of many murderous episodes in imperial history.

APPENDIX 1
Sanctions and Their Effects on Iraq
BRIEF SUMMARY

* August 6, 1990: United Nations Security Council passes Resolution 661, placing sanctions on Iraq to 'restore the authority of the legitimate government of Kuwait'. (That government, 'legitimate' or not, was restored within months. By what criterion is restoration of monarchy ever 'legitimate'? The sheikhs of Kuwait were never required to offer themselves for electoral challenge or even referendum.)

* April 5, 1991: UN Security Council passes Resolution 688 that 'demands that Iraq' end its repression 'of all Iraqi citizens'. (By these standards, virtually every government in the world should have to face similar sanctions.)

* May 20, 1991: President George H. Bush: 'At this juncture, my view is we don't want to lift these sanctions as long as Saddam Hussein is in power'. (The *declared* policy of regime change is as old as that.)

* September 24, 1992: *The New England Journal of Medicine* publishes the findings of Harvard researchers that 46,700 Iraqi children under five have died from the combined effects of war and trade sanctions in the first seven months of 1991.

* May 12, 1996: On *60 Minutes*, Lesley Stahl asks US Secretary of State Madeline Albright: 'We have heard that a half a million children have died. I mean, that's more children than died in Hiroshima. Is the price worth it?' Albright responds: 'I think this is a very hard choice, but the price . . . we think the price is worth it'.

* October 4, 1996: United Nations Children's Fund (UNICEF) releases report on Iraq. 'Around 4,500 children under the age of five are dying here every month from hunger and disease', said Philippe Heffinck, UNICEF's representative for Iraq.

* November 26, 1997: UNICEF reports that 'The most alarming results are those

on malnutrition, with 32 per cent of children under the age of five, some 960,000 children, chronically malnourished – a rise of 72 per cent since 1991. Almost one quarter (around 23 per cent) are underweight – twice as high as the levels found in neighbouring Jordan or Turkey'.

* April 30, 1998: UNICIF reports: 'The increase in mortality reported in public hospitals for children under five years of age (an excess of some 40,000 deaths yearly compared with 1989) is mainly due to diarrhea, pneumonia and malnutrition. In those over five years of age, the increase (an excess of some 50,000 deaths yearly compared with 1989) is associated with heart disease, hypertension, diabetes, cancer, liver or kidney diseases'.

* October 6, 1998: Denis Halliday, who had just resigned as the head of the 'oil-for-food' programme for Iraq, Assistant Secretary General of the UN, gives a speech on Capitol Hill, citing a 'conservative estimate' of 'child mortality for children under five years of age is from five to six thousand per month'.

* In 1995, the UN Food and Agriculture Organization concluded that the embargo and the military attacks on Iraq had been responsible for the deaths of more than 560,000 children. A UNICEF study reached a similar conclusion, finding that 500,000 children had died needlessly between 1991 and 1998.

* Blocked by the US and UK governments, with UN connivance: vaccines, cancer-treatment equipment, pain-killers, plasma bags, food treatment equipment and myriad other items of medical need, over fourteen years, worth $5.4 billion as of July 2002.

* Karl and John Mueller, writing in *Foreign Affairs* ('Sanctions of Mass Destruction', May/June 1999), concluded that the sanctions had killed more Iraqis than had been killed by 'all the weapons of mass destruction in human history'.

APPENDIX 2
Ramsey Clark's Report to UN Security Council

Ramsey Clark: Report to UN Security Council re: Iraq

January 26, 2000

Permanent Mission of the United Kingdom to the United Nations

Dear H.E. Sir Jeremy Greenstock, KCMG,

A delegation of US citizens from twenty states has just returned from Iraq. On January 17, we observed in Baghdad the 9th Anniversary of the beginning of the January 17 - February 28, 1991. U. aircraft flew 110,000 aerial sorties against Iraq, averaging one every 30 seconds, dropping 88,500 tons of explosives, the equivalent of 7 ½ Hiroshima bombs.

This was by far the most intensive bombardment in history. It killed tens of thousands of people, injuring many more. Medicines and medical supplies were exhausted. It devastated water systems from reservoir, pumping station, pipeline, filtration plant to kitchen faucet as well as urban sewage and sanitation systems nationwide. Food production, processing, storage, distribution, and marketing facilities were widely destroyed. Poultry was nearly wiped out by loss of electricity and lack of grain. Animal herds were decimated. Fertilizer and insecticide plants and storage structures were destroyed. Communications systems, telephone, radio, TV, were shattered. Transportation was badly battered. Vital industries were attacked everywhere. Electric power was knocked out across the nation in the first 24 hours of the assault. Petroleum production, refining, storage and distribution from well to service station were attacked across the nation.

The combined effect of this vast destruction of essential goods, services and industries with the most comprehensive economic sanctions of modern times, first imposed on Hiroshima Day, August 6, 1990, has caused more than a million and a half deaths.

Conditions of Life and Death in Iraq

I have traveled to and within Iraq ten times since sanctions were imposed, once during the bombing in 1991. Each year, the death rate has risen radically. The numbers of deaths have been reported internationally regularly and updated each month since 1991. In Iraq, they are palpable. UN agencies, the World Health Organization, the Food and Agriculture Organization, the World Food Programme, UNICEF and others have found and confirmed the deaths time and time again. They must shock the conscience of every sentient human being. Comprehensive reports by UN agencies and other sources are available to you. You are charged with this knowledge. The total numbers of deaths in every segment of the society has risen radically in each of the past nine years under US/UN sanctions.

As a tragic illustration total annual deaths of children in Iraq under the age of five from respiratory infection, diarrhea and gastroenteritis and malnutrition are:

During
1989:	7110	deaths
1991:	27473	
1994:	52905	
1997:	58845	
1998:	71279	
1999 (Jan.- Nov.):	73572	

The annual number of deaths of children under age five grew more than tenfold from 1989 to 1999. Total deaths of children under age five from these selected causes alone during 1990 to November 1999 is 502,492.

While children under age five are the most vulnerable age group, except for the extreme elderly, every age group has suffered radical increases in the numbers of deaths. Members of the population with serious chronic illnesses requiring regular medication, or therapy, suffer the highest percentages of death of any sectors, approaching 100% for some illnesses where survival rates were as high as 95% before sanctions.

The sanctions target to kill, or injure infants, children, the elderly, and the chronically ill.

The Red Crescent and other knowledgeable professional groups believe it will be years after the end of sanctions before the increase in deaths from most causes stops rising because of the cumulative effect of the sanctions on the physical conditions of parents, children, the new born and the overall environment.

Most of those who survive suffer severe physical and mental injury from the sanctions. Indicative of the impact of sanctions is the enormous rise in the percentage of registered births under 2.5 kilograms, a dangerously low birth weight in a nation without adequate food, medicine and medical supplies and equipment. Like death, under weight births have risen radically every year:

Year /	% of live births at weights under 2.5 kilograms
1990:	4.5
1991:	10.8
1994:	21.1
1998:	23.8
1999 (Jan. - Nov.):	24.1

The percentage of live births below 2.5 kg. has increased more than fivefold to one in four registered births. The consequence for the lives of these children is enormous. Many will have underdeveloped organs, mental retardation, remain smaller and weaker than average and be more vulnerable to sickness, malnutrition and bad water. Their life expectancy has been reduced by as much as 30%. Probably 90% of all the infants born in Iraq since 1990 have significantly lower birth weights than they would if there were no sanctions. The effect on lives and health of children with higher birth weights is also drastic. This is why foreign medical teams for five years have referred to a 'stunted generation' in Iraq.

Suggestive of the struggle the children living and dying under sanctions in Iraq face are the following increases since 1990 in treated cases of nutrition related sicknesses and deficiencies.

Year	Number of cases	
Kwashiorkor		
1990:	485	(base)
1991:	12796	26.3 times
1994:	20975	42.6 times
1998:	30232	61.4 times
Marasmus		
1990:	5193	(base)
1991:	96186	18.5 times
1994:	192296	37.0 times
1998:	264468	50.8 times
Protein, Calorie, Vitamin deficiency, Malnutrition		
1990:	96809	(base)
1991:	947974	9.8 times
1994:	1576194	16.3 times
1998:	1910309	19.7 times

Kwashiorkor is an extremely dangerous end product of malnutrition in which the victim wastes and dies without early intensive care. Few doctors in Iraq had ever seen a case before late 1990. From medical school and continuing studies they associated Kwashiorkor with starvation in the poorest regions of Africa and south Asia during periods of war, drought, pestilence and other calamities. Marasmus inflicts a lower death rate than kwashiorkor, but is extremely dangerous, permanently damaging and requires early and extended care for survival. The effects of severe and protracted malnutrition are permanent and life shortening. Common communicable diseases preventable by vaccination which are provided to nearly all children in developed countries and were standard in Iraq before 1990 have increased by multiples. While rates for these diseases fluctuate unlike the death rates and rates for malnutrition related sickness, because of the cyclical nature of their communication, they have been regularly higher, increasingly so, and have afflicted additional hundreds of thousands of children. Increases in 1998 over 1989 were as follows: whooping cough, 3.4 times; measles, 4.5 times (25,818 cases); mumps, 3.7 times (35,881). The Sanctions Committee of the Security Council has failed to approve negotiated contracts for Iraq to purchase vaccines for these and other diseases. Poliomyelitis, which had been virtually extinguished in Iraq, has increased by a multiple ranging from 2 to 18.6 times since 1989. Cholera rose from zero cases in 1989 to 2560 cases in 1998 and conditions in Iraq threaten an epidemic. Amoebic dysentery was 13 times greater in 1998, totaling 264,290 cases, over 1989 and much higher in several earlier years. Typhoid fever was up 10.9 times to 19825 cases in 1998 over 1989. Scabies increased every year from zero cases in 1989 to 43,580 in 1998. Every adult knows the misery, suffering and sometimes heartbreak these preventable communicable diseases cause.

Doctors, nurses, therapists, pharmacists, all persons in health care, work under tragic conditions. Doctors and nurses uniformly state that patients they could easily save under normal conditions die every day. The hospitals are in wretched condition: dark, cold, dirty, stairwells crumbling, walls peeling, beds without sheets, plumbing inoperable, electricity erratic, equipment without parts, medicines, oxygen, anesthetics, antiseptics, antibiotics, x-ray film, catheters, gauze, aspirin, light bulbs, pencils always scarce, often unavailable. Common life saving medicines from dehydration tablets to insulin are never in adequate supply.

In plain numbers without measuring the conditions under which they were performed, or the availability of important equipment and supplies, major surgical operations have declined each year from a monthly average of 15,125 in 1989 to 3823 in November 1999 or by 74.7%. The monthly average number of laboratory investigations has declined from 1,494,050 in 1989 to 454,375 in November 1999, or by 68.6%.

Drastic deterioration in the whole environment, the physical plant, sanitation and the introduction of some 25,000,000 ounces of depleted uranium by US aircraft and missiles have caused enormous increases in illnesses from tuberculosis to leukemia and other cancers, tumors and malformations in fetuses. These conditions will take many years and billions of dollars to restore to 1989 levels. The hundreds of thousands of lives destroyed and the health of millions damaged can never be restored.

Today unemployment is 60%. 95% of the private sector of the economy is shut down. There are no ambulances. 80% of the sanitation trucks from 10 years ago are inoperable. There are no new trucks, cars, tractors, buses, or other vehicles. Food distribution from a comprehensive rationing system controlling staples delivers 1100 calories per day for every person throughout the country, Kurd, Sunni and Shi'ite Muslim, Christian, Jew, rich, poor, alien, with special rations for infants, pregnant women, the severely malnourished, and others with special needs. The poor cannot significantly supplement their food rations. In 1989, daily caloric intake in Iraq averaged 3400.

These brief facts demonstrate the deadly conditions of life deliberately inflicted on the entire population of Iraq, but which inherently impact on infants, children, the elderly and chronically ill first and destroy a vast part of the nation and its overwhelmingly Muslim peoples.

Representative of the attitude of the US government foreign policy makers toward Iraq and the sanctions are the considered remarks of former Secretary of State Henry Kissinger in a syndicated newspaper article published in the second week of January 2000 in which he referred to the 'alleged suffering of the Iraqi people'. Then US Ambassador to the United Nations Madeleine Albright spoke more forthrightly, if more cruelly. She stated in an interview on the top-rated CBS national network magazine show *60 Minutes*, seen by tens of millions of people in the spring of 1997, that she believed the deaths from the sanctions of 585,000 Iraqi children under the age of five as direct result of sanctions reported by the US Food and Agriculture Organization in late 1986 was a price worth paying to maintain the sanctions against Iraq.

The Sanctions Violate the Genocide Convention of 1948

Genocide is defined in the Genocide Convention, in part, as follows:

Article II . . . genocide means any of the following acts committed with the intent to destroy, in whole or in part, a national, ethnical, racial or religious group, as such:

a) Killing members of the group;
b) Causing serious bodily or mental harm to members of the group;
c) Deliberately inflicting on the group conditions of life calculated to bring about its physical destruction in whole or in part;

There can be no doubt that the sanctions against Iraq intentionally destroyed in major part members of a national group and a religious group, as such, killing members of the groups, causing bodily and mental harm to their members and deliberately inflicting conditions of life calculated to bring about their physical destruction, at least, in part. If this is not genocide, what is?

The United States, after decades of resisting, finally ratified the Genocide Convention before these sanctions were imposed. It has frequently accused other governments of genocide, sometimes assaulting them severely with its massive, high tech military weapons against which nearly all nations are defenseless.

The Food for Oil Programme has failed to stop the increased death rates

The Food for Oil programme was approved in December 1996 as a means of maintaining the sanctions against Iraq which were meeting growing opposition in the Security Council. After three years of operation barely six billion dollars in contracts under the programme have been received from 19 billion dollars of oil sales. Despite Iraq's desperate needs, more of the funds from sales of its oil have been turned over to the US, the UN and others making claims against Iraq than have been allocated to contracts approved for purchase of food, medicine, equipment and equipment parts for the people of Iraq. Five billion in contracts for purchases entered into by Iraq has not been approved.

As has been seen the deaths of children and every other segment of the society from the sanctions have continued to rise in 1997, 1998 and 1999. To rebuild the health care system, the food production processing, storage and distribution system and the water systems will cost many billions. Restoring facilities for health, communications, transportation, education, industry and clean up of the environment polluted by the US aerial assaults, including the use of depleted uranium found in extremely dangerous concentrations in parts of Iraq, will cost many tens of billions of dollars.

Iraq was devoting more than 20 billion annually to public facilities, goods and services before 1989. Income from oil sales for 1997-1999 averaged under 2 billion dollars annually, 10% of the amounts available before sanctions. If Iraq devoted all of the funds under the Oil for Food Programme to food, medicine and water, the deaths caused by sanctions would continue to rise and the health of the nation decline. The United States has proceeded to frustrate approval of contracts under the programme in a systematic way to prolong the genocide against Iraq.

United States military aircraft deliberately destroyed Iraq's water storage, distribution and quality control systems during the intensive bombing during January and February 1991. Within two weeks there was no running water in any city or town in Iraq. Many tens of thousands of people in Iraq have died as a direct result of drinking contaminated water.

Iraq has entered into contracts totaling $ 700,000,000 for water and sewage projects. This sum is a very small fraction of current needs. Only $ 65,000,000 has been received, less than 9%. This is done deliberately to continue conditions of life destructive of the population of Iraq. Purchase of chlorine for municipal water treatment, a standard international usage, has been completely rejected. People continue to die at increasing rates from bad water.

Oil production for even the very low levels authorized under the programme, less than 1/3 of the pre-sanctions level, has been difficult to achieve and usually below authorized amounts, because of deteriorated and destroyed facilities and lack of equipment and parts.

Still the sanctions committee has approved only 18% of the tendered contracts for oil production, refining and transport. This is done to prevent Iraq from restoring its ability to save its people through the sales of oil.

Of the $ 207 million sought for communications under the programme, not a penny has been approved. The sanctions committee fears communicated truth will set opinion free and end the sanctions.

The Oil for Food Programme has never been anything more than a means for slowly increasing the rate of destruction of the people of Iraq. Security Council Resolution 1284 is simply a means of starting the process over again. During three years under the programme from 1996 to 1999, well over 200,000 children under age five died in drastically increasing numbers each year at a rate growing from just under 9 to well over 10 times the number who died in 1989. That experience must not be repeated. The sanctions must be ended now.

It is criminal to hold the lives of the people of Iraq hostage to demands of the US against their government, whatever those demands may be. In war it is prohibited to use starvation as a weapon. Medical aid must be given the enemy wounded. Under sanctions an Iraqi is being deliberately killed every two minutes by conditions of life inflicted by the sanctions. Sanctions are the functional equivalent of pointing guns at the heads of Iraq's children and elderly while saying do what we demand to their government, or we will shoot, then pulling a trigger every two minutes, or less.

To save the United Nations in the judgment of history, the Security Council must end the sanctions immediately. They are genocide.

To save itself from the judgment of the people of the world, the US must immediately act to end the sanctions and account for its acts.

Sincerely,
Ramsey Clark
International Action Center
39 West 14th Street, Room 206
New York, NY 10011
email: iacenter@iacenter.org
http://www.iacenter.org
phone: 212 633-6646
fax: 212 633-2889

APPENDIX 3

WMD:
Who Said What When

Every day Saddam remains in power with chemical weapons, biological weapons, and the development of nuclear weapons is a day of danger for the United States.
> Sen. Joseph Lieberman, D-CT, September 4, 2002

Simply stated, there is no doubt that Saddam Hussein now has weapons of mass destruction.
> Dick Cheney August 26, 2002

If we wait for the danger to become clear, it could be too late.
> Sen. Joseph Biden, D-Del., September 4, 2002

Right now, Iraq is expanding and improving facilities that were used for the production of biological weapons.
> George W. Bush September 12, 2002

If he declares he has none, then we will know that Saddam Hussein is once again misleading the world.
> Ari Fleischer December 2, 2002

We know for a fact that there are weapons there.
> Ari Fleischer January 9, 2003

Our intelligence officials estimate that Saddam Hussein had the materials to produce as much as 500 tons of sarin, mustard and VX nerve agent.
> George W. Bush January 28, 2003

We know that Saddam Hussein is determined to keep his weapons of mass destruction, is determined to make more.
> Colin Powell February 5, 2003

Iraq both poses a continuing threat to the national security of the United States and international peace and security in the Persian Gulf region and remains in material and unacceptable breach of its international obligations by, among other things, continuing to possess and develop a significant chemical and biological weapons capability, actively seeking a nuclear weapons capability, and supporting and harbouring terrorist organizations.

Sen. Hillary Clinton, D-NY, February 5, 2003

We have sources that tell us that Saddam Hussein recently authorized Iraqi field commanders to use chemical weapons – the very weapons the dictator tells us he does not have.

George Bush February 8, 2003

So has the strategic decision been made to disarm Iraq of its weapons of mass destruction by the leadership in Baghdad? I think our judgment has to be clearly not.

Colin Powell March 8, 2003

Intelligence gathered by this and other governments leaves no doubt that the Iraq regime continues to possess and conceal some of the most lethal weapons ever devised.

George Bush March 18, 2003

We are asked to accept Saddam decided to destroy those weapons. I say that such a claim is palpably absurd.

Tony Blair, Prime Minister March 18, 2003

Well, there is no question that we have evidence and information that Iraq has weapons of mass destruction, biological and chemical particularly . . . all this will be made clear in the course of the operation, for whatever duration it takes.

Ari Fleisher March 21, 2003

There is no doubt that the regime of Saddam Hussein possesses weapons of mass destruction. As this operation continues, those weapons will be identified, found, along with the people who have produced them and who guard them.

Gen. Tommy Franks March 22, 2003

I have no doubt we're going to find big stores of weapons of mass destruction.

Kenneth Adelman, Defence Policy Board, March 23, 2003

One of our top objectives is to find and destroy the WMD. There are a number of sites.

Pentagon Spokeswoman Victoria Clark March 22, 2003

We know where they are. They are in the area around Tikrit and Baghdad.
Donald Rumsfeld March 30, 2003

Saddam's removal is necessary to eradicate the threat from his weapons of mass destruction
Jack Straw, Foreign Secretary April 2, 2003

Obviously the administration intends to publicize all the weapons of mass destruction US forces find – and there will be plenty.
Neocon scholar Robert Kagan April 9, 2003

I think you have always heard, and you continue to hear from officials, a measure of high confidence that, indeed, the weapons of mass destruction will be found.
Ari Fleischer April 10, 2003

We are learning more as we interrogate or have discussions with Iraqi scientists and people within the Iraqi structure, that perhaps he destroyed some, perhaps he dispersed some. And so we will find them.
George Bush April 24, 2003

Before people crow about the absence of weapons of mass destruction, I suggest they wait a bit.
Tony Blair April 28, 2003

There are people who in large measure have information that we need . . . so that we can track down the weapons of mass destruction in that country.
Donald Rumsfeld April 25, 2003

We'll find them. It'll be a matter of time to do so.
George Bush May 3, 2003

I am confident that we will find evidence that makes it clear he had weapons of mass destruction.
Colin Powell May 4, 2003

I never believed that we'd just tumble over weapons of mass destruction in that country.
Donald Rumsfeld May 4, 2003

I'm not surprised if we begin to uncover the weapons programme of Saddam Hussein – because he had a weapons programme.
George W. Bush May 6, 2003

US officials never expected that 'we were going to open garages and find' weapons of mass destruction.
Condoleeza Rice May 12, 2003

I just don't know whether it was all destroyed years ago – I mean, there's no question that there were chemical weapons years ago – whether they were destroyed right before the war, [or] whether they're still hidden.
Maj. Gen. David Petraeus, Commander 101st Airborne May 13, 2003

Before the war, there's no doubt in my mind that Saddam Hussein had weapons of mass destruction, biological and chemical. I expected them to be found. I still expect them to be found.
Gen. Michael Hagee, Commandant of the Marine Corps May 21, 2003

Given time, given the number of prisoners now that we're interrogating, I'm confident that we're going to find weapons of mass destruction.
Gen. Richard Myers, Chairman Joint Chiefs of Staff May 26, 2003

They may have had time to destroy them, and I don't know the answer.
Donald Rumsfeld May 27, 2003

For bureaucratic reasons, we settled on one issue, weapons of mass destruction [as justification for invading Iraq] because it was the one reason everyone could agree on.
Paul Wolfowitz May 28, 2003

CounterPunch Wire
May 29, 2003
http://counterpunch.org/wmd05292003.html